BMW 3-SERIES

BMW 3-SERIES
Generations 1 and 2 including M3

A collector's guide
by Jeremy Walton

MOTOR RACING PUBLICATIONS LTD
PO Box 108 ORPINGTON BR6 9TJ, England

First published 1992
This softbound edition first published 2001

British Library Cataloguing in Publication Data

Walton Jeremy
   BMW 3-Series Collectors Guide: Generation
   1 and 2 including M3
   I. Title
   629.222

ISBN 1-899870-55-5

Printed in Great Britain by The Amadeus Press, Cleckheaton, West Yorkshire BD19 4TQ

Contents

An impressive line-up of second-generation 3-series BMWs.

Introduction

One of the most versatile front-engine/rear-drive car designs ever produced, the BMW 3-series is the foundation of Bavarian Motor Works' continued expansion.

In this *Collector's Guide* I have concentrated on the first two editions of the Munich manufacturer's smallest offering, not because I consider the current E36-designated 3-series to be unworthy of collection, but because at the time of writing it is still too recent and has yet to grow to full maturity.

The first 3-series (factory-coded E21) from 1975 to 1982 did not try to cater for every need. There was no four-door model, nor any Touring derivative, and the factory blessed the Baur Cabriolet rather than construct one themselves. Yet the series swiftly found a place in hearts conditioned to love its '02' predecessors and conquered new customers when the six-cylinder 320 and 323i performance classic arrived in 1977.

All those omissions in body variants were filled in the second (E30-coded) 3 series, which sold in ever larger numbers. Not only were we offered two, four and five-door bodies, plus the most elegant of four-seater convertibles, but also a bewildering plethora of power plants. These were not all available in RHD form in Britain. Aside from offering 90 to 238bhp in petrol-burning units, BMW also sold successful diesel and turbodiesel variants.

Not even the traditional BMW adherence to rear-wheel drive was sacrosanct in the second 3-series, for the LHD-only 325iX model (available only to special order in Britain) rested on a permanent 4x4 transmission. The sporting summit to the second edition of the 3-series was the (1985–90) M3, and I make no apology for including coverage of the road and competition performances of this enjoyable and effective machine.

World, European and national titles were all secured by these 2.3- and 2.5-litre competitors, which proved as versatile as the 3-series itself. The M3 grasped not just the obvious racing victories, but national rally and rallycross titles as well; even a World Rally Championship event was won by the original M3!

On the road, the point of the 3-series was to provide refined performance and comfort in a compact and durable package, a formula that has found worldwide acceptance and many imitators.

I hope this book does the first two generations of the original BMW 3-series justice.

October 1992   Jeremy Walton

Acknowledgements

I enjoy writing about BMW. It is my favourite subject for a marque history because it features so many aggressive characters, plus competitive products in every dimension of transport – land, sea and air. Yet to present the company and its products in a digestible form to an English-speaking and reading audience is quite a tough assignment.

BMW's factory production records are the best I have encountered. Yet the plethora of engine and body codes, the multinational marketing of individual specifications, the frequently languid RHD introductions and the reservation of many of the model permutations to specific LHD countries make the task a formidable one for any perspiring author.

I could not have written in any detail without insider help and paramount was the input of BMW GB's employee, Frank Sutton. Nobody knows specification and homologation procedures the way that he does, and I spent much of my research time in his patient and quietly humorous company.

Other BMW GB employees who bore the brunt of years of requests were Public Relations personnel Chris Willows, Scott Brownlee and Lorna Arnold. The parent operation in Germany has always been vital to gain any real insight to this proudly Bavarian product, and my particular thanks go to BMW Ag PR Friedbert Holz and to Peter Zollner of the BMW Archiv. BMW Motorsport engineers and executives Paul Rosche, Franz Zinnecker, Karl-Heinz Kalbfell, Karsten Engel and marketing maestro Martin Hainge were also very helpful.

Outside BMW I took much advice from the UK trade, which is acknowledged in the buying section. For a unique chance to experience and discuss the racing M3, my thanks go to Chris Willows, Marc Surer, Steven Soper, Frank Sytner and Altfrid Heger.

Pictorially there is a higher content of non-BMW factory pictures than might be expected, but I must pay tribute to the magnificent company engineering cutaways.

Finally, a particular 'Thank you' to MRP publisher John Blunsden (who kept his word to publish despite the ravages of a recession that scared others away) and his staff who patiently deciphered the manuscript. They were the lucky ones; 'Marilyn' had to read it prior to dispatch to MRP!

Jeremy Walton

CHAPTER 1

Ancestors and heritage

From aviation to '02' series

The BMW 3-series of the Nineties is the third edition of the company's most popular line. It was originated in 1975 (coded E21) to meet the increasing prosperity of Western Germany, being designed specifically to scoop up customers and plant them on an elaborately crafted ladder of numerical status that is now the envy of its rivals. A second generation (E30) of the 3-series emerged in slightly rounded form from 1982–90 followed by the E36-coded '3', begun with a four-door line in 1990. This was augmented by a two-door coupe in 1992 which would evolve as the basis for both convertible and M3 competition car replacement.

Right from the start it should be realized that I am not talking about automotive rarities. BMW easily outstrip Rover production, and the '02' predecessor to the 3-series sold 861,940 units in the decade between May 1966 and July 1976. The first two generations of the 3-series underlined the commercial wisdom of transferring characteristics such as quality, silky six-cylinder engines and four-door bodywork from further up the BMW range. Together, the two opening editions of the '3' sold an amazing 3,584,263 units, of which the first generation accounted for 1,364,038 in seven years, and its successor 2,220,225 in eight sales seasons.

It looks as though BMW calculated everything in advance, and then executed it with legendary Teutonic precision, but the 'numbers game' was not the established part of the BMW marketing arsenal in 1975 that it is today. Then they sold an '02' line and a succession of 2.5, 2.8, 3.0 and 3.2-litre saloons and coupes that had only the logic of a cubic capacity boot lid badge and 'S' for saloon and 'CS' for coupe. It is true that

there was the 5-series (from 1972 onward), and the present 3-series owes much to the inspiration of transferring big car features down a class to succeed the '02' range of 1602/1802 and 2002 products that had become sporting and commercial legends.

For the record, the company currently manufactures 3, 5, 7 and 8-series motor cars. BMWs are made mainly in Bavaria, either at the Munich HQ, or the Bavarian satellite towns of Dingolfing or Regensberg. BMW saloons, coupes and estates (dubbed Touring) escalate from the mild four-cylinder 316i to the fat cat charms of the V12 850i at the top of the 1992 range.

Using 325i as an example, the logic behind the current badging translates thus: the '3' is for 3-series, and '25' represents 2.5 litres capacity. This logic was very rarely broken, but two complications arise: firstly, many LHD buyers delete the badges altogether (a no-cost facility rarely utilized by Britons) and there have been some minor exceptions, particularly in the case of the 316, which has occasionally stayed on sale under that badge whilst sporting a 1.8-litre motor.

There is an 'i' for fuel injection on all petrol BMWs, even though the German name for such equipment would start with an 'e'. BMW have used a small 'e' on their badges, but it stood for 'eta'. This was a Greek word that BMW purloined to designate a particularly slow-revving petrol engine – a 'six' that was aimed at ultimate operating economy. The 325e was not imported to Britain – even though big brother 525e proved quite popular in RHD form

– but was a large volume seller in the USA and Japan, boosted by its low exhaust emission characteristics and amiable driving manners.

Other common suffixes used on the 3-series are 'D' for diesel or 'TD' for its fuel injection, turbocharged, cousin. The prefix 'M' in front of M3 simply stands for Motorsport, which is a separate company within the parent company, has over 400 employees and two major sites, and enjoys a multi-million Deutschemark turnover in its own right.

Entering the Nineties, BMW had reached new popularity peaks. 1989 was the first year in which they manufactured more than half a million motor cars. By far the most saleable items in the BMW warehouse of 'fours', 'sixes' and V12s were the 3-series. Even the Gulf War of 1991 did little to depress the enthusiastic reception accorded to the first four-door examples of the third 3-series generation.

As late as August 1991 the German market was setting new sales records for all seven home manufacturers (BMW,

Road and competitions engines expert Alex von Falkenhausen prepares to launch the BMW four-cylinder racing engine on its initially rocky road to an illustrious career. Its iron block served for over 25 years in both motorsports and two generations of 3-series success.

BMW has a long and emotive tradition in the manufacture of coupes. This selection from the collection of BMW GB Ltd spans, from the right, AFN's RHD version of the prewar 328, a mid-engined M1, the Nineties 850i, a 3.2-litre CSL from the Seventies and a 507, the V8 coupe from the Fifties.

10

Mercedes, Porsche, multinationals Ford and GM-Opel, plus Volkswagen and Audi), staying hot on the pent-up demand from the East that followed the unification of Germany. This process liberated the commercial instincts of Poles, Czechs, Hungarians and many more, for it is unwise to assume that countries such as Poland are too poor to acquire BMWs. Robert Buchelhofer, the 1992 BMW Sales Director, told me that Polish customers bought 100 of the top-line 850i coupes in 1991, whereas in the UK, for all our vaunted free enterprise, our richest citizens coughed up for just 370 such V12 BMWs.

The BMW company was established originally in the aviation business. The BMW initials stand for Bayerische Motoren Werke, of July 20, 1917 formation, but the aero engine company – Bayerische Flugzeugwerke – founded on March 7, 1916, was the true foundation stone of BMW. The company emblem, so proudly displayed today, was designed around the theme of a whirling propeller, and was first used on October 5, 1917 to register a patent name during the Kaiser regime of the First World War.

The most famous BMW engine of that era gave 185bhp and often pulled Manfred von Richthofen ('The Red Baron') into the aerial action that left him on pole position for the number of kills recorded (80) during the 1914–18 conflict. BMW were no less effective in providing aeronautical power units for the Second World War, which made them a prime target for Allied bombing, and therefore the worst afflicted of the German car makers when it came to restarting production.

In 1923 motorcycles had taken BMW into road transportation, with the forefathers of the flat-twin 'boxer' motors that continue in production today in Berlin alongside the four-cylinder K-series. Thus it was appropriate that another motorcycle, the R24, allowed BMW back into production in Munich in 1948.

BMW had started building cars officially in 1928, based on an adaptation of the British Austin 7, but the story starts at the Frankfurt motor show of 1951, before BMW were back in the car business. On display was a single black saloon. Dubbed the 501, the streamlined four-door contained an update of the Thirties 326 inline 'six' (1,971cc/65bhp), but

The rear-engined (boxer two-cylinder) 700 series grew out of BMW's motorcycle past and became a familiar class-winner across European motorsports. The 700 saloon and coupe (illustrated) were important to keep cash flowing before BMW switched to the four-cylinder forefathers of the 3-series. They also previewed the trailing-arm rear suspension that would serve so many four-cylinder BMW saloons.

the designers had created it with an aluminium V8 to follow – Germany's first postwar V8. German sources were rather dismissive of the 501 and its 'weak' old engine and a style reminiscent, they thought, of a period British Austin.

It took BMW about a year, in 1952, to deliver any 501s to customers. At first, cars had to be built around bodies created by Baur in Stuttgart – later to produce their own 3-series convertible – but a tightly financed rebuilding programme for Milbertshofen at Munich saw BMW with their production facilities operable by 1954. The same year saw their advanced V8 make its debut in the 502 at 90bhp and 2,580cc. Basically the same unit lasted – now stretched to 3,168cc – until 1965, and provided up to 160bhp in the 3200CS. The central-camshaft 'eight' powered two classic sportscars along the way: the 503 (150bhp/118mph) and 507 (150bhp/137mph).

Constructing cars that would be judged classics in the Nineties was not to support BMW fortunes of the Fifties. From 1952–58 the company built nearly 9,000 of the 501, a similar number of the 502 and less than 4,000 of the saloons in V8 trim. The sports V8s were even rarer: just 407 of the 1956–59 BMW 503 2+2 and only 252 of the 507. In comparison 450 of the 1978–81 M1 supercar were constructed, and 49 of those were to Procar racing specification.

BMW had developed cheaper models; the Isetta 600 being later developed into the flat-twin-cylinder format that yielded just 19.5bhp at 4,500rpm. Over 161,000 Isetta-BMWs were made, the vehicle being a popular choice in the Fifties and early Sixties in Britain because it could be driven with a motorcycle licence and enjoy road tax rate concessions.

The licensing agreement with Isetta was followed by low-cost BMW development into 35,000 examples of the small 600 saloon with its distinctive narrow rear track and the conventionally tracked 700 saloons. The latter also had twin-cylinder engines, developed from the legendary motorcycle units, but their 697cc engine produced 30–40bhp. These rear-engine saloons, coupes and convertibles earned respect both commercially and competitively.

Some 181,121 of the 700-series were made between 1959–65. It is no exaggeration to say that they – and their 1955–62 Isetta-BMW predecessors – kept the company alive through the years of luxury V8 manufacture. It was obvious

that BMW needed a middleweight saloon of broader appeal to regain their prewar eminence, but first they had to stay financially afloat.

December 9, 1959 was the date of the bleakest Annual General Meeting BMW have on record, for the Deutsche Bank had decided to abandon some of their costly investment in BMW. The bank revealed a 'redevelopment plan' that amounted to a cheap buyout for Daimler Benz. Fortunately, the small BMW shareholders and committed dealers decided to fight under the leadership of Frankfurt lawyer Dr Friedrich Mathern.

The practical recovery was led by the profitable MAN truck concern. Having permission to resume aviation business, MAN management authorized a Dm 30 million loan to the battling BMW shareholders, who matched that amount in loans to BMW themselves. The inevitable resignations during heated exchanges left Deutsche Bank with much less influence over BMW, and the Quandt family (Herbert and brother Harald) with a lot more to say about company fortunes.

Herbert Quandt became the spiritual as well as financial leader that BMW needed to lead them out of the car building wilderness, amassing a fortune estimated at $3.5 *billion* in 1989. Herbert's widow, Johanna, kept a grip on the company shareholdings into the Nineties; the original Quandt stake of 15% had grown to 70%, holding over half the issued share capital from 1969 onward. From 1956–59 BMW had lost Dm 27.7 million. By 1962 they were back in the black on a modest Dm 2.5 million, and have marched forward ever since.

Limited investment during 1960 allowed a devastated BMW to invest in just the middleweight that was needed – a grandfather to the 3-series – the *Neue Klasse* 1500. The 1500 itself had a comparatively short production life (February 1962 to December 1964), but the 23,557 examples manufactured were enormously influential, for this machine defined the small sporting saloon market that BMW 3-series, Mercedes (190) and Audi (80) dominate to this day.

Within the 1500 were the basic elements of so many BMW saloons: a 30-degree slant installation for a tough SOHC motor (which made its debut in 1963 in the 1800), with iron

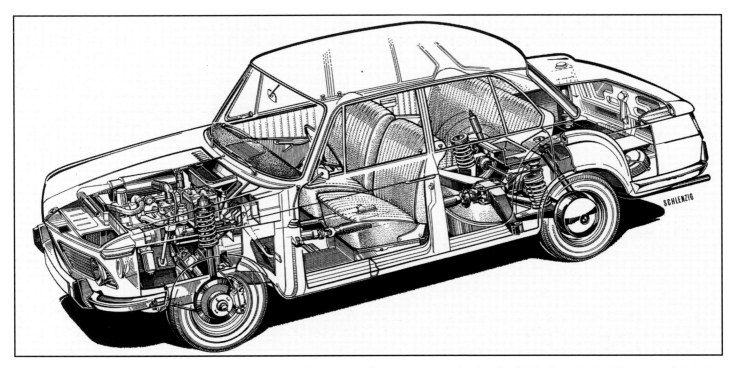

Inside the 'Neue Klasse' four-door saloons announced in 1961 prior to mass production in 1962, the principal features of the first generation of 3-series cars had already been assembled. The SOHC engine was placed upright in the 1500, but slanted to the traditional 30deg from the longer-stroke 1800 descendants onwards. A MacPherson-strut and trailing-arm suspension layout accompanied a disc and drum braking system. The four-door was much more accommodating than the first of the 3-series, a four-door version of which would not become available until 1982.

block and alloy head, trailing-arm rear suspension handing drive to the back wheels, and the faithful MacPherson strut front suspension. A mixed disc (front) and drum (rear) braking layout was employed, but with a generous 10.5in/268mm solid front disc. Other period fittings embraced 4.5 x 14in steel wheels and crossply tyres (165 SR radials were optional). Worm-and-roller steering, which had a faster lock-to-lock action (3.75 turns) than the 1982-90 production 3-series, was a traditional BMW feature until the '3' made its debut with rack and pinion in 1975.

An equal part of the tradition that preceded the 3-series

was BMW's ability to create and produce tough power units. The Sixties four-cylinder started it all, but I would emphasize that the early 'sixes' were simply stretches of their smaller brethren with an extra two cylinders. This also applied to the evolution of the competition 16-valve DOHC motors into 24-valve 'sixes'. That side of the tale has absolute symmetry because these 400bhp-plus competition 'sixes' of CSL racing coupe fame were to be followed by a return to four-cylinder power for the M3.

This happened as a result of the racing CSL unit (M49) inspiring a 277bhp limited-production motor for the M1

mid-engined supercar. Enhanced by further fuel injection development, and wet-sump lubrication, the M635 CSi ('M6' in slang) was also powered by this ex-racing unit. BMW Motorsport engineers then took two cylinders *away* from the inline 'six' for the first prototype M3 motor of the early Eighties!

In engineering the power units of the 3-series, BMW had a magnificent four-cylinder heritage to draw upon from the 1500 to 2000 four-door family and the legendary '02' lineage. The company ensured that the new '3' boasted an engine bay capable of swallowing a new breed of small-capacity 'sixes', but those were not ready for public consumption before 1977, and are the subject of a separate chapter in this *Collector's Guide.*

Therefore it was the tenacious 'fours' that took the load. These 1.5 to 2.0-litre engines were proven not just in terms of

the competition feats, but also in hard public service, so testing durability of a line that stretched back to the original 1500. The motors had appeared in every production guise from 75bhp debutante to 170bhp turbocharged version *before* a single 3-series slipped into European showrooms.

Former BMW engines chief, Alex von Falkenhausen, underlined the sports potential of the counterbalanced crankshaft (five counterweights for the 1500, eight in the 2-litre progression) when he told me in 1978: 'We used quite a light penetration of the nitriding process for these 1500 engines. Today, they still use our steel crankshaft designs for the full racing Formula 2 engines ... But the Nitriding process is heavier for this use at over 9,000rpm; we had designed the original for 6,000 revs.'

Back in the Sixties the production line 'fours' were just beginning to emerge for that *Neue Generation.* The original

Inside the '02' series, the occupants were faced with a 2+2 coupe that looked more like a saloon. Overcoming that lack of rear seat room was to become a 3-series development priority.

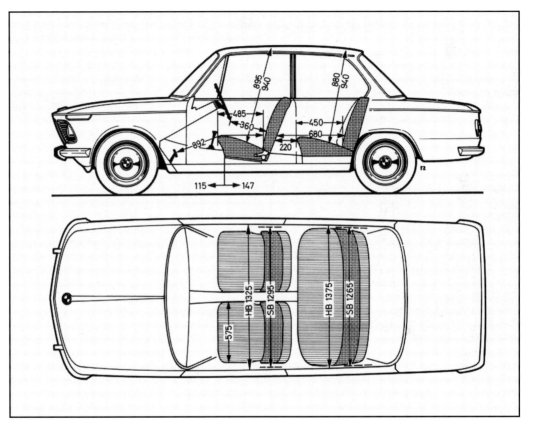

engines of 1961–64 measured 1,499cc (82 x 71mm), but in 1964 came the 1,573cc (84 x 71mm) dimensions that also served the 1602 from 1966 to 1975. More relevantly for our subject matter, this capacity powered the 1.6-litre 316s right up to the M40 motor replacement which became available in Britain in the late summer of 1988. The latter was a much improved machine – as it should have been because that 1,573cc engine had then been made for 24 years! – and it was badged 316i.

In production trim the power progression of the 316's grandfather was thus: for the BMW 1600 of 1964-66 it was rated on 83bhp at 5,500rpm; for the 1602 it was used in both single (85bhp) and twin-carburettor specification, reaching a 9.5:1 compression for the double Solex 40PHH carburettor installation, and realizing 105bhp at 6,000rpm in the 1600Ti of 1967–68.

For the 316 it was presented at 90bhp with a single Solex compound-choke carburettor and an 8.3:1 compression. Like all the first carburated 3-series engines it was capable of running 2-star leaded fuel, whilst the fuel injection engines were set up to demand 97-octane super leaded grades in Europe. A 1981 '315' variant broke the badging rules by retaining 1,573cc (it should have been a 316), and was presented as an economy alternative at 75bhp with a single Pierburg carburettor and a 9.5:1 CR.

Mid-Sixties progress led to another larger-capacity derivative that would avoid the 1500/1600 class, for in this racing class were the very fast Alfa Romeos and Lotus Cortinas. So, for sporting reasons, BMW made a car that could win its European Championship class; it was the 1800TI.

Retaining the 1600 bore of 84mm, a stroke lengthened by 9mm to 80mm brought 1,773cc and 90bhp in single-carburettor 8.6:1 compression form. The 'ti' (*Tourismo Internationale*, looking for reflected Italian glamour) version of the 1800 retained these dimensions, but grew twin Solex carburettors and a 9.5:1 compression for 110bhp during its 1964-66 span. That output was most creditable: a 2-litre Golf GTI in eight-valve, fuel-injected specification was still providing a similar 115bhp in 1992.

The 1800 TI was far from the end of the permutations BMW would wring from 1.8 litres. Initially the competition goal yielded the 1964–65 limited production 1800 TI/SA of 130bhp in 10.5:1CR double Weber carburated road trim (160bhp with easy tuning changes), but the more significant production alteration came in 1968 when the four-door 1800 saloon adopted a 1,766cc unit, which carried the original 1500/1600 steel crankshaft stroke of 71mm in association with a larger cylinder bore of 89mm, a dimension that would become a very familiar BMW statistic within later four- *and* six-cylinder engines.

The 1,766cc unit – apart from the obvious bore and stroke alteration – was statistically similar to the unit it replaced: 90bhp at 5,250rpm and unchanged maximum torque, and it even shared both its Solex carburation and an 8.6:1 compression. So why did BMW change the 1800 in August 1968?

Perhaps it was because they could now utilize common production of the 2-litre block and pistons with the 1600 crankshaft. This was part of the ease-of-production reason, but contemporary German reports also suggest that the later 1800 delivered its unaltered power with greater charm.

Seen from the Nineties, the 2-litre four-cylinders of the first

The 2002 ti was one of the most popular 2002s of all, its 120bhp coming from the 2-litre version of the engine shared with the 2000 line, which had been developed from the original 1500. The ti model was offered only with LHD and was used widely in motorsports.

3-series are ancient history, for they went out of 3-series usage (replaced by the small 'sixes' in 1977), having served only as an interim stopgap while the new 'sixes' were prepared. Nevertheless, it is worth knowing that the 1,990cc utilized that 89mm bore with the 80mm stroke of the first 1800 generation, and served with carburettor and injection within the initial 320 and 320i batches. The proven components combined to make one of the most flexible and powerfully entertaining production power units I have driven. I note that the fuel-injected 300bhp competition cousins of 320i/Formula 2 racing fame also had a broader and more reliable power spread than their contemporaries.

The 2-litre entered production in 1965 on the slant-eyed 2000 C coupes at 100bhp, or 120bhp in CS guise, but was most famous in the 2002 and 2002ti at those single- and twin-carburettor outputs. Even better as a sporting allrounder was the svelte fuel-injected 2000tii of 130bhp. For '02' usage, the von Falkenhausen team certainly explored all possibilities, peaking at 280bhp from 1,990cc, boosted by a KKK turbocharger (no intercooler!) for the 1969 European racing season, which was the first time that a turbocharged saloon had been raced under international regulations by a major manufacturer.

Such pioneering expertise did not lead to any great BMW love affair with the turbocharger for the public. There was the manufacture of 1,672 examples of the low-compression (6.9:1) 170bhp turbo 2002s, and the 1979–83 production of 3,210cc 'big six' engines for the 745i at a low boost (7:1 CR), producing 252bhp. Yet BMW – like Honda – found more prestige through racing 1.5-litre Formula 1 turbo motors than they ever discovered on the production line.

The 1500 came with a capacious four-door body, weighed 1,060kg/2,332lb and gave an initial 80bhp; BMW 1500 performance was the first target for subsequent improvement by emerging specialists such as Alpina at nearby Buchloe.

Factory fresh, 0–62mph took 16 seconds and the maximum was 92mph. Today's customer would also be rather disappointed with an average 25.7mpg to accompany that performance, but it was not far off that of a contemporary VW 1500, which was *much* slower.

Nevertheless, BMW knew their clients would very quickly expect more performance because there were 1.3-litre Alfa Romeos around that managed 95mph. Throughout the Sixties and Seventies BMW management would regard Alfa as *the* opposition in the showroom or on a circuit. Some of the earlier BMW performance derivatives were even marketed as 'ti' models, in the Alfa mould.

There were the inevitable engine enlargements to achieve extra BMW power in the Sixties. A 1,600cc overbore allowed 83bhp for the 1500 in 1964–66, but what really restored the performance saloon reputation were the 1800 and 2000 series of the later Sixties. The 1,773cc of the 1800 proved as rugged and amenable to extra power as any proper BMW power unit should be. Initially rated at 90bhp it was ultimately tweaked to 130bhp. That was in the homologation

The later fuel-injected 2000 tii was sold in RHD form and offered 130bhp. It set world standards for affordable and civilized speed during the early Seventies and BMW had to struggle later to equal its impact when restricted to four-cylinder engines in the 3-series.

The chunky 5-series donated the first 3-series a number of big-car features, particularly a clean dashboard design, with a carefully angled facia to bring controls within reach of the excellent seating. The external picture is of a 1984 218bhp M535i and the cockpit is from a 1985 M5, a car powered by a 286bhp DOHC 24-valve development of the M1 engine.

special 1800 TI/SA, which was enough to provide 116mph for public roads and 0–62mph in 9.0 seconds, figures which were recorded in 1964–65 together with a startling 17.7mpg.

However, the true father of the 3-series was not the four-door 1500 to 2000 series of saloons. Valuable though their elongated 350,729 production run from 1962 to March 1974 was in rebuilding BMW, it was the '02' (for two-door) range that made the idea of a small sporting prestige saloon a profitable proposition.

Unveiled as the 1600-2 at the 1966 Geneva motor show, the cleanly executed four-seaters were transformed when the American importer Max Hoffman had a brilliant idea. He asked for the combination of 'big engine-small car' to be implanted in the low-weight two-door by way of a 2-litre version. The resulting 2002 combined the nimble independent suspension flair of the 1600 with an extra 25bhp and excellent mid-range pulling power.

If any postwar BMW can be said to have 'made' the current BMW reputation for civilized speed, the 2002 and ever faster variants were the uplift that the BMW line needed. The '02' saloons became the Golf GTI symbol of the swinging Sixties

A trio of BMW four-cylinder engines with, on the left, one of the 3.5 million M10/12-based units in the later slant installation. Centre is the legendary M12/7 2-litre Formula 2 engine, which delivered 305bhp compared with the 130bhp of the showroom version, and on the right the Formula 1 turbo development of the M12, which in qualifying trim with the biggest of the KKK turbochargers could wring over 1,200bhp from the iron-block engine. The four-valves-per-cylinder layout shows the central-plug chamber of the M5/M635/M3 four-cylinder engine, one of the multi-valve four and six-cylinder units developed from the Formula 2 engines of the Sixties.

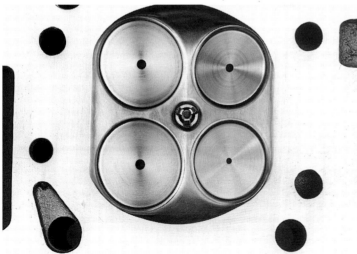

and early Seventies, in ever more unlikely shades of fashionable orange and gaudy (lime) greens as well as simple black and white.

A 2002 *could* be driven sideways through circuit corners at 100mph, just as easily as they could potter to the shop in the highest of four ratios, pulling amiably from 18.5mph and 1,000rpm. The 2002 was no performance poseur. *Motor* testers reached 111.1mph and scrabbled from 0–60mph in 9 seconds with their June 1968 RHD example. Its 100bhp and 116lb/ft of torque showed the benefit of a light kerb weight (2,240lb/1,018kg) by returning a fine 24mpg overall.

The 100bhp 2002 was a natural backbone to BMW's continuing prosperity in the late Sixties and early Seventies. From January 1968 to the summer of 1975 (July 1976 for Federal USA versions) the 2002 was not only a commercial success and a multiple European Touring Car Champion, but also spawned variants that predicted how versatile the following 3-series should become. Of an official 861,940 total

Affordable coupes from BMW have included, from the left, the 700, the '02' line and two generations of two-door 3-series cars. Here they pose behind the two-door coupe version of the E36 third-generation 3-series line.

Motoring into history, the 2002 in its later square tail-lamp turbocharged guise. The model was conceived to compete, but the fuel crisis confined it to limited road use, where its 131mph top speed and 7sec 0–60mph claims were largely unappreciated by a suddenly fuel-conscious public.

'02' production (including 21,753 Touring three-door models), the 2002 itself accounted for nearly 400,000 units, while the 1602 was the other big seller, recording over 260,000 units.

The whole range proved capable of absorbing variants like the Touring and Baur Cabriolet bodies (nearly 4,000 were made on 1602 and 2002 bases), although the numbers of variants sold were far, far, lower than would be the case for the 3-series.

The 2002 provided a race and rally base for further performance that was translated in road variants such as the

120bhp twin-carburettor ti and a 130bhp fuel-injected tii. The 2002 Turbo, Europe's first turbo production car (yes, it preceded the Porsche 911 and Saab), had an exhilarating 170bhp and 130mph capability in 1973. It was the rarest 2002 variant, hitting the fuel crisis head-on and selling only 1,672 copies from a January 1974 to June 1975 production run.

The '02', whether preening itself in the showroom, mastering a circuit, or bounding through a rally special stage, would certainly be the toughest of acts to follow.

CHAPTER 2

The first 3-series

A small sports saloon with big-car features

The two-door that would become the definitive small, sports, prestige saloon was announced to the German press and international LHD markets in the first week of July 1975. The first 3-series was also available in RHD form comparatively early, arriving in Britain during October of the same year carrying 316, 320 and 320i badges and priced from £3,649 to £5,237. The 'fours' exceeded £5,000 by 1976, when the 320i listed at £5,237. It was 1979 before the cheapest model in the range exceeded £5,000; the original 3-series did not breach £10,000 in the UK, except as a Baur Cabriolet 323i, a combination that retailed at £10,547 in 1980.

The first 3-series entered production in Munich under its E21 factory coding in June 1975. Initially, only four-cylinder 316 and 318 (not UK) saloons were made, as the fuel-injected 320i was not constructed until October 1975. That was the official UK debut month, but my factory source, which supplied production history catalogues, list RHD manufacture as beginning in November 1975 and American LHD models from July 1976 (California: September 1976).

It was obvious from the start that BMW engineers had more time and money than could ever have been lavished on their Sixties saloons. The result was that the smallest BMW product was also the most thoroughly developed and it inherited some of its 'instant maturity' from the earlier 5-series. It especially owed a debt to the 5-series in a new family look and what would become the most imitated of car cockpit ergonomics.

In outline the first of the new 3-series sounded much like the '02' series: front engine and strut suspension, rear drive with trailing-arm independent layout. A glance at the larger 3-series body with its more serious attempt to accommodate rear-seat passengers (the 2002 and 1602 were often marketed as coupes) showed the potential for development, particularly in an engine bay that BMW freely admitted would welcome six-cylinder power in subsequent derivatives.

It is worth recalling that a four-door body for the 3-series was not available until the November 1982 body and engine overhaul of the total range. Remember, also, that the first (E21) series continued in low production volumes past its 'sell by' date, or at least the economy-minded 315 was retailed alongside the second (E30) generation for much of the opening sales year and was not dropped from production until 1983.

The 1975 debutante was the product of a five-year development period and an investment of Dm 35 million. The team was headed by Bernhard Osswald, a Swabian. Whereas the '02' series was originally intended to be confined to smaller cars with engines ranging from 1.3 litres upwards, although in the event it was sold with no engine smaller than 1.6 litres, the 3-series was planned to take engines of at least 2 litres and six cylinders from the start.

Overall length was increased by 105mm/4.1in over the '02', totalling 4,355mm/171.5in with a wheelbase of 2,563mm/100.9in. Other 3-series comparisons versus '02' were: wheelbase increased from 2,500mm to 2,563mm; front and rear track went from 1,348mm on the '02' to 1,364mm/1,377mm on all 3-series except the 320i, which ran on a broader 1,386mm/1,399mm stance.

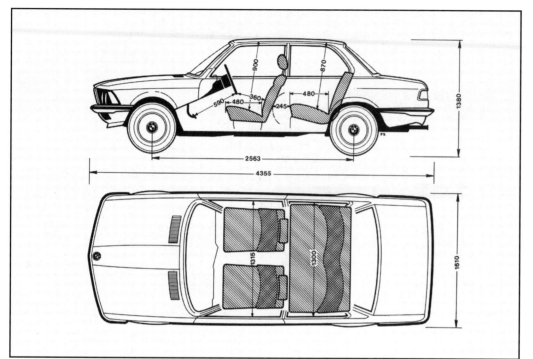

The provision of extra internal space compared with its predecessor, the 2002, was a design priority in the packaging of the 3-series body.

Most of the 3-series' extra length was accounted for by bumpers of increased impact resistance, each bumper extending 40mm beyond that of the '02', or a total of 80mm in all. Thus BMW worked with very similar body dimensions to the '02', but managed to extract a full inch (25mm) in the seating breadth, although the total body fattening was only 20mm/0.78in. Overall height was lofty by sports saloon standards, totalling 1,380mm/54.3in. This was within fractions of the front track dimensions (1,387mm/54.6in), but the back was wider still at 1,396mm/55in.

Such gains naturally imposed a weight penalty, but were nothing compared with those that would be seen from Audi Volkswagen in the early Nineties. The original 1602 weighed in at 920kg/2,024lb, but the last test 1502 for *Auto Motor und Sport* had accrued 1,020kg/2,244lb. The starter model of the

new 3-series range, sharing the 1.6-litre capacity of the two examples quoted (a 1502 betrayed BMW nomenclature, running at 1.6 litres rather than the logical 1.5 litres) came in at exactly 1,020kg. This was a fine engineering achievement for a body that was showing strength gains of close to 20% in prototype trim.

BMW gave the 3-series a conservative sporting demeanour whilst continuing their rigid family class system. The kidney grille and central section and the hooked surround to the rear side glass were important to preserve corporate identity, while the 316, 318, 320 and 320i badges identified the three carburated models and one with injection. The adoption of four headlamps on 2-litre cars and just two headlamps for the 1.6- and 1.8-litre models ensured an instant status rating.

Anti-corrosion work was evident from the first of the 3-

The smaller four-cylinder 3-series cars, the 316 and 318, were awarded single-headlamp status, double units being reserved for the more powerful 320 and 320i variants.

The original line-up, in the original script, covering all the initial four-cylinder manufacture.

series. Looking over a 10-year-old 3-series you will see that BMW claims for extended durability are justified, some British street-domiciled decade-old machines showing more showroom gloss than three-year-old examples of brand X.

Taken overall, the concept of the first generation of the 3-series was unremarkable in engineering terms, but beautifully executed. BMW believed they enjoyed a quartet of plus points over their legendary '02' line. These were safety, comparative silence, space and aerodynamics. What they did not know was that the 3-series would mature so successfully that BMW would prise open a unique section of the market, leading to proliferation of clones and vast profits.

The smallest advance of the 3-series over an '02' was the combination of increased space and bluffer frontal area. There was, at best, a marginal gain on the aerodynamic front from 0.44/0.45Cd to 0.43, the 320 front spoiler bringing the fat-wheeled '02' and the 3-series to parity in this respect.

Safety was emphasized by the BMW engineering assertion

Clean-cut outline of the first 3-series generation was unmatched by any rival, as was the durability of the overhead-camshaft engines with chain drive, mileages beyond 200,000 having since been reported.

that banishing the fuel tank to beneath the rear seat had increased the available crumple zone by some 74% compared with an '02'. The quoted bodyshell resistance to torsional forces was increased by 18%.

Thankfully one tradition was maintained, and remains with all BMW cars to this day: the best of toolkits was located in a bootlid compartment. Within it was a BMW selec-tion of grips, spanners, pliers, screwdrivers and assorted quality repair tools.

Another BMW tradition that was maintained throughout the first two editions of the 3-series was the forward-hinged bonnet. I think this is the safest antidote to an unlatched bonnet being airlifted over the screen. Yet BMW have now eliminated its effective linkages and struts in favour of a conventional rear-hinged bonnet for post-1990 3-series cars.

The inside story was dominated by the theme of taking big-car features and transplanting them at the beginning of the range. There was a four-spoke steering wheel like that of the '5', and quadruple black and white dials were the standard issue for the first 3-series. For the 320 these lined up as a large speedometer (120mph, RHD; 200km/h in LHD) and matching tachometer, with the redline beginning around 6,500 for most variants.

Flanking the primary display in each corner were the fuel and water temperature dials. An analogue clock sat in the centre. Both dash panel and facia were aligned to bring the driver a feeling of being totally in command, rather in the manner of a simplified light aeroplane. Each dial or control was apparently equidistant and within a hand span of prompt response.

A quartet of separate quadrant heater/ventilation controls were backed by a rotary knob to set fan speed, whilst the cigarette lighter and aforesaid quartz clock curved around to the left of a British driver. The heating and ventilation capability of the 3-series was succinctly summarized by Clive Richardson of *Motor Sport*: 'as splendid as that of the 2002 was poor.'

The 5-series seat transplant, usually in cloth with high-quality plastic surrounds outside the centre panels, was also praised by many as 'typically BMW: firm but with support where the body demands it, and so relaxing in conjunction with a good driving position.'

The cleverly combined head/side/facia light cum rheostat pull/twist switch sat on the right, along with the heated rear screen switch. Such facia lighting was also widely copied because it hinted at aeronautical pretensions, offering a soft orange glow that was much kinder to the eyes than white light.

The gains in 'comparative silence' on the first 3-series were to increase cabin comfort significantly. These could be summarized as primarily benefiting rear-seat passengers for they received some soundproofing attention that had been totally absent on the '02' line! Quantified, BMW said they had offered a 68% bonus in sound absorbent materials and that the interior noise level had dropped between six and eight decibels: subjectively this amounts to a virtual halving in perceived sound levels. The biggest contribution to defeating the annoyances of living with the lovable '02' was the efficient sealing of the side glass to eliminate the hiss displayed by an '02' at serious speeds.

The dynamic philosophy for the 3-series was tilted toward comfort over ultimate handling, but the principles of strut front suspension and trailing-arm rear remained in place, to be overhauled in conscientious detail. The most obvious replacement felt through the driver's palms was the imposition of the now almost standard mass-production feature: rack-and-pinion steering.

BMW recognized the inevitable, and switched to a ZahnradFabrik (ZF) rack-and-pinion system geared at 21:1. This was considerably slower than the gearing offered on the 2002 (17.3:1), and became a life-long bugbear on all 3-series, outside the M3, demanding a shuffle of more than four turns lock-to-lock. Admittedly, the steering was light enough to park, but it became a chore in sports motoring or tight manoeuvres.

The Germanic four-spoke steering wheel was actually smaller than that of its predecessor at 380mm/15in instead of 400mm/15.75in. Power steering and slightly swifter ratios

Front and rear views of the 320 provide a reminder that a front badge was not thought necessary, but one at the back was a (frequently deleted) feature. The 320 had a slightly more muscular version of the single exhaust than the smaller four-cylinder models.

Steel wheels were a far more common standard feature on LHD cars in continental Europe than in the UK, but all the first 3-series cars retained two doors and the 'dogleg' outline of the rear windows.

The 3-series set new standards in instrumentation clarity, driver comfort and logical layout. The analogue clock was to make its reappearance after a spell flirting with digital timekeeping in the Eighties.

(19:1) were first offered on post-1977 six-cylinder models.

Also new was the braking system, comprising a mixed disc/drum layout on the 1975–83 four-cylinder models. The German press were not impressed by the abandonment of double for single calipers in the transition from '02' to 3-series, but nobody ever seriously complained that the 3-series was under-braked. The four-cylinders all shared a 250mm/9.8in front disc and 255mm/10in rear drum (only the rears being significantly larger than those of the '02'). There was no ABS for small cars in those days, and rear disc brakes were reserved for the subsequent 323i in the first 3-series.

Compared with its predecessor, the strut/trailing arms system was substantially revised. The front struts, with their eccentrically mounted coil springs, were raked rearward at the top mount, and the bottom wishbones were forged instead of pressed steel. An anti-rollbar was incorporated on *all* models instead of the '02' restriction to higher performance models. A simplified bar layout was used that was cheaper than the optional unit of the '02' series.

The rear axle progressed from separated coil spring and

The engine bay of the carburettor 'fours' was as logically laid out as the cockpit. A useful feature, widely imitated, was the transparent fuse-box (visible at the nearside of the engine bay). The linkage for the forward-hinged bonnet is a mechanism that survived the second-generation 3-series, but not the 1990 E36 edition.

telescopic damper units (the shock absorbers aft of the springs) to a combined spring/strut layout that was based on stronger semi-trailing arms. These were backed by a differential brace that fought rear-wheel steering tendencies.

British road test comment tended toward acidic on the 'softly, softly' suspension philosophy. *Motor Sport* in February 1977 stated of the recently arrived RHD 320i: 'the front is now far too soft and the rear too stiff. The 320i wallows soggily at its front end and when pushed really hard, exhibits considerable body roll. At the same time the rear roll stiffness, increased over both 2002 and 320, causes the inside rear wheel to pick up far too easily, resulting in pretty abysmal traction in most circumstances.'

Elongated springs were a feature of this softened BMW

approach to sports motoring. At the front BMW travelled from the '02' figure of 180mm/7.1in to 192mm/7.6in, whilst the backs were stretched to 208mm/8.2in from the '02' statistic of 170mm/6.7in. BMW attributed these spring changes and unspecified damper setting modifications to a 25% overall drop in front end suspension stiffness, allied to a dramatic 40% escalation of rear rates compared with the '02'.

Significantly, BMW uprated the suspension for 1977. Front spring rates rose, along with firmer damper settings and rollbar thickness. Conversely, the back rates were dropped 10%, the accent being on bump settings rather than rebound. This was also claimed by BMW to 'reduce road noise transmission to the bodywork'.

Seen from the Nineties, the power train engineering was

The 1975 interior combined typical BMW virtues of durability and function with a pronounced extra effort towards enhancing safety. Despite the priority given to increasing interior space, the back bench area was still cramped to the level where the two-door was frequently described as a coupe.

quite advanced, BMW being very aware about the needs of their home market in regard to lower-octane and, finally, low-lead fuels.

For the 1975–77 span, only four-cylinder engines were supplied and all had been overhauled from earlier BMW lives. Dominating the development programme was the increasing availability of low-lead fuels with consequently deflated octane ratings. All the 3-series models were designed with unleaded fuels in mind for their LHD environment, such petrol becoming widely available in Germany during 1976. In the UK the leaded/unleaded fuel picture was not quite so simple, as unleaded fuels did not become a serious factor until the late Eighties and a second generation of 3-series.

Expect at least an ignition adjustment to be necessary before any of the original 3-series cars can safely be run on cheaper unleaded petrols. There were good technical reasons for suggesting that customers used unleaded in BMWs manufactured prior to September 1984, but I took the precaution of a leaded tankful at every fourth fill-up.

28

For Britain, the 3-series was a welcome P-plate arrival. This is the range's starting point, a carburated 316, a badge which later also covered carburettor versions of the 1.8-litre engine.

BMW engine development of three single overhead camshaft (SOHC) carburated motors (1.6, 1.8 and 2.0 litres) and the ex-BMW 520i K-Jetronic fuelled 2-litre concentrated on lowered compression ratios and modestly elevated peak rpm to compensate. The injected engine was actually the only unit to survive with its previous compression (9.3:1) intact, the product of a later design period.

Illustrating the extended rpm were statistics for the 2002 and its 320 spiritual successor. Both were officially rated at 16Mkg/116lb/ft torque, but the earlier car was peaking at 3,500rpm whereas the 320 needed 3,700rpm. It was much the same story in power, but here the low-compression (8:1) 320 was 9bhp better off than the 2002, hitting a 5,800rpm peak rather than 5,500. The 320 gained much of its power advantage with a compound Solex 32/32 DIDTA carburettor.

The higher-rpm new generation of BMWs were liable to extract a fuel consumption penalty when compared with their predecessors. The 320 was a good example, its final drive numerically raised from 3.64 to 3.9:1 (partially to compensate for unexpected weight gains of more than 224lb compared with the equivalent 2002). Some magazines recorded 21 to 23mpg, which was close to the 22.2 Urban mpg recorded by BMW engineers in testing.

Autocar managed nearly 25mpg overall in the first 320 they tested, took 9.8 seconds on sprinting from rest to 60mph and recorded 111mph. The fuel-injected 320i, intended to assuage the performance demand until the six-cylinder 320i/323i could be readied (see following chapter), recorded a lower 0–60mph time of 9.6 seconds and a modest gain in maximum speed to 113mph.

By comparison, the same magazine had recorded maxima of 107 and 116mph for the 2002 and its fuel-injected 2002tii cousin, and to 10.1 and 8.3 seconds for the 0–60mph runs. The 2002 returned 25.5mpg, and 25.4mpg was the reward for fuel injection in the 2002tii. Therefore it was no wonder that the first four-cylinder 320i was seen only as an understudy that awaited the six-cylinder touch.

In the wake of the winter 1973/74 fuel crisis, privately owned BMW Concessionaires GB Ltd (the factory waited until January 1980 to take over the company completely)

Detail aerodynamics on the first 3-series included the abbreviated black spoiler and under-bumper air intakes.

were impatient to have the 3-series. At that time the 1602 began the UK range at £2,099 and the efficient 2002tii cost £3,445. These were stiffish prices, as a Mini was still less than £1,000 at the time and a Jaguar E-type S3 with V12 power was not much more expensive than the fuel-injected 2002, costing just £3,743.

By October 1975 the UK concessionaires, then owned by Tozer Kemsley & Milbourn, were ready to market three model lines in the common two-door body. They were the 316 at an initial £3,429, the carburated 320 at £4,039, and the 320i was – temporarily – assigned flagship duties for a price tag of £4,749, a figure which says a little about inflationary forces of the period.

Tackling the thorny question of how to succeed an already much loved '02' range, Raymond Playfoot, manager of the

UK press department, said in his briefing: 'although retaining the classic combination of efficiency and performance that made the 2002 a model that will live in motoring history, the '3' models are another 10-year step forward in development. With their improved engines, better steering and handling, greater interior space and luxury, and advanced safety techniques, the new compact range possess the virtues of the larger BMWs, but with these virtues further refined and adapted.' BMW themselves had this all neatly summarized as: 'not a larger small car, but a smaller large car.'

Despite the prices, the 3-series soon found acceptance in Britain, and a number of significant running changes should be noted. August 1977 saw important production improvements that filtered through to the UK from January 1978. Amongst these were an enlarged fuel tank (58 litres/13 UK gallons) and replacement cloth trims, including a swap from Gentian Blue to Marine (the imagination boggles) and 'additional interior equipment colour cloth and leatherette fern green, door covering and panelling with changed pattern,' the export department told BMW Concessionaires, adding that the optional limited-slip differential now had a locking value of 40% rather than the mild 25% that existed prior to June 1977 production.

As production numbers increased, the number of models proliferated, but running changes were minimal through the late Seventies. The 1978 break saw a number of fine detail changes within. Nearly every BMW from 316 to 635CSi was bequeathed 'front seats with strengthened backrests and seat cushion area of improved shape on 3- and 5-series.'

There was also the promise of 'more comfortable springing, enlarged back support area and greater lateral lumbar support.' It was at this August 1978 point that rear headrests were adopted from 316 to 323i. Other internal progressions embraced scissors-type winding mechanisms for the notably smooth-moving windows and an enlarged internal rear-view mirror. Incidentally, electric window options then picked up a manual failsafe auxiliary fitting.

Externally, the biggest change was to flatten and blacken the model emblems throughout the BMW line. Potentially the most important development for customers at this stage was the adoption of a disc brake pad monitor. The warning light was installed on the 3-series in place of a low fuel warning. For the four-cylinder models the sensor was mounted on the front left brake unit.

For April 1980 the British importers built increased value into the 3-series, which now spanned £5,300 to nearly £8,000. They equipped all 3-series cars with an electric door mirror, tinted glass, and locking for both the fuel filler cap and the glove box. In September 1980 (W-plate) BMW improved,

Ignore the cheeky child and note the fuel flap for the filler orifice or look at the finely detailed toolkit that is still a feature of contemporary BMWs.

and confused, the 316. It was now made with the LHD 318 engine (1,766cc/90bhp/single Solex carburettor), yet the badge remained resolutely '316'. The other good news for Britons was that the price also remained static at £5,355.

The company claimed 'a top speed of more than 100mph and a 0–60mph time of 12.2 seconds'. BMW supplied fuel consumption figures for both the standard four-speed and the £274 optional five-speed gearbox. Those consumption figures were 25.7 Urban mpg; 41.5mpg at 56mph for the four-speed (45.6mpg for the overdrive-equipped five-speed). At 75mph BMW quoted 30.4mpg for the four-speed and 34mpg from the five-speed model.

The five-speed transmission became standard in January 1983. *Autocar* returned 101mph, 0–60mph in 12.1 seconds and an overall 26.7mpg from a five-speed version. All this made the larger-engine 316 less of a performance embarrassment in the UK versus the breed of hot new hatchbacks.

There was one further development of the 316 that was aimed purely at the UK market. In January 1983 a special batch of starter 316i hybrids was made that allied RHD with the popular LHD 318i motor (1,766cc/105bhp/Bosch K-Jetronic) and the E21 body. This shared the UK market price lists briefly with the later (E30) 3-series, priced at £6,250 in January 1983. The 316i was dropped from production in September 1983. As for 106,312 other examples of the 3-series, it was made in Dingolfing, whilst the majority (1.25 million) of the first series came from Munich.

In four-cylinder guise, the 3-series was not the most vivid of motor cars that Munich created, but it sold more strongly than its predecessor. Including the six-cylinder variants, which we detail in the following chapter, over 1.36 million were made.

The most popular '3s' were those run under the 316 title (337,034), but the 318 was closer at more than 192,000 than we might have expected with only short run availability in the UK. If the 318i is added, some 285,773 were manufactured.

BMW found the car sales land of milk and honey with the original 3-series an unexplored high-profit niche. At launch time the 3-series really had no direct opposition in Germany as the Mercedes 190 would not be available until November 1982. It made its debut with four doors rather than two, but by that time BMW had the second-generation 3-series ready with the promise of four doors in 1983.

Indeed, the original 3-series' peak production year of 1981 hit the kind of 220,000-plus annual output that would interest Ford, or any other volume European manufacturer, particularly at the profitable prices BMW could demand for their unique cocktail of quality, pace and accessible prestige. It would be 1984 before the second-generation 3-series exceeded that rate of annual production.

CHAPTER 3

The six-cylinder 3-series

A smooth way of expanding the class

When BMW deliberately engineered a six-cylinder future for their smallest car, they created a new class that outflanked their principal home market rivals, and one that has never been completely understood by those rivals who have sought to emulate the BMW formula for profit.

Writing this in 1992 it was obvious that Mercedes had tried to respond with their 190E-2.6, but they missed the essential point: the BMW small 'six' was specifically engineered for BMW's most diminutive offering, not transplanted from middleweight duties.

This would matter to the customer because the tailor-made BMW motor was manufactured to fit the 3-series engine bay and had the smallest external dimensions possible for that duty. If BMW had wanted to insert one of their large 'sixes', it would have meant compromising the balance of the 3-series, as well as accepting the kind of squeeze on underbonnet space that is a characteristic of some aftermarket conversions (often badged as 335i). Even the best of them – and I talk after experience of an Alpina E30 with some 260bhp – lose the essential agility that is part of 3-series appeal.

That appeal was certainly realized by the introduction of the carburated 320 (often referred to as the 320-6, to delineate between it and the preceding 320/320i four-cylinders) and the fuel-injected 323i. Taking the 320 as an example, its best production year (1977) was but 53,560 examples whereas the 323i exceeded that figure in 1978 with 61,402 cars and peaked at 65,369 the following year.

At the top of the range the 320i-4 and the 323i were not dissimilar in their best production years – both exceeding 30,000 pa – but the four-cylinder enjoyed only one year above 30,000 (32,322 in 1977) whereas the 323i stayed above 31,000 for three years (1980 was the best year, when 36,424 were made) and performed strongly into the Eighties until it was replaced by the 1982 E30 outline.

It is worth recalling that BMW were making 200,000 *less* vehicles per annum than they were at the dawn of the Nineties, so every 3-series variety provided a welcome broadening of appeal on the road to 500,000 pa production.

In August 1977 production began of a completely new BMW six-cylinder breed, its power unit known by the motor code M60 and later it evolved into the M20. It was the first BMW engine to use a belt to drive an overhead camshaft, and the first truly new BMW engine since 1961. The larger 'sixes' were developed from the 'fours' and closely followed some of their key dimensions. BMW have only trusted belt drive for some recent single-overhead-camshaft layouts, reserving chain drive for the DOHC (M50) successor that is now installed in the current 320i/325i. Chain-driven cams were specified for the M42 unit of the old 318is saloon, the 1992 Coupe, the old M3 and all SOHC big-capacity (3.0 to 3.5 litres) 'sixes', plus the 5-litre V12.

For the 3-series the arrival of a new six-cylinder in 2-litre carburated and 2.3-litre fuel-injected guises was crucial to the planned expansion of BMW output. The 320-6 was never intended as a performance substitute for a 323i, yielding 122.4bhp versus 143bhp and losing nearly 30% on the torque curve.

In the Eighties, further derivatives of the inline 'six' would be

The engine bay of the E21 3-series always had six cylinders in mind. This is the 320i version with drum rear brakes, quadruple lamps and a carburated version of the M60 SOHC engine. Note the use of angled front struts and coaxial rear coil spring/damper units on the first 3-series cars.

seen which would yield both of the respected 2.4-litre diesels (the turbocharged version following a normally aspirated unit) and the bold 'eta' energy conservation petrol unit: a 2.7-litre which brought the six-cylinder and 3-series together for the first time in American and Japanese showrooms, but which was not officially imported into the UK.

The first incarnation M60 motor was not a revolution in its 1977 guise. An iron block and alloy SOHC head construction were wrapped around 12-valve principles, but it undeniably set new standards of smooth power delivery. The slant 'six' (still tilted at 30 degrees to the right) was to feature in the 3- and 5-series, although in the latter case it was initially only provided in carburated 2-litre form. The 2.3-litre was reserved as the sporting apogee of the 3-series, intended to 'consign even the successful 2002tii to obscurity', in BMW PR prose.

Developed through the Seventies by a team that included Motorsport legend Paul Rosche, the M60 was asked to produce over 60bhp per litre on super fuel grades, and compression ratios of 9.2:1 (320) and 9.5:1 for the 323i. The crossflow aluminium head retained the V-formation of two valves per cylinder (it would be the Nineties before the long anticipated four-valve layout made its debut in the small 'sixes', and then only the 5-series had such power units initially) but the single camshaft - like the spheroidal cast-iron crankshaft - enjoyed the luxury of running in seven bearings.

The crankshaft was superbly counterbalanced by the action of 12 counterweights, and it seemed as suave at 6,500rpm as at half that crankshaft speed. Induction for the 320 was by a single Solex 4A1 carburettor whilst Bosch K-Jetronic fuel injection served the 323i unit during its 1977–82 initial span. As a direct comparison, the 1,990cc short-stroke (80 x 66mm) M60 developed 13bhp more than its carburated 89 x 80mm 2-litre predecessor and only 3bhp less than the fuel-injected 320i-4.

Such a short-stroke bias showed up particularly strongly at 2 litres on the torque curves. The four-cylinder offered a bonus of 127lb/ft at 5,500rpm versus 118lb/ft at 4,000rpm for the new 'six'. Naturally, the 2,315cc and its elongated (76.8mm) stroke disposed of the four-cylinder torque superiority, yielding 140lb/ft.

To accommodate the inline 'six', a smaller but more efficiently cored, crossflow radiator was adopted, carrying an electric fan in front of it. That was the implication of the launch, but subsequent research leads me to believe that a viscous coupled fan was thermostatically controlled for the majority of 320/323s sold.

The electrical system was also uprated, taking a 65 ampere alternator and 44 amp/hour battery. Incidentally, most UK vehicles should have transistorized ignition, although the 320-6 did not adopt this feature in LHD until August 1978.

Despite BMW claims at the launch of the new 'sixes', it was found that there was also a fuel consumption penalty in operating a 'six' instead of one of those well-proven 'fours'. It was this fuel appetite that prevented the arrival in the Eighties of a small performance 'six' in the 3-series for Americans. BMW just could not afford to upset the fuel consumption balance of their range in the USA, so it was with a 325e that the company belatedly offered North Americans something

more than 1.8 litres and four cylinders in 1984 (it entered production in October 1983).

Transmission changes to suit six cylinders included a larger Fichtel and Sachs clutch, and replacement, beefier gears for the standard four-speed; in Britain it was 1981 before an overdrive five-speed was offered, and there is always the later possibility of an optional close-ratio set being installed, identified by a direct (1:1) fifth. From the start an optional ZF HP22 three-speed automatic was available and, as for the initial standard manual four-speed gearbox, ratios were shared between the 2- and 2.3-litre small 'sixes'. An overall difference in gearing resulted from a 3.64:1 final drive for the 320-6 and 3.45 for the 323i. As in the case of the gearboxes, much of the transmission technology could be traced back to '02' ancestry, particularly the ratios employed.

The ZF automatic transmission proved a reasonably popular option, representing fractionally under 51% of all the 320-6s made in RHD. Not all were for the UK, but the October 1978-September 1982 totals of 320-6 RHD output

The tidy 323i in original LHD trim with steel wheels and no sunroof. Visual identification clues included the grille badge and oversize 185/70 HR-13 tyres on 5.5J wheel rims.

The 320 was reborn as a carburated six-cylinder for the British market. This picture illustrates the small under-bumper blade-style spoiler, slotted 5.5 x 13in steel wheels and 185 tyres, all shared with the 323i. Also note the wide use of chrome surrounds and the effective side rubbing strips with tough rubber inlays.

showed that 9,960 Getrag manual gearbox models were accompanied by 5,036 ZF automatics.

The 323i entered LHD manufacture in January 1978 and RHD was initiated in March of that year; it was on sale by May 1978. BMW collectors might like to note that 1977 saw 35 LHD pilot-built examples, plus a pair of RHD fore-runners. Output naturally ran some way behind the 320-6, but from 1979 to 81, when the factory production lines were up to full speed, the sales ratio between 320 and 323 was roughly 2:1. Some 137,107 of the 323i were made between 1977 and 1982 compared with 270,445 of the 320-6.

The 320-6 arrived in Britain first, retailing at £4,999; it was made in Munich from October 1978 and sold in the UK from January 1979. The 320-6 was trimmed to much the same level as the 320i-4, but it is worth noting that the company started to offer power steering as an option that may be valued in any secondhand purchase. The standard layout was a ZF 21:1 rack-and-pinion that called for a cumbersome 4.05 turns lock-to-lock.

Specification differences between ostensibly similar inline six-cylinder 3-series were that the original 320-6 did not offer rear disc brakes (the 323i always did) and that the 320-6 was not fuel-injected. The first 320-6 of the 3-series were carburated by a complex four-barrel Solex 4 A1, rather than the Bosch K-Jetronic of the 323i, so both fuel consumption and service bills for the 320-6 were higher than necessary.

At less than £5,000, the 320-6 carried a great deal of detail engineering that enabled it to face up to British market opposition, which was then headed by an Alfa Romeo Alfetta 2000 at £4,800, £4,168 for a Ford RS2000, and £4,898 for a Triumph Dolomite Sprint.

For the 'sixes', front disc brakes grew approximately half an inch and were the same diameter as the 323i front units at around 10in (255mm). Yet the 323i used a fully vented unit of 22mm/0.87in thickness, whereas the 320-6 retained a solid unit of 12.7mm (half an inch) depth. A 320-6 used rear drums rather than discs, commanded via a 9in Mastervac servo. They shared their 10.16in diameter with all but the 316.

Running what were referred to simply as uprated springs and dampers, the 320-6 and 323i were given replacement 5.5J x 13in standard steel wheels which boosted the rear track by a notional 3mm. There were also front and rear anti-rollbars slightly thickened at the back - to restrain body lean on both the 'sixes'; in fact BMW factory literature no longer showed a rear anti-rollbar for the four-cylinder models, reserving it as standard equipment on the 320-6 and 323i, whilst noting that the front bar on the 320-6 was 'stiffened.'

Standard 185/70 HR rubber promised more grip than the four-cylinder set-up of 165-section tyres on the previous 320, although it is worth noting that the 320i did sport 185-section covers. Experienced from the Nineties, neither grip nor manners were a patch on the ubiquitous Hot Hatches, or the current E36, but it is possible to make significant improvements at reasonable cost and preserve the period look of these significant 'sixes'.

A six-cylinder 3-series showed natural weight gains, but approximately 50lb of that was due to the extra two cylinders in the engine bay, which it countered by elevated spring and damper rates in the nose. Compared with the 320-4, the 320-6 was heavier by 95kg/209lb at the kerb.

Full *Autocar & Motor* performance figures are given in the appendix, but BMW claims were realistic. They are reproduced in full below. For comparison, *Autocar* results of the Seventies can be summarized as: 111mph maximum speed, 0–60mph in 9.8 seconds and 24.6mpg overall.

BMW CLAIMED PERFORMANCE: 320-6
(Autumn 1977, four-speed manual)

Km/h	Mph	Seconds
0–50	31	3.4
0–80	50	7.2
0–100	62	10.7
0–120	75	15.8
0–140	87	22.7
0–400 metres		17.4

Max speed: 112mph
DIN fuel consumption, converted to mpg, was 29.7.

The 323i in more usual British trim with optional BBS alloy wheels to the fore. The largest changes were hidden away, including the K-Jetronic fuel-injected engine with a claimed 143bhp. A quartet of disc brakes were installed and the suspension was uprated, particularly at the front (using 7-series damping rates), and anti-rollbars were enlarged front and rear.

My own driving experience included the debut of the 320-6 in France. I noted that it had a very accessible torque curve, 'in fact 93.5lb/ft torque, or more, is provided between 2,000 and 6,200rpm, and it is this flexible power that dominated our drive.' I concluded: 'The complete 320-6 is very, *very* good value at £5,000. Look at what you get for £5,000 today and I think this small "six" is a very attractive sporting proposition.'

The smaller 'sixes' prompted a larger (58-litre) fuel tank on all models. Petrol was now stored under the seats and within a designated crumple zone for enhanced safety over the original design. Replacement door and seat trims were also introduced at this point.

By February 1979 Munich were listing the availability of the overdrive (0.813) five-speed gearbox and claiming a bonus of 1.4mpg at a constant 75mph (28 versus 29.4mpg with the standard four-speed) for the 320-6. Performance claims for the automatic were more pessimistic than usual. Munich reported 0-62mph in 13.6 seconds and more than 19 seconds for 0-75mph as against 15.8 seconds with the manual four-speed gearbox.

A digital time display had replaced the neat analogue central clock by early 1979, its red digits displayed beneath the tachometer of LHD models. Fuel economy concerns were acknowledged by BMW with a narrowing green section to the low end of the rev-counter to encourage fuel-consciousness. On the 1982 version of the 323, the band thinned dramatically at 4,000rpm and expired at 5,500. This meant the harmony of BMW instrumentation was temporarily interrupted, for the red section began just below 6,500rpm, leading to a most uncharacteristic riot of colour. Black and white order was soon back in place, but a formal 'econometer' has been a feature of most subsequent 3-series bar the M3. The analogue clock also returned for later 3-series editions. Incidentally, 3-series gained extensive interior trim changes and head restraints in time for autumn 1980 sales, all inspired by the example of the 7-series.

Baur of Stuttgart convertible bodywork came to Britain for September 1980, this being one of the early models brought in by the new factory management in January 1980.

An official factory convertible was produced in the second generation, but the Baur body was a halfway house between Targa and full convertible styles. It had plastic roof panels separated from a fabric rear hood section by an elegant, but safety-conscious hoop. Baur continued to be involved in the second-series convertible business. In Britain, six-cylinder E30 convertibles had the factory's full convertible style, but four-cylinder E30s came from Baur.

The five-speed gearbox became a showroom item that was only previewed in June 1982. A factory letter advised us that 'as of works holiday '82, all six-cylinder (manual) models will be fitted with the five-speed overdrive as standard equipment.' Helpfully it added that the five-speed could also be optionally ordered for the less powerful four-cylinders. At this point the redline on the 320-6 was reduced by 200rpm and was reflected on the tachometers of vehicles built after August 1982. The original thin red warning band was from 6,400 to 6,800rpm.

UK customers generally opted for the highest possible specification. The factory reaction was a July 1982 'special' that foretold the subsequent successful spread of the 'SE' extra-equipment marketing designation down the range from its initial 7-series appearance.

The 3-series UK-market specials consisted of manual and automatic variants of the 320-6 and 323i. The extra equipment was offered for a £8,317 total on the 320, and some £9,063 in automatic guise. The specials represented good value in contemporary terms, for the basic 320-6 exceeded £8,000 during 1982. A customer could not duplicate such equipment at equally low cost using the previously widely accepted luxury packs.

The specification of 1982 SE derivatives comprised a manual sliding steel roof and multiple-spoke BMW Accessory alloy wheels in an opal green. These matched the body/interior combination of opal green metallic, hitched to a pine green interior based on the velour look of the 7-series. For the 320-6 SE the door mirrors were also colour-coded in green, and rear seat head restraints and a sports steering wheel were included. Only automatic transmission specials boasted standard power steering.

These 1982 specials are an obvious target for classic car collectors as the UK order was for just 400 of the 320-6; less than half that number were requested in 323i trim.

These Baur 323i Cabriolets in Germany (side view) and Britain (model holding the separate roof panel) represent a modern rendition of the partly closed, true cabriolet, not the often misquoted translation of convertible. True BMW drop-top convertibles came with the second-generation 3-series, or in the rare 1967–71 Baur version of the 2002. The latter model was also produced as a partly closed Baur Cabriolet … in a deliberate attempt to confuse British authors?

The 323i story: performance and specification

The 323i was a very serious effort finally to eclipse the embarrassing 2002tii sporting legend. A BMW press briefing in 1977 stated, 'the new 2.3-litre six-cylinder develops 143bhp; it replaces the four-cylinder 320i (125bhp) and could well consign even the successful 2002tii to obscurity. In any case its unique conception will soon thrust it into a position of leadership.'

In fact, the 323i established a new level of compact, high-quality performance. Its straight-line abilities were enough to cope with the Golf GTI, and its balance between speed and economy was biased most firmly towards performance. Much of the extra horsepower came from its unique camshaft, plus the enlarged cylinder head and exhaust porting to complement the use of K-Jetronic injection and a slight elevation of compression (9.5:1 versus 9.2:1) compared with the 320-6. A bonus of 325cc over the 320-6 was obtained via a 10.8mm elongation of stroke, both engines sharing an 80mm bore.

BMW performance claims for a machine that had 143bhp

and 140lb/ft of torque were modest and are appended below; they were easily surpassed by independent testers in Britain and matched by those in LHD markets. As an additional comparison, the results of the French weekly, *AUTOhebdo* are listed alongside the BMW claims; the full *Autocar* statistics are given in the performance appendix, but in outline they include 0–60mph in 8.3 seconds; maximum speed 126mph; test fuel consumption 19.7mpg.

323i CLAIMED PERFORMANCE

Km/h	Mph	Seconds	*AUTOhebdo*
0–50	31	2.8	—
0–80	50	6.4	6.3
0–100	62	9.5	9.1
0–120	75	13.6	13.3
0–140	87	18.5	19.2
0–160	100	—	28.6
0–400 metres		16.7	17.2
0–1000 metres		30.9	31.6
Max speed 118.00mph			120.1mph

DIN fuel consumption quoted by BMW
was equivalent to 30.7mpg.

Chassis changes on the 323i were headed by the change to rear disc brakes (supported by 160mm/6.25in drums for the handbrake) and vented front units. The suspension was also further enhanced beyond the 320-6 specification. A 'sports tuned' layout translated as further stiffening of the front strut damper inserts on the progressive principles found in 7-series cars, and BMW announced 'the anti-rollbars have been enlarged.'

In 1978, *Autocar* felt 'our preference would be for an even stiffer set-up with this type of performance. It was quite common for the car to feel rather soft.'

Other running changes were described in the section on the 320-6, but it is worth pointing out that the taller (3.45) final drive allowed nearly 20mph per 1,000rpm from the 323i. That meant the maximum speed was recorded at 6,350rpm in fourth, rather than the official rev limit of 6,600rpm.

External identification of the 323i flagship to the 3-series

was confined to front and rear badges, plus twin exhausts (one per side).

The 323i cost £6,249 in April 1978, but there was a long list of options installed to the May 1978 *Autocar* demonstrator that pumped up the price to a significant £8,386 – nearly enough for a 528i at the time. The listed options embraced electric mirrors at £222, plus electric windows for £264. Power steering was not installed on that press car, but was sold for another £482.

It was August 1978 when the minor change of a brake pad wear indicator was incorporated on the 323i. As for the 320-6, a Baur convertible was offered from September 1980, by which time the basic UK cost of a 323i amounted to £7,550. Options now embraced the vital 1990 standard feature of central locking at £342 on all 3-series. Naturally, costs kept escalating, but it was left to the second-generation 323i coyly to crack £10,000, or the special equipment derivatives described below. The last of the basic 323i breed in the original body was listed at £8,940, minus options.

The 1982 season was important for the post-factory holiday switch to standard five-speed gearbox fitment (as noted on the 320-6) and the UK specials. These cost £9,867 in manual trim and tested the list price waters beyond £10,000. This was for a 3-series, with £10,613 demanded for the automatic cousin which, as for the 320-6, incorporated power steering as a package.

The 323i version was even more collectable than the 320-6 because just 175 were ordered, and they were very distinctive in two-tone paint. Tints of grey were the order of the day: Ascot for the higher levels (wing mirrors and all) and Graphite for the lower panels.

Within, an Anthracite-labelled cloth was installed and complemented by Recaro sports front seats, head restraints and the inevitable sporty steering wheel. Dynamic changes were more serious than for the 320-6: gas-damped sports suspension listed along with front and rear spoilers, the forward one in matching Graphite and the back in standard black. The options list contributed the manual steel sliding roof panel and BBS alloy wheels carrying standard Michelins.

Were the Seventies claims of the BMW factory justified? After all they asserted, 'these new engines succeed the 2-litre

Officially billed as 'last of the line', one of the special-edition 323i models which came complete with two-tone grey paint and multiple-spoke alloy wheels, replacement under-bumper apron-cum-spoiler and bootlid airdam.

The special-edition 'run out' six-cylinder 320/323i previewed the many profitable marketing twists BMW GB Ltd would wring from later 3-series cars, especially in SE and Sport guises. This 320i was not treated to a replacement front spoiler, but it did boast of Opal Green paint and 7-series cloth trim interior as part of its special-edition specification.

This rear airdam was a frequently chosen optional addition to British BMWs, but the car was best identified from the back by its unique use of separated twin-pipe exhausts.

four-cylinder engine of the BMW 320 (two-door) and BMW 520 (four-door) and put the new model BMW 323i at the top of the compact class.' Certainly, there were independent sources who agreed on the unique appeal of this BMW six-cylinder initiative.

Autocar got this new breed of compact 'sixes' right. In their May 1978 summary of the 323i they felt, 'BMW's top small car is not without its faults, but it is a very enjoyable way of getting about. It will readily turn aggressive or docile according to the driver's whim. It is more sporting than many cars with more sporting pretensions, yet it is more practical than they are into the bargain. Expensive? Yes – but (it) is bound to carve a niche for itself amongst the richish, youngish individualists.'

The same weekly magazine also identified the individuality of these 'sixes' when they said, 'the 323i is a shrewd marketing exercise. It outperforms a number of more expensive BMWs. On price, performance and type it does not really compete head on with another model.'

The M60 'six' was to provide a sound base for BMW to build a veritable host of petrol and diesel options, but what of the car it powered in its original guise?

'Fast but flawed' would be my epitaph with the benefit of 15 years' hindsight. The 320-6 carburation was as unsatisfactory as many other contemporary and complex multichoke compound carburation arrangements favoured by BMW: heavy on fuel and demanding of frequent, expensive, service. They can be persuaded to run beautifully, but even those whose priority is not performance will probably find themselves better served by the 323i. The latter has the consideration of a competition pedigree and range-leading status that helps preserve prices over the long run, besides the standard fitment of four-wheel disc braking that was exclusive to this model in the E21 era.

It would be wrong if I did not mention that the 323i did have one major setback: the handling. Even when it was promoted via the UK County Championship race series it was obvious that a priority had been to tame its tail-happiness, a trait that suspended its sales while the model was investigated by the Swedish safety authorities. I have known plenty of skilled drivers who simply revelled in 323i handling manners – Tiff Needell and Barry Williams spring to mind in Britain – but both of those characters love sliding around circuits on opposite lock, trying to get the rear wheels to kiss the fronts under power – and it may not be your cup of Bavarian tea. Personally I thought the rear-end grip so limited as to be ludicrous and time-wasting, but by the standards of the rear-drive period it was no more inefficient and potentially troublesome than its bigger brothers, or machines such as the V6 Ford Capris.

My conclusion is that, despite the handling traits which can catch out the unwary in adverse conditions, the 323i was a fine BMW. It represented an original thought, was faster than any obvious rival and was built to quality levels that were emphasized by the provision of a six-year anti-rust pledge in the early Eighties.

CHAPTER 4

The second generation

A smoother style and a four-door option

Developed over a six-year period as part of a multi-million pound programme, the later 3-series was presented against a November 27, 1982 embargo in Germany. Then the four-door model was merely a static exhibit to emphasize that an increasing number of body alternatives would be proffered during the eight-year production span of this foundation, to further BMW production growth.

The second edition was to prove the most popular 3-series to date, the factory-coded E30 range surpassing 2.2 million units when it handed over to the current E36. Even then it was not eliminated completely, convertible and Touring bodies remaining in manufacture for several years alongside the aerodynamic generation of 3-series cars.

The secret of its success is built on a character that should particularly have appeal on the secondhand/collector's car market. The basic concept was of an exclusive, yet more affordable car, for the increasing wealth of export and home market customers. A compactly crafted conventional saloon car outline (only the 1.3in increase in width was significantly different) had been honed to unbelievable quality standards.

Appeal was also generated by the fact that nobody else provided a front-engine, rear-drive layout that housed power plants from 86bhp diesel to a 238bhp Evolution M3. At a price premium all-wheel drive was an option in the same basic layout, but supply was limited (even in the UK) to LHD, a remark that also applied to the production M3.

Key E30 developments included considerably more convincing standards of adhesion, lower noise levels and the installation of items from bigger models, such as a complex computer, analogue fuel economy pointer and service interval indicator. Diesel engines and ABS anti-lock brakes were mentioned at the 1982 presentation, and were delivered.

These sophistications were to be realized with an average range weight *loss* of a claimed 40kg/88lb. Independent performance tests tended to confirm this surprising engineering feat. For example, the first 323i weighed in at 1,190kg for *Autocar* whilst the better equipped 325i in the E30 shell recorded 1,048kg. BMW attributed the weight loss to a better understanding of the body construction, through stress analysis.

Gradually, a plethora of bodies became available for the 1982–90 generation of 3-series. These ranged beyond the two- and four-door saloons to encompass a factory convertible (though Baur continued to supply some special needs, even in the UK), plus a five-door Touring. Then there were the radically modified panels of the competition car basis provided in the M3 homologation variant, and such derivatives are dealt with in later chapters.

Initially there were just the two-door RHD saloons for sale in Britain from March 1983, contrasting with the four-door-only Mercedes 190 line. Measurements for both BMW two- and four-door derivatives (autumn 1983 for the UK four-door) were the same. A 101.2in wheelbase (2,570mm, up just 7mm on the original) lay within a modestly diminished overall length of 170.3in (4,325mm compared with the 4,355mm of its predecessor).

Front and rear tracks were within fractions of each other at

Conscientiously constructed and equally carefully drawn. Under the skin of the 323i, the 1982 leader of the E30 range. Extended front spoiler and associated air ducting are emphasized, along with four-wheel disc braking and the revised rear suspension, the coil spring being separated from the telescopic damper by the halfshaft.

1,407 and 1,415mm respectively (55.4 and 55.7in), compared with the 1,386 and 1,399mm of the six-cylinder originals. Height was set at 1,380mm (54.3in) for most derivatives, much as before. Width was up more obviously, by 35mm, now measuring a total of 1,645mm/64.5in across the body.

Aerodynamically, BMW engineers were still in the Dark Ages as compared with Audi. Citing lack of stability, mark identity and roadholding as black points against aero innovation, they executed a mild restyle, especially around the front lip of the bonnet. The result was a quoted 15% reduction in drag factor to an overall 0.37/38Cd, depending on tyre widths.

Even fatter tyres was a natural step, the four-cylinders being sold on the home market with 175/70 HR rubber; the inline small 'sixes' came on a minimum of 195/60 VR tyres. BMW also went up an inch on wheel diameters for all post-1982 3-series, settling on 14in for all but later Eighties

sporting options.

Rim widths were not fixed upon the automatic 'fatter is better' philosophy. Instead of a 5.5J x 13in standard range fitment that existed in the later days of the first 3-series, BMW adopted 5J x 14in for four-cylinder and 5.5J x 14in to suit the 'sixes'. All were in steel from the German factory, but national markets adopted alloys on special edition models, particularly in Britain.

Both front and rear suspensions were revamped, based on the principles of MacPherson-strut front, trailing-arm rear. The front anti-rollbar had been removed to a position aft of the front axle line. Previously BMW had employed the bar as part of the lower front wishbone. The relocated rollbar measured 18.5mm, compared with 23.5mm of the first 3-series, and was asked to co-operate with slightly slimmer front coil springs (130mm versus 152mm).

The later 3-series also had replacement front wishbones,

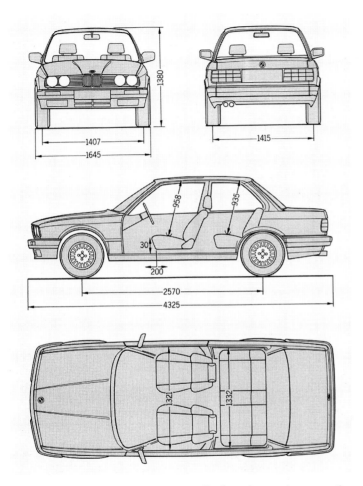

There were plenty of press people ready to tell BMW they had not changed the 3-series enough to keep pace with rivals such as the aerodynamic Audi. Yet more 3-series cars than ever were sold during the E30's eight-year sales life. Although the outline was little changed, the number of variants offered increased.

Dimensionally little different externally from its predecessor, the E30 line did offer a little more rear seating room and there were modest aerodynamic gains.

arms formed in the shape of a crescent instead of the previous single link. The new items were located by a single ball mounting. The complete suspension/steering mounting subframe was biased for low noise levels rather than location,

hence the use of two large rubber-bushed mountings. Even in 1982 BMW were using the limited deformation of rubber bushing to provide the 'elasto-kinematics' that became so fashionable in rear axle work from others in the later Eighties.

Although the ratio of the rack-and-pinion did not alter perceptibly from the lamentably slow original (officially reported as 21:1 to 21.45:1), hydraulic power assistance was optionally available. The power steering did allow a little relief, dropping to 20.51:1, but the practical feel at the wheel was still that of a four-turn shuffle.

At the back trailing arms, the fundamental alteration was to mount the arms at an angle of 20 degrees rather than the original 15. The said arms attaching above the rear transverse subframe at four points were also said to provide a resistance to suspension squat forces under heavy acceleration. BMW reverted to mounting the coil spring and damper separately, the long telescopic dampers now positioned behind the driveshafts.

A rear anti-rollbar was listed as a German market option for all but the 323i, which used a 12mm bar in place of the 16mm (318i/320) and 17mm (previous 323i) items of its predecessors. Only one track dimension, front and rear (1,407mm and 1,415mm), was listed for Generation II introduction, whereas a variety of figures were proffered for the old E21 line. The E30, a lot tamer in its handling, through a rather uninspired initial understeer – this was most pronounced in the six-cylinder models – reluctantly gave way to the traditional tail-out BMW stance under duress.

The big braking news was the availability of Bosch ABS anti-lock brakes as an option for the first time on a 3-series, but only if it was agreed to pay for the four-wheel disc braking system, standard only on the 323i. All models gained an inch diameter from the Mastervac braking servo-assistance, now totalling 10in girth.

The inch on wheel diameters allowed a modest increase in brake disc diameters, just 5mm/0.2in for a total of 260mm.

The front units were served by single-piston calipers described as 'fully floating' and 'space-saving', as opposed to the double-piston units previously installed. Only the 320i and 323i had ventilated front discs, a vital feature for the 320i, as the older, carburated, 320-6 did not have vented front discs.

Rear brakes on all but the 323i were of the drum type with adjustment provided to take up any slack activated by reversing. The original 3-series did not have this useful feature, but did have 250mm/9.8in drums as against the later car's 228.5mm/9in. The later 323i used non-ventilated discs of an unchanged 258mm/10.2in.

The clutches were unchanged, but new manual gearboxes and final drives demanded enlarged casings. The move to larger diameter wheels was accompanied by lowered – numerically – final drives. For example, the 323i went down from 3.45 to 3.25:1 and the 316 graduated from the E21 differential of 3.91 to 3.64:1. The effect of these gearing changes and the enlarged wheels, increased soundproofing and the rounded exterior, was a notably quieter BMW 3-series.

Now the 323i rear-end identity clue came from the bootlid spoiler rather than the separated dual exhausts; twin pipes were now packaged together on the nearside. The blacked-out centre pillar gave a hint of the coupe style on the original two-door models.

The quality of the 3-series cabin was a primary reason for the car's enduring appeal. Robot assembly standards of the Eighties allowed both surrounding body and associated fittings a precision assembly which coachbuilders could not match consistently at mass-production rates. The LHD automatic is from the original stock with a fuel consumption indicator built into the lower half of the tachometer and a service interval indicator – ideas that have survived into the Nineties. The computer option was not added to LHD cars until late in 1983. The manual RHD car is a facelifted 316i. Note that the steering wheel and most of the controls remained the same throughout, but the original digital clock went in favour of the RHD (F-plate registration) car's analogue quartz clock.

The major power train change was to switch all but the basic 1,766cc/90bhp 'four' over to fuel injection. In the German range the next step was a 105bhp Bosch K-Jetronic 318i, but that was not sold in Britain until October 1983. The new line featured a pair of fuel-injected 'sixes', the 2-litre and 2.3-litre M60 units sharing L-Jetronic. Power was quoted as 125 and 139bhp, the latter a slight drop over the first 323i figure of 143bhp. That was due to a change in fuel injection from the mechanically effective K-Jetronic to the fuel economy-biased electronic L-Jetronic. This loss was apparent despite a modest elevation in compression, from 9.5 to 9.8:1; similarly the fuel-injected 320-6 moved from 9.2:1 to 9.8:1.

Initially, Britain took all but the fuel-injected 318i, continuing to badge 1.8-litres misleadingly as a 316. The initial UK 3-series supply began in September 1982. Output of the RHD 323i and 320i began in December 1982, and it took a further month before the 90bhp RHD 316 was being assembled. This meant a three-model range of two-doors was ready for sale in Britain from March 1983, when they were

The LHD four-door version arrived early in 1983 and, like the two-door, was available as a 316 (carburated, 90bhp), 318i (L-Jetronic fuel-injected, 105bhp), 320i (L-Jetronic, 125bhp) and a range-leading 323i. In Munich this was credited with 150bhp with the L-Jetronic motor, rather than the 139bhp quoted at launch time. This meant that factory 323i power modifications were available very rapidly in LHD production.

received warmly by press and public alike.

Priced at £6,995, the 316 was initially available within the Y-plate UK registration plate period, as were the £8,595 new 320i and the first of the rebodied 323i E30 models. The latter in basic form cost £9,935; it would be the last year of a sub-£10,000 323i as the list price increased by over £500 for 1984.

All UK models had the following items as standard showroom equipment: electric mirror adjustment; service interval indicator; height-adjustable front seats. The 320i added velour carpeting to match the usual cloth trim, and a rev-counter, while the 323i had all the mechanical improvements detailed earlier, plus twin exhausts, auxiliary foglamps and a rear spoiler.

An £8,600 320i could be bought with an optional manual steel sunroof (£391), a ZF limited-slip differential (£277) and green tinted glass (£91). Items such as electric operation of the front side windows required another £274, and central locking an additional £145. Thus an £8,600 BMW 320i had become a £9,773 automobile, and in-car entertainment

would push a 320i beyond £10,000.

In 1983 the chief opposition to BMW 320i was the Alfa Romeo Alfetta (£8,150), Audi 80 CD (£8,356), Ford Capri 2.8i injection (£8,356), Lancia HPE 2000ie (£7,691) and the Saab 900 Turbos, which started at £10,995. Just two of those brands turned out to provide effective long-term opposition from a British perspective: Audi and Saab.

The 3-series was almost bound to succeed with the combination of what *Autocar* called in a February 1983 summary of the 119mph 320i, its 'incomparable levels of mechanical refinement. The engine is a jewel,' bubbled the weekly and added: 'It is fast, exceptionally efficient and generally quiet. It is amongst the best built cars in this class, and it now has better – if not perfect – handling.'

Output of the later 3-series multiplied rapidly in 1983, and variations on a theme were exported fairly promptly. The four-door derivative, in which the central B-post was moved eight inches forward to accommodate the rear door set, was most significant.

Initially the four- and two-door derivatives sold in equal

The four-door arrived in Britain for January 1984 sale, this 323i having an unpopular combination of optional sunroof and standard steel wheels.

numbers, ex-factory, but at the end of E30 production Sales Director Robert Buchelhofer told me, 'the four-door was the more successful, at between 60 and 70% of all sales. This was mostly because diesels were confined to four-doors only.' The diesel, an inline six-cylinder, was available from September 1985 in LHD form and achieved 20% of the total production of the BMW 3-series at the peak of its popularity.

The major marketing change in the first year of UK sales was packaged and assembled as a 1984 model. In August 1983 a BMW (GB) Ltd dealer circular summarized the four-door specification and prices, plus the introduction of the fuel-injected 318i as follows: 'the 318i at £7,950 estimated price falls neatly between the 316 and 320i and shares the 316 specification, except for a standard five-speed overdrive gearbox.

'The four-door models share the same standard specification as their two-door counterparts except that they have fully retractable rear windows and rear compartment heating. The price difference of £350 for these models will ensure very strong demand.'

Also introduced in the autumn of 1983 was the optional four-speed ZF automatic transmission, priced around £600 and confined solely to the six-cylinder 320i/323i. Another detail change was the adoption of electronic control systems on the carburated 316 which provided fuel economy benefits together with a fuel cut-off facility.

The line now stretched from a two-door 316 at £6,995 to a four-door 323i in automatic transmission guise at £10,885, and was badged as 316, 318i, 320i and 323i. Automatic transmission and the four-door body were available on all derivatives. The range in Britain now included £9,945 to £13,485 prices for cabriolet versions of the every 3-series. These were the Baur conversions rather than the subsequent factory convertible. BMW offered 'cabriolet conversions' at £2,950 extra, on two-door cars only.

Extra horsepower for the RHD 323i came to Britain in October 1984 and reflected an important gain in performance for 323i buyers. Using the extra production facilities of satellite Bavarian factories, BMW uprated the 323i from an official 143bhp (139bhp in emission-conscious

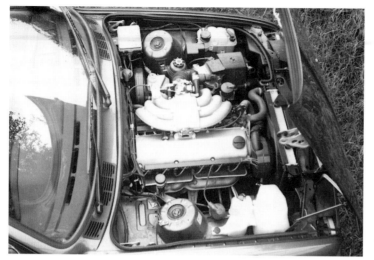

markets such as Switzerland) to 150bhp. Changes included replacement of camshaft, distributor and inlet manifold. *Autocar* recorded 0-60mph in 8.3 seconds, 122mph and an overall 23.1mpg but, fuel consumption aside, these were not improvements on their results for the first of the 323i 3-series in the old body.

September 1984 saw the introduction of the first British market special, a 320i, built over a 300-strong run, that was sold only in Diamond Black with Anthracite interior trim. The £10,750 320i was made in November and December 1984 and could be identified by the standard rear spoiler and side stripes from the 6-series coupe. BMW GB felt there was a value of £649 expended in standard extras, including a manual operation steel sunroof, alloy wheels shod by Pirelli P6 tyres, M Technic suspension, standard alloy wheels and a number of colour-coded zones, such as the bumpers and mirrors.

In October 1984, some of the smaller running changes

The L-Jetronic fuel-injected M60 six-cylinder engine of the 323i, the traditional slant installation of BMW's first belt-driven SOHC motor being clearly visible. The picture is of the 12-valve 325i variant, which was available throughout the later life of the E30. The original 323i set world standards for smooth power delivery, but the 325i fed such accessible torque and power that the 24-valve engines which eventually replaced them had to be driven harder to match them in British traffic conditions.

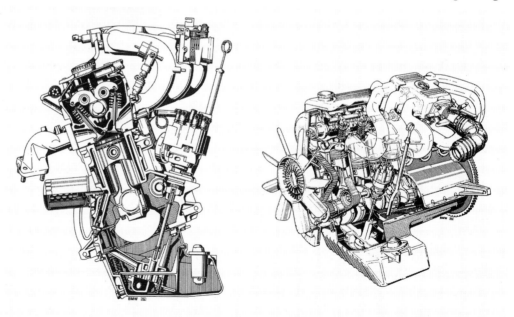

from German production made it to Britain. These included the four-speed automatic for four-cylinder derivatives, and a retrimmed back seat, said to offer badly needed extra space.

The 325i for Britain made a September production debut. Its improved ability was based on a power unit that had gained 7.7% cubic capacity for a gain of 21bhp – an extra 14.5%. A 1984 BMW internal briefing stated that the objective had been 'once again to become the absolute leader in terms of performance in the compact saloon class.' Another objective was 'to have a genuine successor to the 2002 Tii, or the E21 323i, and to establish a greater lead over the 320i.'

The British 325i arrived at £11,495 on a 1984–85 C-plate. By then the 316 had escalated to £7,750, but had a standard five-speed gearbox. Best British seller at this point was the 105bhp 318i, a machine whose basic price (£8,595) was not too dissimilar to contemporary premium Ford Sierras and Vauxhall Cavaliers.

A number of changes had arrived throughout the UK line, particularly some subtle aerodynamic detailing. Fewer grille bars were featured, an engine undertray was installed, and the leading edge of the lower front spoiler also had fewer apertures. Other 3-series alterations in the autumn of 1985 allowed a 4bhp bonus for the 320i, taking it to a quoted 129bhp that remained official until the close of production.

On all 1986 model year 3-series cars, beefier steering locks, enhanced lateral support for the seats, and a return to an analogue black and white clock were in evidence. The 325i auxiliary equipment beside the obvious power augmentation started with hydraulic twin-tube shock absorbing as part of an uprated suspension specification, and an oil cooler that demanded an opening in the lower front apron/spoiler. As for the rest of the range, aerodynamic updates reduced the number of grille bar apertures and an engine undertray appeared.

At introduction, ABS anti-lock braking was a £1,000-plus option, so it is worth looking for in earlier used car buys. Foglamps and twin exhausts continued on British-market 325i models, but the back spoiler was now finished in body colour on those machines specified with metallic paint. Otherwise the small rear spoiler was left in Diamond Black,

although concours competitors may care to argue with the judges if their example is in Gazelle Beige, in which case BMW have quoted Sable as the pigment adopted for the said spoiler. Standard interior trim was a cloth combination dubbed County, which was shared with the 320i and covered slightly larger seats.

Another minor, but useful change was the uprated capacity of the battery, up from the 320i's 50 amp/hour rating to 66Ah, plus an 80Ah alternator delivering 1,120 Watts. Because the battery was mounted in the boot, luggage capacity dropped on VDA calculation from 425 to 404 litres. The compensation was a modest redistribution of the kerb weight of over 2,400lb, which could have assisted rear traction.

Mechanical changes to the running gear of the 325i also extended to a replacement twin-pipe exhaust system of larger diameter, increased clamping loads for the clutch plate – derived from 325e and diesel – plus heavy-duty driveshafts and wheel bearings. Automatic transmission was specified by many 325i owners, and it now offered three settings, including sports or economy motoring.

In time for the 1986 summer was a proper factory convertible, which is more fully detailed in the following chapter. The soft-top was the 325i at £16,495 initially. In 1992 the old convertible was still being sold, promoted chiefly upon the cost benefits of the 318i base.

There was also a 1986 UK market special, the 325i Sport, which proved very popular and could sell in hot hatchback numbers at the peak of its sales graph, even though it cost twice as much as most of them! The 325iS was introduced at £14,095 for a five-speed manual gearbox version or £15,081 when it came complete with the multiple driving programme automatic ZF gearbox.

Standard Sport goodies were headed by the BMW Motorsport-developed M Technic aero kit. This comprised a distinctive front and rear spoiler, the rear allied to a pronounced curvature in the rear bootlid airdam. BMW Motorsport told me at the spring 1986 Geneva show that 'the whole kit makes a big improvement for the car through the air'. Other items of aerodynamic origin were the side skirt extensions and a deeper rear apron.

M Technic branding was also applied to the sports suspension: replacement gas-filled dampers, stiffer springs and thickened front and rear anti-rollbars, plus M Technic leather-rimmed three-spoke steering wheel and leather gaiter for the gear-lever. More obvious was the employment of BBS alloy rims (6.5J x 14in), but from September 1986 these were very swiftly widened to 7J x 15s. These filled up the arches and happily carried 205/55 VR-15s. The spare was mounted on the usual 5.5J x 14in steel, clasping a 195/65 cover.

A limited-slip differential joined the fatter tyres to assist traction and handling properties on the Sport. The net result was a far better 325i, but it was no M3. The big failing was in the steering feedback and low gearing of the production '3' in

comparison with the M3, but the six-cylinder engine was far better to live with than the 16v 'four'. I have known customers start with a 325i, buy an M3, then revert to a 325i Sport. Handling aside, the Sport is a much better everyday option.

Ancillary items in this British-market 325i Sport package were green-tinted glass – which reduced the optional cost of air conditioning to just over £1,000 – sports seats and 635 coupe twin side stripes. The body colours offered initially were Diamond Black, Polaris Silver and Dolphin. Lachs Silver was added from September 1986.

More Special Equipment (SE) UK luxury and ABS for 1986 were the 3-series headlines of that season. Good news

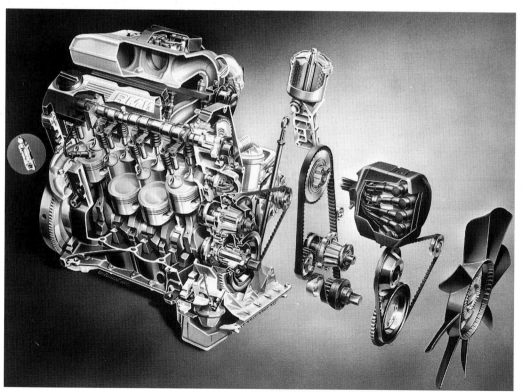

Inside the important M40 four-cylinder, introduced in late 1987 to end the long life of the Sixties M10/12 engines. In Britain the 318i version became available in 1987, the 316i from September 1988. The main innovation was belt drive for the single overhead camshaft. The units were well packaged and ran discernibly more smoothly, although some engine repairers do not speak well of their longevity in comparison with the earlier chain-driven SOHC units.

Spot the difference. The 1987 facelift was extremely mild, being identified mainly by the deletion of many chrome areas (especially surrounding the side glass) and the use of plastic bumpers.

for the September 1986 sale was the inclusion of ABS anti-lock braking as standard on all 325i derivatives; by then, that meant the basic specification 325i saloon in two- or four-door forms (with manual wide or close ratio, or automatic gearboxes), 325i Sport and 325i convertible.

Logically, BMW (GB) went for the SE operation on their smallest saloons, which was an idea that had worked exceptionally well in the British 7-series. The SE specification was introduced on two- and four-door machines at prices from £13,675 for the 320i and £16,395 on a 325i base. Features on 320i included power steering, power front and – for four-door models – rear windows, BMW alloy wheels (rather than BBS options), computer, headlamp wash/wipe, rear roller blind and electric operation of the steel sunroof. For the 1987 model year (September 1986 onward) central locking had become standard throughout the UK 3-series line, with a slight price premium imposed for 316/318i. Autumn 1986 also marked the introduction of fashionable asbestos-free braking pads and linings to the UK 3-series.

SE items for a 325i joined a standard specification that was improved via an official letter of August 1986. At that point ABS electronic anti-lock braking became standard on this model only. The occasional steel-wheeled example (the standard specification) gained a new wheel cover, and it is

worth noting that the production 325i tyre sizing was changed from 60-series 195s to 195/65 following the factory summer holidays of 1985. The additional SE items for a 325i were the same as for 320i, centred upon 'power everything'.

I have devoted subsequent chapters to the 4x4 (325iX), convertible and M3 variations on a 3-series theme, but it makes chronological sense at least to mark their UK arrival. In April 1987, these LHD-only machines were sold at £23,550 for the 2.3-litre M3 (then rated at 200bhp), and either £17,850 for the two-door 4x4 or £18,345, to cover a four-door 325iX equivalent. A 325i power plant was now rated at exactly 170bhp in the catalytic convertor-prepared engine that was mandatory in this LHD Special Order model.

However, even without the exhaust cleanser, in September 1987 the power of the 2.5-litre 'six' sold in the UK dropped slightly because the compression ratio was lowered to 9.4:1 and the Motronic management adjusted accordingly to co-operate with unleaded fuels. The same ratio change was also made for 320i derivatives.

A significant long-term change for the 1988 model year was the introduction on the 318i of the 1,795cc/115bhp M40 engine, a fine development of existing BMW SOHC themes into a brand new four-cylinder line that initially featured a simple SOHC/eight-valve cylinder head.

The M42-coded DOHC 16-valve engine of the 1990 model-year 318is was beautifully packaged, hiding even the spark plugs behind screw-top covers. Chain drive was reinstated for the double overhead camshafts and the unit developed 136bhp

This unit also spawned a DOHC, 16-valve development that became the heart of the subsequent 318iS, BMW's closest opposition to the hot hatchback set. That handling and grip were a little more important to BMW in 1987 than they had been in 1977 can be judged from the fact that this four-cylinder gained the previous six-cylinder standard 195/65 tyre dimensions, but the wheels remained steel units within plastic cappings unless an alloy was specified optionally.

The SOHC M40 engine transformed the best-selling 318i into a desirable machine, balancing BMW smoothness with a claimed maximum of 117mph and an entirely competitive 0–62mph time of 10.8 seconds for manual models, and 11.9 seconds for the automatic. Independent testing showed the top speed to be justified and the 0–60mph potential to be under 10 seconds, whilst returning 27.4mpg of the unleaded fuel that it was designed to consume, rather than it being converted in the manner of older BMW power units.

The 1988 model year revamp in autumn 1987 included more visual manoeuvring than usual, removing chrome in favour of matt black. This encompassed the front and rear screen surrounds, plus the side glass encasements, but the rain channel and outer window capping remained in chrome. Side rubbing strips lost their chrome highlights, and a black plastic insert was placed between the now enlarged and raised rear light clusters. All models, bar M3 and convertibles, gained side rear panels that deepened their approach to the

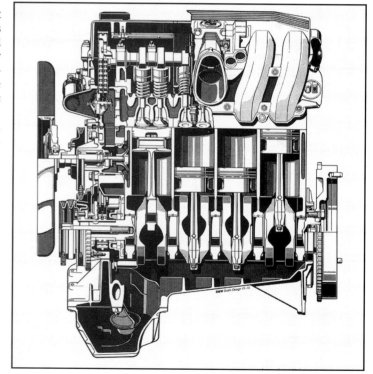

The 318is was a comparatively short-run sporting option in the main E30 range, being available in LHD form from September 1989 to December 1990. It may well be worth a collector's attention, especially as it is great fun to drive. Exterior decoration was modest, just front and rear spoiler extensions and the remaining chrome blacked out. Those cross-spoke BBS alloy wheels were an option, as was an ABS monitored system for the ex-325i four-wheel disc brakes.

back wheels and tyres, so visually closing the gap between rear tyre and arch. Neither the M3 nor the convertible gained 2.5mph impact absorbing bumpers – initially in contrasting colour with the body – and associated smaller spoiler lips found in the main range.

Mechanically the most influential change was the adoption of variable-ratio steering from the 316 upward. This feature had made its presence first felt on the 325i, and had spread downward to the 1988 four-cylinders. The objective was lighter steering without a power option necessity at parking speeds, but it did no favours to sporting customers of the 3-series in its lack of feedback.

Another notable mechanical change was the provision of up to 64 litres/14.08 imperial gallons in the fuel tanks of six-cylinder models, which had previously managed a maximum of 55 litres. Also effective was the use of ellipsoid outer headlamps for all 3-series, which also gained that rather classy green tinted glass from top to bottom of the line. Hidden away was a worthwhile change to the 320i, which gained twin-sleeve gas dampers at this point, a feature which

A popular model in the UK in its own right, the 325i was dressed up with an M Technic body kit and oversize alloys to create the 325i Sport.

had previously taken much of the 'joggle' out of the ride of sportier BMWs. Incidentally, the sportiest 325i Sport package was rested during the UK 1988 model year (roughly September 1987 onwards), but was reinstated for 1989, when a new M Technic body was made ready.

In Germany the public had to be told about the benefits of the most extensive range changes since 1982, *and* introduce them to a choice amongst 14 engines – never mind a choice of bodies that covered two- and four-door saloons, the M3 modified two-door, a line of two-door convertibles and the return of a Touring (five-door).

In the autumn of 1987 BMW were adding the turbocharged version of an M60 (originally, the 320/323 'six' family), a diesel 'six', plus the refinement of electronic fuel injection, and 5-series parentage, to manufacture a quickly economical 324td of 115bhp. This engine was not confined merely to saloons, but also popped up in the Touring derivatives, but it was not sold to the British – a fact deplored in many quarters, as it has a fine reputation.

The 90bhp carburettor motor was ditched for the 1989 model year on the 316 (dealers were told in June 1988) and that meant the entire petrol line was now fuel-injected. The superior M40 four-cylinders of 1,596cc supplied 102bhp, enough to allow the 316i to exceed 110mph, almost break the 10-second barrier from 0–60mph and return over 25mpg in harsh use.

The 316i was sold from September 1988 in the UK at £10,750, but this should be seen in the perspective of the 325i beyond £17,500 and its SE cousin, nearing £20,000. Once again equipment levels were raised: from the 316i upwards the specification covered preparation of the engine for catalytic convertors – so a retrofit could be executed to meet 1992 European legislation – power steering, electric operation of front windows, and a tachometer, the latter already standard in the UK. These joined items such as central locking, that had been on the showroom list for some years.

For the 318i, £11,880 was justified by the bonus in power, plus the electric windows and power steering, and 195/65 HR rubber in place of 175/70 TR covers for the 316i. The 320i and SE alternatives commanded around £14,000 and

Many 3-series derivatives failed to make it to Britain in the E30 body, including this 324td turbo diesel. Another big seller elsewhere but absent from the UK was the earlier 325e with a slow-revving petrol engine.

This side view of the 325i Sport specification in 1991 emphasizes the body alterations and cross-spoke alloy wheels that were part of a £20,000-plus deal in Britain. This car was actually an Alpina hybrid and when sampled in a back-to-back test with the E36 3-series in Scotland was thought by some to be a valid choice against its 325i successor.

£15,400, and the specification continued to feature much the same items as in previous years, although the range changes gave the basic 320i front foglamps, electric windows (front only) and power steering – and thus removed some of the appeal from the 320i SE package. The same applied at the 325i SE level. Power steering and electric windows had also arrived from the option list for the standard model, the two-door now costing £17,540 and four-door SE variants closing on £19,000.

The 325i Sport was another candidate for the 3-series £20,000-plus club, but was reintroduced after a year's sabbatical at £19,945, in two-door form only. Standard Sport equipment remained a package based on the revised M Technic aero kit, suspension, sports seats and steering wheel. Naturally all the later 325i standard features were included, and the 170bhp engine was mated to the close-ratio Getrag gearbox – first isolated and furthest from the RHD driver – plus a 3.91 axle. Britons were unable to find a real performance bonus in this close-ratio gear set, but the fanatical found comfort in *Autocar & Motor* figures that revealed

0–60mph in 6.8 seconds (7.4 seconds was usual for a later 325i) and 0–100mph in 18.8 seconds in place of the usual 19.9 seconds. Top speed remained at 132mph and fuel consumption shrunk from over 24mpg to 22.4mpg overall.

The 1989 UK updates were minimal and the range-wide alteration was simply to delete the UK 'dim-dip' feature, which could be met by a headlamp levelling system that provided the benefit of load adjustment. Catalytic convertors were offered for every UK BMW that sales season, all based on an optional cost of £350. A warning triangle and first aid kit were now firm commitments on the standard specification list from BMW (GB).

Shortly before Christmas 1989, British BMW dealers were advised of an important sporting addition, the M42 (DOHC, 16-valve) version of the 318i taking on the S-suffix as well as the benefits of a 136bhp power plant. The 1.8-litre engine devel-oped nearly 76bhp a litre, second only to the fabled M3 in the generation of power per litre.

Visually, a front and rear spoiler set, sports seats, M Technic steering wheel and suspension, plus a black satin

Racing Dynamics, marketed from Dreamwheelers at Milton Keynes, showed their knowledge of chassis engineering as well as engine power for the E30 'sixes'. Attractive styling options came with this 2.8-litre version of the 325i, which was warmly received in Germany.

An Alpina BMW, in this case the C2 2.5, usually provides enough action to keep its driver wide awake, which suggests that journalist Steve Cropley was seriously blasé as he eased on some opposite lock during a mid-Eighties test!

finish for the surviving external chrome were used to identify the model.

Complete with independently assessed 125mph ability, 0–60mph in 9.3 seconds and an overall 27.5mpg – fractionally *better* than the 318i – the 318iS became very popular. It was not over-priced, being pitched initially just under £15,000 against the £12,000 or so from Volkswagen and Vauxhall GTI/GTE warriors, but that BMW £14,750 offer was without ABS or the alloy wheels that so many owners opted for. A co-operative suspension system allowed reasonable grip from 195/65 rubber, but the back-up of ABS to prevent a tyre locking up was desirable.

The 318iS shared many range features. This meant that power steering, electric front windows, a rev-counter, central locking and green tinted glass were all included. Standard colours were Alpine White (exceptionally popular), Brilliant Red and the metallic shades of Diamond Black, Laser Blue and Sterling Silver. A chequered interior cloth trim provided a suitably sporty note, but leather was always an option.

The last major British marketing move outside the sporting

The BMW Z1 sportscar used the existing 3-series 12-valve SOHC 325i engine and various items including the central control axle that were reworked for the E36 models of the Nineties. The stylish work of BMW Technic, the Z1 soon died, but a cheaper four-cylinder sportscar – again using some 3-series technology – was a strong possibility for the mid-Nineties.

318 and other models continued beyond the introduction of the E36 was to try to shift a few more four-cylinders under a package dubbed Lux and make it available for 316i and 318i. At this point (February 1990 UK sales start) BMW (GB) also overhauled specifications for the SE six-cylinders.

The 316i/318i Lux took on moody blacks – even the exhaust trim! – but they also gained a 62-litre fuel tank and the upholstery grades previously allocated to 'sixes'. Enticements embraced the usual power steering and electric windows up front, but the models could also be identified by 6J x 14in BMW alloys, a manual sliding steel sunroof and a rear spoiler, plus a sportier steering wheel. An outside temperature display was incorporated.

The uprated 320i/325i SE contained all the trim moves mentioned on 'fours', but also took up the 730i cloth trim panels that incorporated pinstripes. The handbrake gaiter

was in leatherette, leather was used for the manual gear-lever knob and a 'leather insert' was employed for automatics.

The showroom SE features were enlarged and cross-spoke 6.5J x 14in alloys helped identify them over their predecessors. Main gains were an electric sliding roof, computer, sports steering wheel and rear electric windows for four-door models. By the advent of the 1990 G-plate even the two-door version of the 325i SE cost £21,460.

The second generation of 3-series, coded E30, brought an even warmer glow to the financial men than the 1.36 million examples of the first 3-series. Its successor, during its eight-year span from 1982 to 1990, brought production at Munich and – latterly – Regensberg of this generation to more than 2.2 million, although 2.4 million looked like being the final total when the convertible and Touring had finished their early Nineties after-life.

CHAPTER 5

Convertible, Touring and 4x4

Versatility based on a 2.5-litre 'six'

Versatility from one basic design is an accepted facet to mass-production saloons these days, but BMW carried it to new heights of effectiveness in the mid-Eighties with the 3-series. There were 17 listed 3-series derivatives by September 1989, but I devote this chapter to recalling three significant factory offspring: Touring (a small 't' for touring in factory language, but a large 'T' from the British importers!), Cabriolet and the 4x4 325iX.

All three factory 3-series were initially based on the availability of the 325i engine, its enlargement over the 323i base featuring some careful cylinder head work that permitted a 170bhp catalyst version of the engine.

What progress was made between 323i (coded M60) and M20-coded 325i inline 'sixes'? The obvious benefit was that of peak torque, though not all of it was down to an 8% growth in cubic capacity. Bosch Digital Motor Electronics assisted considerably in promoting the broad spread of power that is such a noticeable benefit of a 325i unit when compared with the earlier 323i. In percentage terms, torque was up a maximum of 10% and power 15% but the lower speed torque was the most obvious improvement when at the wheel. In the mid-Eighties the power output per litre was prodigious by SOHC, two-valves-per-cylinder standards. At 68.7bhp per litre, a company internal memorandum spoke of the 2.5-litre engine taking up 'the pole position' in a comparison with rivals of the period. More relevantly for the customers, fuel consumption was little affected, and the legendary suave power delivery remained in the same sweet league as its predecessor.

How was the 325i engine developed? Its basic exterior 'slant-six' dimensions were those of the 323i, but using the 2.7-litre 'eta' cylinder block – as had so many aftermarket conversions – allowed an 84mm bore to co-operate with a new 75mm stroke of the cast-iron crankshaft to provide 2,494cc, a distinct shift in emphasis from the original 2,316cc (80 x 76.8mm). The lead-free era had truly arrived, for compression was dropped to 8.8:1 from 9.8:1.

The enlarged 'six' allowed BMW a very hearty core to the derivatives described in this chapter, but later convertibles would work right down to a fuel-injected 1.8-litre car, and the Touring would finally list motors down to 1.6 litres. By contrast, a 325iX 4x4 model was always based on 2.5 litres. The grippy all-wheel-drive 325i, like the M3, was always confined to LHD.

I was surprised to find that factory records (to December 1990) reveal an output of 29,553 of the 4x4 3-series and 101,332 convertibles – over 72,000 of those the 320i-based machine. The rarest convertible was the Motorsport-assembled M3, and less than 800 such soft-tops were manufactured. The Touring remained in production alongside the new 3-series, as was the convertible, so the Touring total of 61,569 was also set to increase. There was no Touring derivative until the second 3-series, although the 2002 and cousins had been available with such bodywork. It had proved very unpopular on the home market but very fashionable in export countries such as Britain.

Baur of Stuttgart created the first 3-series convertible conversions from late 1977 onward, these being equipped

The 325i was the first of what would become a full engine line-up for the convertible. Over 101,000 BMW convertibles had been made by 1990, the 320i variant being the most numerous (some 72,000) and the M3 the rarest (under 800).

with the central rollover section, framed side glass and two separate opening sections; the soft rear folding roof was complicated by a single glassfibre lift-out panel. Conversion cost was some £1,600 for a new car in the UK. By January 1989 Baur bodies cost an additional £4,300; by then Baur versions of fresh air motoring were listed for 316i, 318i, 32i and 325i.

Despite the availability of the factory convertible with six cylinders, 16 UK customers chose Baur bodies for their 325i in 1989, 25 went for the 320i, 30 opted for a Baur 318i and 36 took the cheapest 316i – which exceeded £15,400 in total during January 1989.

Such Baur conversions were made available with increased BMW blessing in Britain through the Eighties, principally to

cover the gaps left by the lack of a four-cylinder convertible in the factory line. In my view they are no match for the factory convertibles, and I find Baur bodies more complex to live with than the disappearing hood design of BMW themselves.

First of the important 1983–90 3-series factory derivatives to materialize was their Cabriolet – 'convertible' to English language readers – which entered LHD production during January 1986. By June 1986, RHD cars were coming off the BMW lines, but although all prototypes were built at Dingolfing (11 cars in 1985) production convertibles were also made at Regensberg to take the pressure away from routine 3-assembly at Munich.

Karmann and Baur were both tried in the search for a convincing hood, but it took the design efforts of Shaer

Waechter, of Dusseldorf, to come up with a sufficiently superior and ingenious solution that would satisfy BMW. Shaer Waechter dubbed the BMW 325i hood action 'top dead centre', and had to support the hood frame with six transverse hood bars and seven per side. A total of 28 bearings were used to smooth out the action, seated in Teflon inserts for a claimed maintenance-free life. Those bars exerted sufficient tension on the frame and its triple-layer cloth hood to obviate the need for any clamps or studs to secure the hood against water leaks. Work was reinforced by the triple-layer laminate structure, which carried artificial fibres externally, cotton within, and mid-mounted rubber sandwich.

For the M3, BMW Motorsport engineers added the refinement of an electric motor, which was activated literally at the touch of the button, and allowed the top to disappear into the usual rear compartment, complete with 'flip top' lid.

How did they compensate for the loss of two-door saloon-type sheet metal beyond the front A pillar? A direct kerb weight comparison of the 325i two-door and a 325i Cabriolet shows an appreciation from 1,200 to 1,310kg, representing a gain of 110kg or 242lb. The bulk of this extra weight went into basic body building, including the competition car practice of seam welding.

The steel reinforcement of the topless 3-series body was concentrated on the scuttle and structure beneath the dashboard; an extra bar from steering column to transmission tunnel; extra panels to add muscle to the junction of side sills and front roof pillars; and internal strengthening of the rear side panels by an extra plate joining them to the wheelarches. There were side sills beneath the doors, plus additional members within the sills. Thickness of steel was also enhanced for the transmission tunnel and two skins were provided for the rear seat floor panel, which extended to the partition between the rear seats and the boot.

Even the front wheelarches had reinforcing panels. The folding roof compartment was anchored to the back wheelarches, but most reassuring was the heavier-gauge metal windscreen frame.

To lower the cloth top it was necessary to ensure that the

The 318i started the convertible model line in the surviving E30-bodied cars for Britain during the Nineties. From February 1991 these carried the later tail-light clusters and under-bumper aprons.

Even though the E36 body was well established in the UK in 1992, the 325i convertible in the old body could command a list price of nearly £24,000 without embarrassment.

electric side glass was lowered, then release two locking levers on the top screen rail and pull the studless hood away from front and rear tension. A safety catch in the nearside hood compartment released the lid. Then the hood could be folded away, the lid pressed shut and the car driven off.

Claimed performance was little different from the saloons in maximum speed, but lagged over 0–62mph. BMW reported 134mph for the 325i Cabriolet and 121mph for the 320i, plus 0–62mph times of 8.7 and 11.5 seconds respectively. In truth *Autocar* exceeded the 323i claims marginally (135mph, 0–60mph in 8.1 seconds) and returned 26.5mpg into the bargain.

The only problem was that one had to remember that the bootlid and hood compartment cover could not be raised at the same time. The other drawback was the inevitable price penalty. The compensation – at least on the 325i – was an excellent level of standard equipment: multiple-spoke alloys, central locking, anti-theft alarm with deadlocks, all-electric

windows, uprated suspension, sports steering wheel, green-tinted glass and sports front seats. The 320i shared all these features, but lacked the 325i's standard ABS braking.

The 325i cabrio began life in the UK at £16,495 in 1986 (on a C-registration plate) and took only two years (E-plate) to reach £23,990 and be on sale in Britain alongside the new 3-series in September 1991. The similar looking 318i and 320i Cabriolets were also still on sale, with only the 1.8-litre model under £20,000, at £18,220. The M3 convertible, whose import was never planned to exceed 40 examples in 1989, was a wallet-bashing £37,250. At the time, the 325i convertible was approximately £17,000 less and an M3 saloon some £14,000 cheaper. The combined effect of the recession and those vicious prices made the M3 convertible a true rarity in Britain.

Most potentially valuable of the less powerful examples were the 1990 325i Motorsport convertibles. They featured an electro-mechanical hood assistance system as opposed to

These views of LHD and RHD cabins show how tidily BMW packed away the hood beneath its hard tonneau. What cannot be conveyed is the sheer fresh-air pleasures that await the lucky drivers and their passengers.

the usual double hydraulic struts. The price was a hefty £28,950, which included £725 for the assisted hood and over £5,000 on the Motorsport-branded items.

Only 250 325iM cabrios were built in a choice of two colours: Sebring Grey or Macao Blue, similarly allied to black or silver leather for the upholstery, and the choice of black or blue for the hood. Sebring Grey was scheduled for the black trim and hood treatments.

Individually itemized, the Motorsport element majored on an M Technic body kit that provided a front spoiler, rear skirts and side sills. For less expensive 3-series convertibles no rear spoiler was offered, optionally or otherwise. A BMW (GB) salesman's bulletin identified unique convertible body features as principally devoted to the front and rear aprons (below the bumper line), the installation of a black panel between the rear lights, and the use of colour coding for bumpers and mirrors.

M Technic branding was also imposed on uprated suspension and the steering wheel, supporting 7J x 15in cross-spoke alloys with Nogaro Black sprayed centres, as

The rare M3 convertible was an even more protected species in Britain, where prices nudged to near double those of the already costly 325i convertible. This unregistered 1989 example was waiting to leave BMW Motorsport at Garching when the writer spotted it.

The leather-trimmed 1986 convertible was one of the few RHD Alpina-modified cars to offer 2.7 litres and more power than the contemporary M3 to the British public.

found on some M3 editions. Rubber was also the same as for some past M3 models: 205/55 R-15.

Within, a Napa-Tex woven cloth/leather finish – similar to that of the M5 – was applied to the seating. There was an extensive use of leather trim to outer parts of the seats, doors and side panels, and centre and tunnel consoles. Further showroom seductions embraced lining the bootlid, a computer, a graduated tint on the windscreen and black satin chrome finishes. Body colour was applied to mirrors and bumpers.

Mechanically, aside from the suspension changes, the power train was pure catalytic convertor 325i, and the EH-coded automatic gearbox was offered for approximately a further £500. The specification was fairly generous, comprising items such as four-wheel disc brakes and all-round electric side glass operation. Yet the wheels for the cheaper 318i derivatives were confined to 5.5 x 14in steel. These were covered by 195/65 R-14 rubber, whereas the later design convertibles of 1991 had alloy wheels and substantially uprated interior trim.

In December 1990, BMW (GB) heralded a price-cutting 1.8-litre derivative of the 3-series convertible, and this was followed in April 1991 by a BMW Motorsport exercise that was officially named 318i Design Convertible. The 318i convertible was £17,840 in late 1990, and an automatic transmission variant cost almost another £1,000. The specification revolved around the usual 115bhp 1,796cc engine in both cases, and the 1,220kg/2,690lb machines were rated as capable of 116mph in a body measured at 0.37Cd with the roof raised. Acceleration from 0–62mph took 12 seconds, around 27mpg could be expected in urban use, or there was a thirstier automatic cousin.

I loved the factory 3-series convertible, but do not take my word for its excellence. *Autocar* said in their September 24, 1986 road test summary of their press demonstrator, 'convertibles based on existing saloon models are always difficult to engineer and do not usually sell in very great numbers. BMW started from scratch to ensure a high quality end-product, and the main criticism of the 325i convertible

The sections in white are the new pieces of hardware needed to change an E30 325i into a 4x4 BMW 325iX. Less than 30,000 such cars were made, and by 1992 the 5-series was providing BMW's 4x4 model.

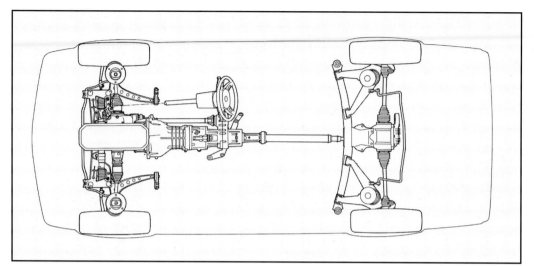

Top view of the LHD 325iX showing how standard was the rear and how much modification was necessary to squeeze front-drive into a 3-series. The central differential shaft drive to the forward diff can be seen running alongside the five-speed gearbox, disappearing at the bellhousing.

would seem to be the amount of time a potential customer has to wait to take delivery of what is destined to be a classic of its kind.'

The BMW 325i Touring made its debut at the Frankfurt motor show in September 1987, but manufacture did not begin until the following spring. The 3-series Touring differed from its slow-selling 2002 and 1802 predecessors by being based upon the four-door saloon – a feature not available in the all-two-door '02' days, but it seems that the factory was not satisfied with the profits generated at this end of the market, hence the 1992 emphasis on a new 5-series Touring.

BMW concentrated on three areas to achieve acceptable driving manners: body strength, aerodynamics and suspension. There was a 90kg weight penalty (1,270kg compared with 1,180kg) with the 325i Touring against the equivalent saloon, but wider side sills and an integral rear spoiler allowed the same 0.36Cd aerodynamic drag factor. BMW claimed that lift forces on front and rear axles had been cut significantly.

Body changes beyond the full-depth 'fifth door/hatchback' enhanced the rear end considerably at much the same weight increment as that suffered by the convertibles. A new roof and modified side panels were supported by longitudinal and transverse support members. BMW said these 'have been substantially reinforced for extra rigidity. New intersecting panels and load bearing structures, as well as bonded side and rear windows, also help to provide greater stiffness.'

A quartet of disc brakes were standard specification for all the heavier-bodied Touring models, with 10.2in diameter the minimum even on the later 318i. ABS was a British option on all but the 325i Touring, which like its saloon sister had standard ABS.

Basic 3-series weight distribution remained equally split front and rear. Coil springs and damping were uplifted in recognition of an average extra 45kg (200lb) weight gain, most at the back. There was the German option of self-levelling suspension, and this was also listed in the UK, retailing at £721 in 1989. The system worked in combination with sports suspension settings and power steering. The hydropneumatic layout required no additional power source, taking an auxiliary line from the oil circulation system of the power steering via a tandem pump.

The fifth door was operated with assistance from two low pressure gas spring struts, and the number-plate panel was contoured as a hand grip. The fifth door stretched down between the rear light clusters to provide a flattish loading sill. Yet space was constricted by the sloping rear window line – a similar problem to that inflicted on the original Audi 100 Avant/estate. The Touring back seats could be individually folded, and the rear seat cushion removed for a small bonus in vertical carrying capacity. Payload was increased to a maximum 480kg/1,058lb.

The overall finish of the luggage compartment was superbly detailed, including four points at which loads could be lashed down and a roller blind to cover contents. A safety net between the luggage compartment and occupants was originally listed as an option. Stowage 'caves' in the side panels also helped security, whilst rear speakers were located in these panels along with the battery on 4x4 and diesel Touring models.

Production of LHD and RHD examples was not undertaken until March 1988; the RHD 320I Touring was made from September 1988 onward. By then BMW had the 324 turbo diesel derivative, but, as for every other BMW diesel, this model was not offered in Britain. Another feature to escape the UK was the 4x4 (325iX) running gear beneath Touring coachwork.

A 318i Touring followed at a distance, at least as far as the UK was concerned, and was offered for sale in June 1989. At the close of 1989 BMW (GB) had sold 1,023 318i Tourings, 1,391 of the 320i equivalent and a profitable 1,494 of the 325i Touring.

Standard equipment, ex-factory on the original 325i, was sensible in embracing vented rear discs for the 4x4 derivative and solid discs otherwise. British 325i-specification Tourings came with ABS as standard, but then one could hardly have expected less as its saloon brother listed ABS as standard in the Eighties. A 320i Touring went without ABS in the UK, priced at close to £700 as an option in 1989.

For the 320/325i-based Touring models 6J x 14in multi-spoke alloy wheels wore standard (for 325i) 195/65 rubber, whereas the 325iX had Michelin TD 200/60 VR-365 tyres on appropriate 365 x 150 TD alloy wheels.

Touring goodies comprised five-door central locking that

A 325iX being subjected to a salt spray test. Only the bootlid badge and subtle bodywork appendages identified the 4x4 version of the 3-series.

This 1971 predecessor of the 3-series Touring, a model which was derided in Germany, had three-door bodywork based on the '02' line. At the time it was badged as a BMW Touring 2000 tii. Its 2-litre engine, with mechanical fuel injection, developed 130bhp and was credited with 0–62mph in 9.2sec and a maximum of 118mph.

not only covered the rear hatch, but also the fuel filler cap. A sports steering wheel, halogen auxiliary driving lights and the BMW headlight wiper-based cleaning system were also featured on the six-cylinder UK-market Touring. Subtle details like colour coding, the use of green tinted glass and the introduction of satin black for chrome were extended to the Touring.

Introduced at £13,470 in June 1989, the 318i specification in the UK – compared with a 325i Touring – lost ABS anti-lock braking, alloy wheels, headlight wash/wipe, sports steering wheel and those halogen front foglamps. All of these items could be made up on the option list, so try to secure alloy wheels and ABS on any secondhand purchase.

Compared with the six-cylinder models, the 318i Touring was rather frenetic, a 4.27:1 final drive being necessary to shift 1,180kg/2,601lb respectively. Fortunately the M40 motor was a more sophisticated 1.8-litre than its predecessors. Performance was adequate in manual transmission trim, reaching 0–62mph in a claimed 11.5 seconds, but the automatic was markedly slower. Top speed was rated at

117mph, or 116mph for the auto. Urban fuel consumption was acceptable at a listed 27mpg for both transmissions.

Autocar highlighted the 325i Touring's limitations and strengths most succinctly when it commented, 'Open the tailgate … and you will not find an easily loaded platform to take your freezer. Instead, you will have a struggle to lift it up over the rear lamp clusters, hoping that there is sufficient vertical space to accept it. Close ratio Getrag gearbox and 170bhp engine give performance characteristics which would have been rare in almost any car, saloon or otherwise, 10 or even five years ago. It will sprint to 60mph in 7.6 seconds and can squirt from 50 to 70mph in third gear in just 4.5 seconds. Top speed is a little over 130mph.'

New to the public at Frankfurt in 1985, the 4x4 325 saw a suave brand of 4x4 motoring based on the two- and subsequently four-door E30 saloon body, although inevitably the car's LHD status tightly restricted UK sales; BMW at Bracknell took 43 examples during 1989 and the model was dropped in 1990. But elsewhere sales were significant and 30,000 were made between 1985–90. My information points

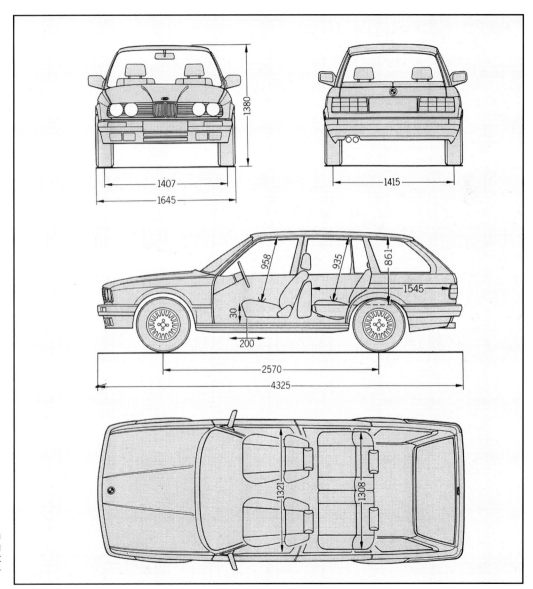

Dimensionally little changed from its saloon car base, the E30 Touring was significantly heavier as a result of the useful five-door configuration.

to the USA taking nearly two thirds of that total.

BMW engineers had experimented with front drive between '02' and 3-series and dismissed it as out of character for their products. But the 4x4 challenge was not to be ignored, as Audi at Ingolstadt had presented their stunning 4x4 turbo quattro coupe at the March 1980 Geneva motor show. The original quattro's impact upon performance motoring continues to this day. Most manufacturers were forced to adopt 4x4 in the wake of the Audi quattro, not for sales volume throughout the range, but to earn a technical halo. BMW were not interested in Audi's World Championship rally success, but they *were* concerned about their increasing lack of technology, in the public domain at least, particularly in the fields of aerodynamics and 4x4 traction.

In altering an existing front-engine, rear-drive, middleweight saloon with strut front and trailing-arm rear suspension to 4x4 configuration, BMW unwittingly found itself with a new rival at launch time. Ford had experience of a British Ferguson-patented system in the Seventies and had determined to put into production an XR4x4 version of the Sierra

in 1985. BMW also wanted a 1985 production debut, and the Ferguson system, incorporating a central viscous coupling, was made available for mass production through an Anglo-German co-operative.

The Ford Sierra XR4x4, Scorpio 4x4, Sierra RS Cosworth four-door and Escort Cosworth RS all shared their basic 4x4 hardware with the BMW 325i, including a power split broadly defined as one third front, two thirds rear (37% fore, 63% aft). In fact Ford were marginally more conservative over feeding power to the front wheels, splitting at 34% and 64% but the principle of rear-drive handling in a 4x4 car remained.

The big difference between BMW and Ford was that Ford specified *optional* anti-lock braking from Alfred Teves a few months after the introduction of their 4x4 whereas BMW went straight ahead with their version of a Teves 3-series ABS system. BMW selected much stiffer settings in their viscous coupling (VC) differentials, a move eventually echoed by Ford when the Escort Cosworth arrived in 1992. BMW also took a couple of basic precautions to improve slippery surface

The harmony of line is preserved by the sloping rear hatchback. Such lines, however, rob useful vertical storage space aft of the back seat in a manner not tolerated by manufacturers of more focused assaults on the estate car market. The 325i, nevertheless, could carry a useful load at up to 130mph with unmatched smoothness.

The load area was superbly finished, with useful side compartments, but loading could be a fiddle through the U-section for the tailgate. A rear cover (retracted in this picture) was incorporated to cover the shorter contents of the load area.

behaviour of the ABS. These concerned reprogrammed electronic parameters which reduced yaw momentum; a longitudinal acceleration sensor to distinguish between low and high friction coefficients, and a slight boost to tickover speeds. This is applied directly at the throttle butterfly by an extra electronic control circuit tied into the longitudinal sensor, and avoids the embarrassment of locking all four wheels at very low speeds on the iciest inclines.

Based at Schwabisch, Viscodrive GmbH undertook production runs of more than 5,000 on behalf of the British Ferguson patent holders in Coventry, who dealt with small-run prototypes and competition requirements of the period. Viscodrive was established as a 50-50 partnership between GKN in Britain and transmission specialists ZF (Zahnradfabrik of Friedrichshafen). ZF have always been a major supplier to BMW, and these days are best known for

automatic and manual gearboxes, plus power steering and rear differentials.

Adding 4x4 to the base of a rear-drive 325i involved fitting a central differential/transfer box with planetary gears and a viscous coupling placed aft of the gearbox. Rear drive was assembled in the usual manner – albeit a VC limited-slip differential was utilized at the back as well slipping through a 3.91:1 final drive, or one with a 3.73:1 ratio when used in association with the sports five-speed gearbox.

Power was fed forward by an external shaft from the central differential gear set, the shaft motivated by a multiple-row Morse chain. BMW fed power forward on the opposite side to Ford (the nearside front in British terms) but faced the same installation problems. Thus a new cast aluminium sump pan allows the passage of the offside driveshaft and the BMW front has many new components.

Luxury trim is at odds with a role as a supposed load carrier, but BMW had to offer a prestigious alternative to the conventional estate car. Here the split seat action is demonstrated, a vital feature in order to store taller objects, given the line of the tailgate.

The 318i version of the Touring arrived in the UK in June 1989 at £13,470. It was the entry point of the five-door range until September 1991, when the Touring version of the 316i made its debut at £13,750. Both remained on offer a year later, but by then cost £13,840 and £15,840, by which time a 325i Touring nudged £22,000.

The BMW 3-series 'hot hatchbacks' were the Alpina-modified Tourings, the 190bhp 2.5-litre C2.5 and the 210bhp C2 2.7, in appropriately modified chassis.

BMW reworked their E30 suspension around new aluminium lower wishbones and a replacement subframe. For the first time negative offset front geometry was selected. This was achieved by remounting the front strut and altering the kingpin inclination, an attitude of 2.9mm/0.11in negative being adopted in place of positive, and the track stretched. Standard power steering and anti-rollbar were repositioned, reflecting the fact that the front cross-member had travelled forward to accommodate all the new hardware, everything being positioned so as to give the front driveshafts a straight run.

Compared with a conventional 325i, the 'iX' was stretched by 13mm at the front to 1,470mm/57.9in but was just a millimetre wider at the back. Wheelbase, overall length and other vital statistics – apart from the extra weight – remained the same as for the rear-drive models, which also provided standard steering and gearbox (choice of automatic, manual or close-ratio five-speed), plus sundry other hardware.

The 325iX had replacement spring strut supports and an enlarged central transmission tunnel and wheelarches to accommodate the revised ride height. The standard wheel and tyre combination was a steel 6J x 14in wheel with the usual 195/65 VR tyre dimensions, but the Michelin TD system was available in alloy: 150 TD 365 plus 200/60 VR-365 rubber.

BMW claims were realistic for the extra kerb weight incurred by the factory 4x4 conversion. The gain quoted for the 325iX over the equivalent saloon was 90kg/198lb. An internal memo in Germany warned of performance losses due to that extra weight, plus the additional gear sets, bearings, seals and joints, and a loss in aerodynamic values caused by the modestly raised body height.

The same memo quoted the top speed of the 325iX as 212km/h (131.6mph), and 0–100km/h (62mph) was recorded by company testers as 9 seconds. That meant a company-estimated loss of 5km/h top speed, plus 0.7 seconds on the 0–100km/h drag. A 10.3 second time in fifth between 50 and 75mph (80 and 120km/h) was reckoned to be 1.4 seconds adrift of the rear-drive 325i. The 325iX did not fulfil BMW objectives for either sales or profit in an E30 suit. Neither the 325iX nor the Touring 3-series had firm introduction dates in the Nineties E36 body. By contrast, a new convertible – again with the cleanest of hood and body lines – seemed a certainty for the early Nineties, constructed on E36 foundations.

CHAPTER 6

Foundation for sports success

The development of the M3 road car

BMW Motorsport GmbH, a company-within-a-company that has been trading since 1972, created the M3 to uphold the BMW reputation for unbeatable saloon car performance, on road or track. They succeeded not just in creating a race and rally track victor, but also an outstanding example of how to make a profit whilst supplying sporting excellence. Some 17,184 M3 saloons were built between 1986 and its cessation of production in December 1990. For comparison, the Sapphire Cosworth 4x4 hit approximately 12,000 units between 1990 and 1992, Lancia Delta 4x4 and integrale series from 1985–91 had exceeded 30,000 units when the final version was announced.

A winner of national, European and World Championship racing titles, the BMW M3 also proved a doughty performer in tarmac rallying, and won the World Championship qualifier in Corsica. In this section I examine the development of the road car that had to be made at the rate of 5,000 vehicles a year in order to earn international recognition (the homologation process for Groups A and N) from the Paris-based sporting authority, FISA.

Every major aspect of the M3 that could increase its competitive potential was examined, but not all such features had to be built into the road cars. Braking and handling were improved, but not to serious competition standards, for that was not a requirement of the authorities.

As for any BMW, the heart was its engine – in this case a massively overbored four-cylinder, built along traditional BMW DOHC, 16v competition engine lines. It had immense strength in both durability and potential horsepower, but

aerodynamics were also critical for BMW competition aspirations. These were not just confined to the obvious spoilers, for the rear bootlid height was elevated and the back window raked. Cutting aerodynamic axle lift and harnessing modest downforce energy would be priorities throughout the M3 career. Specifically, such aerodynamics contributed to racing stability at 160mph and a drag figure of 0.33Cd for the road car, which was not bad for such a boxy outline.

Basic engine research started in the summer of 1981, and the first principle to establish was the worth of a light and simple 16-valve four-cylinder over the BMW 3-series performance option for the public of an inline six-cylinder (320i/325i). The company finally did have to follow the latter route with the M3's E36 successor, owing to changes in international regulations and marketing priorities.

To this end, the iron-block slant 'four', itself a development of the 1.5-litre from 1961 that has served BMW in so many forms – including GP racing – was mated to a sawn-off six-cylinder head for initial trials! That was the DOHC, four-valve-per-cylinder layout used in the earlier M635/M5 and descended from the mid-engine M1 of 1978–81. The resulting engine was coded S14, and was stamped on the block as 23 4 for all 2.3-litres, which is a point worth remembering when analyzing motor and chassis codes.

Paul Rosche recalls the 'modification' with dismissive laughter: 'You know how we make the first M3 engine in 1981? I tell you. We slice the end from an M635 24-valve; two cylinders are removed and water passages closed off. Yes, now we have a cylinder head to put on the iron block "four".

The emotive 'M' for Motorsport badge and '3' for 3-series were united in a memorable driving experience, even before production began. This picture, taken in spring 1986, records an oversteering exuberance that no longer finds its way into press material for the sombre Nineties.

The additional body panels for an M3 involved a plethora of modifications, but BMW reaped their reward by making over 17,100 saloons in Munich and nearly 800 convertibles at assorted sites. Standards of paint match and finish mirrored those of the parent factory, which was recommendation enough for most owners.

The M3 at the Ismaning test centre before launch. It revealed a standard of finish that integrated the bulges, flares and spoilers in harmony.

That's what we needed to show us the M3 could work!' All the vital dimensions – bore and stroke, valves – were set to be those of the M1 motor, according to the then project leader, Werner Frowein.

Why not a six-cylinder?

Paul Rosche recollects: 'Most important was our experience with four-valve-per-cylinder Formula 2, the M1 and M635. We had proved the large cylinder bore (93.4mm) for motor racing and production; the cylinder head design of the M635 looked so good for us that we did the first development work in two weeks by cutting up the head for a six-cylinder head and fitting it to a 2-litre 'four'. It worked

The rear was distinguished by the pure hoop spoiler, twin exhaust and under-bumper extended apron. Rear glass was substantially reworked in pursuit of more air feed to the back spoiler. A significant reduction in the aero factor from 0.36 to 0.33Cd was a credit to such a fat-wheeled, boxy design.

well, straight away. However, a six-cylinder motor would have been just too heavy for the best race handling of a front-engine car, and the crankshaft is longer than we would like. The "four" is a more compact engine, and we knew it better.'

In February 1983 BMW Motorsport became much more serious about the M3 project as the racing replacement for the 528i/635i saloons and coupes that they were being forced to use in the early and mid-Eighties under Group A international rules. BMW had more suitable equipment – notably the M635 CSi with another production development of the 24v inline 'six' rated at a mighty 286 street horsepower – but production was never enough for the car to become eligible. If BMW had been a prominent British company, the

M635 CSi would have been homologated, but neither the German authorities nor the parent company would stand for it, so the M3 had racing rationale firmly reinforced as its reason for living.

An enlargement to 2,302cc for the production engine for maximum effect in the 2.5-litre racing class was possible via a steel crankshaft and an 84mm stroke to accompany a 93.4mm bore. The bore and stroke remained true to the M1 for all but 600 examples of the final 2.5-litre Sport Evolution, which had an even bigger bore (95mm) and an 87mm stroke to produce 2,467cc.

What Paul Rosche did not reveal, but which is obvious talking to those who have to meet his standards and those of the parent company, is that the subsequent road version of the engine and chassis then had literally millions of Deutsche-marks and thousands of hours expended in durability and refinement running. This aspect was reinforced for me by a story I gathered at the launch – and the knowledge that the M3 had to go through all the usual factory durability tests, but in a far shorter span than normal, to meet homologation and consequent production schedules.

First, the launch story. I gave a BMW M3 development engineer a ride around Mugello in a Sierra Cosworth prototype that *Performance Car* had arranged, to meet the BMW newcomers at the Italian launch. As the Ford had just been welded up in the exhaust department by BMW engineers, I apologized to my travelling companion for not demonstrating its full potential, particularly as the spanner and arc-welding men of Munich had impressed on me that they were not diving under that 'blank' Ford to weld the exhaust again! My companion nodded solemnly and reported that BMW Motorsport had 'the same problem for M3. Took us nearly another year, many more development miles, and much more money to fix it, but they made us do it.'

Secondary development tales told me that the M3 spent its time in all the usual durability tests for hot and cold climates, was crash-tested and also had to go through a pretty severe emissions control panic when the decision was taken to make a catalytic convertor version available at launch. As for most BMWs there were numerous proving sessions at Nurburgring.

In fact the M3 racked up at least 6,200 miles at this historic

Chief M3 clues within were the sports seats, a first gear isolated closest to the (LHD) driver, M Technic sports steering wheel and the provision of an oil temperature gauge within the 8,000rpm tachometer. Note the central (between speedometer and tachometer) colour-striped 'M' logo, the optional computer to the right of the radio, and the standard use of electric windows with central locking.

venue, relying on the famous old track sections to prove the suspension under duress from October 1984 onward. The toughest tests were three flat-out sessions held on the Southern toe of Italy. The Nardo speed bowl saw the M3 hurtle round at more than 140mph for a minimum of 31,000 miles.

Another obstacle that had to be overcome with the parent company was that of producing a car on normal production lines with so many plastics. Steel was used for the extended wheelarches, which were designed to accommodate racing wheel rim widths of up to 10in. Otherwise the Motorsport engineers were able to use more plastics than had been seen in a production 3-series. The fact that steel would be used for

the main body meant that development time for the body really was minimal owing to the need to get the body-in-steel tooling prepared.

The chunky M3 made a static debut at the 1985 Frankfurt show. The show reactions were predictably warm, some right over the top in the German-language press. BMW Motorsport needed this kind of support as there were alternative projects that I was not aware of, such as the inevitable 3-series/3.5-litre marriage that specialists such as Alpina were to profit from when the factory decided to steer a more manoeuvrable M3 course.

Another 1985 internal hurdle that was overcome was to satisfy high-level management of its public road abilities.

Between the lines of sunlight and shadow can be seen the historically important and correct front and rear cloth trim of the BMW sports seats (with height and squab adjustment).

This was in a direct comparison with the 325i and the Mercedes 2.3-16. After the toughest test yet, management were convinced, and the Type Approval reference machines could be built, following managerial sign-off.

The project received new impetus in 1985 when Thomas Ammerschläger, competition engineer on the Cologne/Zakspeed Capris before he moved to Audi and worked on the quattro chassis, entered BMW Motorsport. Thomas assumed overall responsibility for developing a product to be mass-produced by the mainstream BMW AG in Munich.

M3 motors were built in a Munich factory corner, alongside the V12s, by the highest paid hourly workers in BMW AG; even 'tea-breaks' were streamlined, with girls bringing these aristocrats of the engine building craft their beverages. It would waste too much time if they downed tools!

New engineering influences were most pronounced in the modified strut front suspension, as the geometry was altogether new. I was told that there was triple the castor of 3-series and a quicker power-assisted rack, ratio 19:6:1, all in a successful effort to increase feel and high-speed stability to a point unmatched by any contemporary production car.

New front and rear rollbars of sturdy girth were associated with new pivot points to increase effectiveness, and twin-tube Boge gas dampers – Bilstein on the racing cars – were installed. However, the basic layout of the rear axle, with 15-degree raked semi-trailing arms, was retained, albeit with stiffer springs.

As to why BMW never put the effective M3 chassis work at the disposal of less happy handlers in the 3-series, I learned more during the 1990 launch of the 850i. A BMW engineer, who declined to be named, revealed, 'all the M3 suspension parts can be fitted to less expensive 3-series.' Indeed, the basic mounting points are the same. However, it was very expensive to make this change and he continued, 'the parts were more expensive to produce than the standard ones. I think this was another good reason why they were not adopted for any other 3-series in production.' On record, he would do no more than nod at the suggestion that BMW mainstream managers were unconvinced that a machine like the 325i was bought by a clientele sufficiently appreciative of vehicle handling to justify the expense of a change to a system created via Motorsport, rather than mainstream, BMW engineers.

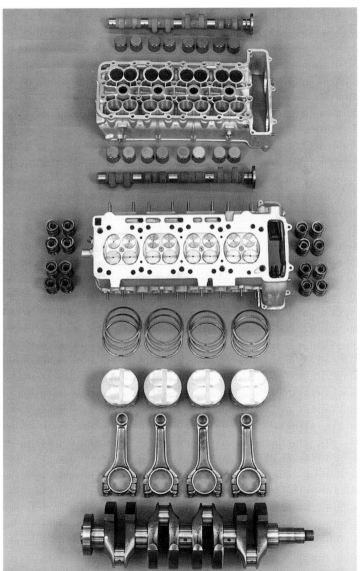

The M3 S14-coded engine was a magnificent piece of work that proved durable, even though it was originally a hurried conversion from the S38-coded six-cylinder units of M5/M635 CSi fame. The 93.4mm bores were also siamesed like the 3.5-litre six-cylinders and each branch of the intake manifolding had its own butterfly. The 84mm-stroke crankshaft was a new steel forging carrying eight balance weights and a vibration damper. Despite a stiffening shell between the engine block and gearbox casing 'to reduce vibration and resonance', this 2.3-litre was rough in comparison with any contemporary BMW unit. Some of the Evolution versions revved encouragingly in the 5,000 to 7,000rpm band on the road and the engine was regularly and successfully asked to withstand nearly 10,000rpm in competition.

Front and rear suspension adhered to the principles of 3-series running gear, but were extensively modified and featured fresh geometry to enhance performance on wider wheels and tyres. Note the front strut linkage for the thickened anti-rollbar and the retention of the divorced telescopic damper (more truly a strut length, aft of the halfshaft) and coil spring; twin-tube dampers enhanced the ride considerably.

Radical bodywork changes were finally allowed by the parent company, including raking the enlarged rear window to provide better airflow to the 40mm/1.6in raised SMC plastic rear bootlid/spoiler assembly. Hard plastics also complete the side and front spoiler 'body kit', but the square wings *a la* quattro are, as discussed, in steel. Incidentally, standards of finish and paint were all that would be expected of BMW; I have now seen 55,000-mile examples that have resisted the ravages of British weather and traffic creditably.

The cabin was completed with the BMW-built sports seats that are optional on lesser 3-series, and a tough three-spoke Motorsport steering wheel was added to the solid air of the grey-toned environment. The seats were adjustable via three levers and knobs to cater for height, thigh support, backrest rake, legroom and tilt.

Standard equipment within the German price covered a sporting version of Bosch ABS that reacted to nothing but the hardest shove on the centre pedal. Also included was a ZF multi-plate limited-slip differential, torqued to a soft 25%, a bigger 70-litre/15.4-gallon fuel tank, tinted glass, electric twin mirrors and a Getrag five-speeder, with first isolated closest to the LHD pilot. For racing purposes the bigger Getrag used in the 6-Series coupe was initially employed, six speeds appearing as the astonishing M3 motored into the racing history of the early Nineties.

Original options included a simplified on-board computer (I managed 26.9mpg in 93 road miles at the launch). Air conditioning, power windows, central locking, leather trim and the usual plethora of in-car entertainment possibilities were also offered.

The usual BMW 'command post' driving position highlighted the switches and instrumentation as an object lesson in comprehensible clarity. The 260km/h (161mph) speedometer was matched by an 8,000rpm tachometer with a 7,300 redline. The rev-counter carried an oil temperature gauge instead of an econometer.

BMW Motorsport had two substantial factory sites at Munich and Garching and employed over 400 people, some of them to create the M3. However, with the exception of the convertible, it was built on the Munich production lines. The soft-top rarity (less than 1,000 made) was made at Garching.

BMW Motorsport actually hand-made convertible M3s from 1988 to June 1991, constructing a strictly controlled number. To pursue this and other assembly projects, the sports department was subdivided and expanded to embrace a 1986 factory at Garching. Still within Munich's outer environs, Garching was planned to accommodate the complete vehicle engineering staff (ie, not the engine men of

---

Brief specification: 1986 BMW M3, LHD only
(amended where 1991 information improved)

Engine: Inline DOHC four with 16v and Bosch ML Motronic injection/ignition. Bore x stroke, 93.4mm x 84mm (2,302cc). Compression, 10.5:1. Power, 200bhp @ 6,750rpm and 176lb/ft torque @ 4,750rpm.
Bhp per litre: 86.8
Option: 195bhp with catalyst at 6,750rpm
170lb/ft (catalyst) at 4,750rpm

Transmission: Five-speed with Borg-Warner synchronization, 3.25 final drive, rear drive and limited slip. *Ratios:* 1st, 3.72; 2nd, 2.40; 3rd, 1.77; 4th, 1.26; 5th, 1.0. Final drive: 3.25:1

Body: Basic unitary steel 3-series augmented by SMC plastic bootlid/spoiler and body kit; front and rear bonded glass. Glassfibre-reinforced resin 3-piece bumper/spoiler with foam filling, also used polyurethane skins. Rear bumper, same construction and side sills. Cd 0.33.
Dimensions: Wheelbase: 2,562mm/100.9in (2,564mm with 225/45 VR 16 option); overall length: 4,360mm/171.7in; width: 1,675mm/65.9in; height: 1,365mm/53.7in.

Weight: Full tank of fuel (70 litres), no extras; 1,200kg/2,640lb.

Brakes: Based on current 5-series (vented fronts) discs + ABS. *Sizes:* Vented fronts had 284mm diameter; solid rears, 250mm. Single piston calipers.

Wheels & tyres: Alloy BBS 7J x 15in; Uniroyal or Pirelli P700, both 205/55 VR.

Suspension: Uprated strut/trailing arms, uprated 15-degree trail angle for trailing arms. Boge twin-tube gas pressurized shock absorbers and inserts, unique coil springs. Anti-rollbar has twice standard leverage, pivot point outside spring/strut axis. Replacement stub axles encase 5-series wheel bearings. *Steering:* Rack-and-pinion: 19.6:1 ratio, servo-assisted.

Performance: (BMW figs) max 146mph; 0–62mph 6.7s; 50–75mph in fifth, 7.1s. Catalyst: max 143mph; 0–62mph 6.7 sec; 50–75mph 7.5 sec.

Fuel consumption: Urban, 24.3mpg; @ 56mph, 48.6mpg; @ 75mph, 37.6mpg.

Price: Dm58,000 without options, equivalent to £18,125 at press time. LHD only.

Utilizing some 5-series components, the braking system of the M3 was enhanced to the point where BMW could claim a 35% increase of effective front and rear brake friction areas.

Preussenstrasse), a design studio, sales department, stores and car production. Output of cars had been planned at a ceiling of approximately 1,000 units a year, but Motorsport managed to double and triple that in 1989–90. This production capacity obviously could not be absorbed by the M3 convertible alone, which reached a total output of 786.

In fact the M3 convertible almost did not make it into 1988

production as a four-cylinder at all, for the first show car had a 4x4 drive train hitched to the usual BMW 325i power plant. This became a one-off when the realists persuaded management to opt for the four-cylinder M3 unit and rear drive. The model has never sold in large numbers, but this was never intended.

According to factory sources, the M3 saloon was actually rendered in one 1985 pre-production example. It went into full manufacture from July 1986, but a batch of 20–30 very accurate production replicas were finished to meet the press at Mugello in May 1986. Some 2,396 M3s were built in 1986 and it was recognized for competition in Groups A and N (5,000 examples being built in one year) by March 1, 1987. The panel below shows how production then fared and reached its peak in 1987.

M3 SALOON PRODUCTION
(excluding Motorsport prototypes, Munich)

1985	1
1986	2,396
1987	6,396
1988	3,426
1989	2,541
1990	2,424
TOTAL	*17,184*

M3 CABRIOLET PRODUCTION
(BMW Motorsport, Garching)

1988	130
1989	180
1990	176
1991	300
TOTAL	*786*

Performance and prices

Some 6,750rpm and 200bhp – or 195bhp in catalytic convertor trim – were the figures quoted for the M3, which was sold only in LHD form to the public. This output was enough to claim up to 146mph and 0–62mph in comfortably under seven seconds, with or without a clean exhaust. Independent tests in Britain showed that the M3, in any trim, was substantially the fastest of the E30-bodied 3-series.

Autocar & Motor ran three 2.3-litre versions, including a brace of 200bhp examples (one convertible, one saloon) and reckoned they were good for up to 146mph, with 0–60mph in the six to seven second bracket and 0–100mph occupying less than 20 seconds. In fact *Autocar's* most consistent results came from the 1988 220bhp Evolution version that will be discussed later.

For the secondhand buyer, the following M3 variant identification tips may be useful: the first Evolution model (200bhp) had an 'E' punched onto the cast eye of the cylinder head, which is underneath the fourth cylinder throttle housing, and it can only be seen by using a mirror! Externally it was identified by extended front and rear spoilers, and used a lightweight bootlid. This model gave no practical road benefits except a slight increase in stability at higher speeds.

The M3 was a comparative rarity on British roads, especially an officially imported example such as this car. The model was first imported (in LHD only) in April 1987 and sales in the UK never exceeded 100 units a year.

The 1988 first Evolution BMW for the road did not mean much to customers, but it provided the racing teams with enhanced aerodynamic forces, thanks to an extended front spoiler and double-blade rear wing. An alternative exhaust manifold had already been recognized by the racing authorities at this stage.

Evolution II carried an air collector and valve cover in white, also painted with Motorsport stripes. The motor generated 220bhp, still peaking at 6,750rpm (using replacement camshafts, pistons, lightened flywheel, air intake trunk and Bosch Motronic chip). It was mated to a slightly taller final drive (3.15:1), and BMW claimed a substantial increase in performance.

Usual M3 figures were 146mph and 0–62mph in 6.7 seconds. For the Evolution II, BMW recorded 152mph and 0–60mph in 6.7 seconds, and *Autocar & Motor* certainly found an improvement over their 200bhp M3 test experience. Instead of recording 7.1 seconds for 0–60mph and 19 seconds for the 0–100mph drag, they returned 6.6 and 17.8 seconds respectively. They timed themselves at 148mph around the Millbrook bowl, which equates to an honest 150mph; and their best M3 overall fuel consumption was 26mpg.

I liked the 220bhp level as the best road M3 as it was smoother than the later 2.5 and practically as fast, so long as the revs were kept in the 5–7,000rpm band. The chassis, running Pirelli P700s of 225/45 section on 7.5 x 16in BBS alloys, never seemed to run out of dry road grip, understeering if overdriven. In the wet, of course, it would still slide if the full 7,300rpm redline was employed in second or third.

Evolution II also sported additional spoilers, carrying front brake ducts and the extra lip on the rear wing. These rested on a lightweight bootlid, further weight-saving being achieved through the material thickness for the rear wing, bumper supports, back screen and rear side windows. Altogether the factory expected to save 10kg/22lb to lower the racing weight.

Identification clues on the Ravaglia/Cecotto machines included the Evolution II spoilers and the use of body colour for the air collector and rocker cover, which meant either Misano Red or Nogaro Silver. My test car bore a plaque inside that announced it was 'M3 73/508 1989 BMW Motorsport GmbH'. Cars from these series should be signed either by Roberto Ravaglia (UK only) or Johnny Cecotto.

A recollection from 1986 seems appropriate. At the introduction time I was lucky enough to attend the epic Italian launch on and around the Mugello race, and reported for *Motoring News*: 'The engine idles with Teutonic-Motronic precision, has plenty of torque from 2,500 and marches through the close ratios with resonances galore around 4,500 which is particularly annoying and ultimately tiring in motorway use – but it is a real joy from 5,000 to 7,000. Then it struts into real power production, comfortably outpacing the Mercedes Cosworth alliance, by 15bhp.

'The gearchange is naturally super for the track, but less attractive when you are shifting between first and second, across the gate. After three full-throttle departures, this knack was acquired once more, providing a good example of the normally obstructive competition shift layout. This Getrag also has the advantage of being perfect for use out of town, within the second-to-fifth H-pattern.

'The 5/6-series-derived brakes – and wheel bearings for that matter – were superb on circuit or road. On track the ABS acted only when provoked, from 125mph in fifth, into a U-shaped 65–70mph curve that required third.

'As anticipated the chassis proved memorable. It will cope with four-wheel circuit drifts, usually preferring to understeer when pushed too hard, but capable of holding a third gear tail slide over a particularly greasy section.

'On the road it's even better and would have saved BMW a lot of past criticism regarding the oversteer of the former 3-Series … The ride is outstanding by sports saloon standards; the steering is informative and the whole plot works better than we have any right to expect of a conventional saloon: 10/10.'

This was my conclusion for *Motoring News* upon the international debut of the M3 that May. 'The 2.3-litre M3 amounts to a 146mph package of old and new BMW goodies that sets new standards of pace and chassis grace amongst rear-drive saloons, but wins no prizes for four-cylinder engine refinement or UK availability. Currently, this is a model that will be seen everywhere but the UK. Even the USA get the marginally less powerful catalyst model in 1987. Thus, the UK personal importers will have to settle for LHD and a price currently equivalent to £18,125.'

As an official Special Order-status import, the M3 was a comparatively rare sight on British roads. Just 55 of the original M3 saloons were brought in for 1987 registration, and 58 in 1988. The peak UK M3 sales year was a princely 62 M3 saloons in 1989. The importers also had a convertible (19 examples sold for 1989) and by 1988 there was also the 2.5 Evolution to register. At the close of 1990 just 211 of the 2.3-litre saloons, 32 convertibles and 38 of the 2.5-litre saloons had been officially imported, which explains why the car remained on Special Order status throughout its UK life.

Of the rarer evolutionary models, the official UK importation documentation supports the existence of only seven Evolution 1 and 51 Evolution II. None of the 1988 'Europa Meister 88' (195bhp KAT/full leather trim, each signed by Roberto Ravaglia, but not to be confused with the later UK-bound special 215bhp) models, were handled by BMW GB. Britain was not on the unleaded pace that season. The official Roberto Ravaglia (Cecotto on the Continent) model reached 25 UK copies, and I am told approximately 51 of the final Evolution Sport 2.5-litre were ordered, though sales figures recorded 38 sales to August 1991.

The initial German price was the equivalent of £18,125, but British Special Order M3s always exceeded £20,000 from the official network, and held their value, even in LHD, until the Nineties recession took prices of older models down to less than £10,000.

The first M3s came to Britain in April 1987 via the official importers, nearly a year after their LHD announcement. The initial price on a D-plate was £23,550, and that was maintained until the 1988 E-plate examples.

Standard equipment included the 7J x 15in alloy wheels, limited-slip differential, power steering, the sports seats and electronic ABS anti-lock braking; but extra had to be paid for commonly fitted items such as a power roof and windows, on-board computer and – on later M3s – EDC (Electronic Damper Control). The latter offered three settings that corresponded to Sport, Comfort and the compromise that engineers would have selected for all situations without this gimmickry. I conscientiously tried to remember its use. I would occasionally select the soft setting in town, but the compromise setting was in use for 90% of my UK mileage.

For 1988 the standard 200bhp M3 was supplanted for UK purposes by a supply of 51 220bhp Evolution models that

Detail of the front and rear spoilers for the Ravaglia limited edition reveals the extended front blade and secondary (lower) airdam on the bootlid.

Inside the Ravaglia limited edition can be seen the unique Motorsport striped seat and door trim, leather-edged for the seating.

were retailed for £26,960. Showroom features centred upon the uprated 220bhp engine – detailed in the section on evolutionary M3s – and revised aerodynamics, identified by an additional tail spoiler flap and brake ducting to the front device.

Similarly priced, but officially 5bhp less powerful, was the 25-off (for UK) Roberto Ravaglia edition of signed specials, which cost £26,850 in July 1989. At this point, all officially UK-imported BMW M3s, including the small run of Ravaglia specials, had three-way catalytic convertors.

All the Ravaglia cars for Britain came with gaudy seat inlays, leather surrounds, and some other interior parts were coated in silver. Front electric windows and an on-board computer were added to the standard fitments listed earlier for M3, including anti-lock brakes. External identification is aided by black centres for the 7.5J x 16in alloys – half an inch up on the original car – carrying extremely effective Pirelli P700-Z covers in the 225/45 size.

2.5-litre Evolution Sport

The 2.5-litre Evolution (Evo III to its parents) was sold in the UK at more than £30,000, but only 38 were shifted in 1990 at that cost. The recession, plus LHD, prevented these extraordinary road rockets doing much more than acting as extremely good PR for the importers whenever another road tester dived into ecstasy about their brutally rapid characters. One such car was placed in the company collection at Bracknell, to live out its days alongside the immortal BMWs ranging from the Thirties 328 to the Seventies CSL.

The final competition-prompted twist to the 2.5-litre

theme was produced only briefly (for three months and 600 examples). This derivative was launched in Germany at the equivalent of £29,820, and cost £34,500 when it arrived in Britain.

In summary, the main changes were: a capacity increase from 2,302cc to 2,467cc via an elongated crankshaft throw and plumper bores; a consequent gain of 18bhp and 10Nm, plus a radical rethink of aerodynamics: both front and rear spoilers could be adjusted; there was a degree of ground effect; the front wheelarches were enlarged; the front suspension was lowered and the interior overhauled to feature a distinctive Motorsport appearance, along with a suede look to the leather steering wheel rim, gear knob and handbrake grip.

The story behind the M3 Sport Evo was far from the 'bigger is better' manufacturer development trail. The 2.5-litre had been conceived purely as the basis of a more effective weapon against Mercedes in the German Touring Car Championship. It was announced against a backdrop of BMW Christmas Motorsport Conference celebrations, as the company had won the national title again in 1989 – quite unexpectedly – and intended to hang on to that advantage.

Even though Mercedes had been equipped with full production 2.5-litres – plus subsequent short-stroke evolutions – BMW felt they wanted to offer such a big four-cylinder to compete right up to the capacity limit.

German TV watched as the menacing black 2.5-litre M3 Sport Evolution was literally exposed from under wraps. Truth to tell there was not much to see externally, just the bolt-adjustable wing set, and the hint of serious intent given by the lowered front end and enlarged wheelarches, to take the 18in diameter wheels forecast for general Group A employment.

Before the 1990 season, loyal BMW engines engineer Franz Zinnecker commented, 'for the 2.5-litre M3 I had rejoined BMW Motorsport, whilst Paul Rosche was moved onto another project that I cannot discuss (probably the McLaren V12/48v – J.W.). Our priorities were to keep on increasing the competition potential of the 2.3-litres – I think that unit went from 295bhp to a best of 317bhp before we added another 5bhp with another 500rpm.

'That took us up to 9,800 competition rpm, but we did not think we could gain more under the regulations without an increase in capacity, so we make the 2.5-litre. Now I think we

The 1989/90 winter revealed the final twist to the M3 of the four-cylinder racing breed. The 2.5-litre engine and adjustable aerodynamics were imitated in 600 examples for the road, all made in 1990. The car was raced by the factory until the close of 1992, its badged successor being a totally different six-cylinder Coupe.

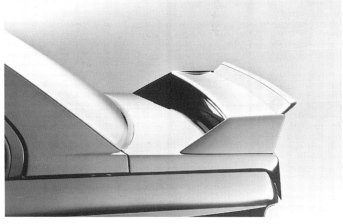

The Evolution 2.5-litre brought with it three-position adjustable aerodynamics. The rear-end picture also illustrates clearly the original raised bootlid profile of the M3.

Originally used in Motorsport training cars, the heavily moulded 2.5 M3 seats also took on a fuzzy stripe pattern in the standard cloth trim (leather was an option along with air conditioning) for door panels and rear seats. The aperture in the top of the seat backs apes that for a racing safety harness.

may have to come back to an 8,800rpm limit, but we have more power and new crankshaft balance weights to increase in the future.'

By the 1990 racing season the 2.5-litre Sport Evolution III was regularly credited with 330bhp at 9,500rpm, but it had started the year at 9,200rpm. More of that in the competition chapter, but it can be seen that the 2.5-litre did the job that was intended and, courtesy of Franz Zinnecker, I can also pick up on a previously forbidden BMW engines engineering topic: 'Originally von Falkenhausen would not let us have siamese bores. This rule was broken with the bigger six-cylinders and, therefore, we have this feature on all M3 motors as well.' The 95mm bore of the 2.5 Evo III is the biggest the writer knows of for a four-cylinder outside the Porsche 3-litre (104mm).

Building on a reputation for constructing engines that give the ultimate in bhp per litre in normally aspirated, catalytic convertor-equipped vehicles, BMW Motorsport went close to the elusive 100bhp per litre. Honda subsequently claim to have exceeded this figure with the V-TEC series of smaller Civic engines.

These road car statistics were achieved in the M3 2.5-litre by installing oversize inlet valves (38.5mm/1.52in) instead of the usual M3 sizing of 38mm/1.5in. Camshaft timings went from a duration of 264 degrees to 282. Compression ratio was *not* raised, but dropped from the 10.5:1 of the series M3 to 10.2:1. Internal engine modifications included sodium-cooled exhaust valves – the head diameters as before – and oil injection jets to spray beneath the pistons.

Externally few engine clues were given as to the overhauled interior: just red for the spark plug caps and a polished exhaust pipe.

BMW performance claims were not accompanied by establishment *Autocar & Motor* figures in Britain. The company credibly claimed a 154mph maximum and 0–62mph in 6.5 seconds. There was a reduction of the standing kilometre

The original M3 2.5 Sport steering wheel. Like the seats, it is an odd marriage between race practice and road safety, but both items were amongst the best the writer has experienced in a production saloon. The gear-lever knob and handbrake were trimmed in the same scuffed suede.

A British press demonstrator 2.5 Sport Evolution outside the Spa-Francorchamps circuit in Belgium, the scene of so many BMW 24-hour triumphs. Even in 1992 the 2.5 M3 proved capable of defeating Porsche and Nissan to score a 1-2-3 in the Belgian classic.

time to 26.7 seconds rather than the 2.3-litre model's 27.3 seconds. The Evolution's final drive did few favours to the fifth-gear acceleration – which was slower than a 2.3-litre model – but fourth gear let the engine rev a little and returned a reasonable 7.6 seconds from 50 to 75mph.

In my experience, and according to the claims of the factory, fuel consumption is excellent. The factory claimed 22.6 Urban mpg; I achieved 22.68mpg as an average over 2,000 miles of the 1990 Pirelli Marathon, which included a long session in the company of an AMG-modified Mercedes 190E 25-16 at speeds in the 145–155mph bracket.

The 2.5-litre chassis was refined in detail. From a racing viewpoint the most significant alteration was a new front and rear wing set that could be adjusted – albeit slowly and carefully for the private owner – via soft metal bolts to provide three basic positions fore-and-aft, or nine permutations.

The aerodynamic progression was from fully retracted – front spoiler in, rear laid almost flat – to a full extension of the front lip, and a distinctly GP 'flipper' look to the back blade.

The effect was to maintain the usual 0.33Cd in the retracted position, cutting front-end lift and allowing only slight lift forces on the back. Fully extended, BMW claimed virtually zero lift fore and slight downforces at the rear. A Venturi-principle spoiler was integrated forward, artificially accelerating the flow of air beneath the car by means of a V-shaped wind deflection profile. 'As a result, the air flowing beneath the car accelerates to a higher speed and creates an under pressure, the car being literally sucked onto the road,' explained BMW breathlessly.

The front spoiler also deleted the usual auxiliary lamps in favour of extra brake ducting, and the friction materials – but not front discs or calipers – were replaced with further uprated heat-resistant pads. Other front-end changes included lowered suspension ride height (10mm/0.4in), a further flare to the wheelarches to accommodate ever larger diameter racing slicks – racing 18in now allowed by virtue of production 16in diameters – and yet more attention to close up the lattices of the front 'kidney' grille. All front-end openings were additionally streamlined (headlight mountings, front grille attachment areas and surrounds to the bonnet), usually using rubber fillings, which were raced in 1988.

Kerb weight remained quoted as before (1,200kg) but that had meant much additional lightening to offset the extra engine capacity effects and generous standard equipment. Specifically the company attacked the fuel tank capacity, substituting the 320i/325i unit of 62 litres/13.64 gallons instead of the usual M3 reservoir of 70 litres. Other dietary requirements were to carve more out of the front and rear bumpers and rear bootlid, thus reducing the depth of rear

and side glass, just as it did for the original Evolution M3. Similarly, deletion of the roof grab handles and map reading lights helped.

Lower and ever wider, Michelin MXX covers of 225/45 ZR 16 dimensions were accompanied by 7.5J x 16in cross-spoke alloys with Nogaro Silver hub and spoke finish. Grip, on all but the most slippery of surfaces, was prodigious.

Showroom trim changes allowed only Jet Black or the snappy Brilliant Red body colour, each contrasted by red or black bumper insets. A green band was tinted prominently into the front screen. The interior was overhauled with that

'For the joy of driving' (Freude am Fahren) is an old BMW advertising motto, one that seems particularly relevant when at the wheel of an original M3.

suede leather look for steering rim, gear-lever and handbrake handle, plus red seat belts. The door trim panels were also unique, and an M3 logo was placed on the door instep.

Motorsport seats were new to BMW and extremely effective, but no Recaro option was offered on this model, thus seat heating was also unavailable. The seats were normally finished in Anthracite cloths and wore Motorsport striping; black leather was an expensive option in Britain, as was air conditioning. On one demonstrator I tried the conditioning cut in, showing that the engine did not run cleanly through day-time temperatures of 90 degrees.

These Sport Evo details may prove relevant to UK collectors. The retail price in June 1990 was £34,500, but that did not include the following items, which I have listed with the extra cost in brackets: electric sliding roof (£745); front electric windows (£413); black leather seats (£901); Electronic Damper Control (EDC) at £1,494; venting rear windows (£119); air conditioning (£1,341); on-board computer (£363); anti-theft locking (£397); headlight wash-wipe (£310) and electronic heating control (£160). Such an M3 would have retailed at £40,743 with some £6,243 of options installed.

The M3, whether as an original or the final Sport Evolution 2.5, was a magnificent reminder of the simple pleasure of effectively developed rear-drive motoring. It had rough, gruff, habits as the big 'four' worked through its broad rpm range, but I cannot recall more driving pleasure from the production saloon car ranks. Even so, the track versions of the next chapter wrung yet more magic from the M Power formula.

CHAPTER 7

The competition 3-series

From Junior charger to M3

When the 3-series replaced the '02' range in 1975, there were plenty of pundits who claimed that the more civilized newcomer would not make a worthy sports successor. It was indeed a formidable task to follow the race and rally exploits of the 2002 Ti, tii and turbocharged pioneers, but the 3-series did prove equal to the task, albeit in far more specialized form than was permissible in the Sixties and Seventies.

Although the sporting prestige of the road car range has lain with the six-cylinder 3-series, in small capacity competition it was always about four-cylinder units until the autumn 1992 advent of the replacement M3. Such experience divides into production-based Group 2/one-marque saloons (1976 Eggenberger 320i/4 with 220bhp and TWR County Championship 323i of 1979 with 170bhp); and the radical 305 to 620bhp Junior Team/World Group 5 Championship/IMSA American racing 320i and 320T machines of 1977–80. The best known was the angular aggressiveness of the 1986–92 M3, which evolved from 285 to 340bhp in normally aspirated 2.3 and 2.5-litre competition specifications.

Whilst the steel-bodied conversions of the Seventies 3-series never amounted to major forces in international competition, the wild glassfibre and gutted steel '320i', with its Formula 2 M12/7 racing engines delivering over 300bhp, were an immediate German and international Group 5 success. Unfortunately they could do no more than win classes at World Championship level – there were too many pesky Porsche 911 turbochargers about for outright wins – and the 2-litre class was also the limit of their German Championship aspirations. So BMW Motorsport went back to their roots, took a leaf out of the Porsche book, and turbocharged the Formula 2-engined 320 racers.

The result was a minimum of 500bhp and a sprint race maximum beyond 600bhp, but such cars were never as reliable as the normally aspirated 320i competitor. Most outright success was found in the USA IMSA series, where David Hobbs and McLaren North America were key factors in the never-ending struggle to pull a few outright wins from Porsche in 1977–79; the best season was that of 1979, when Hobbs won four events and the car finished third in the IMSA series.

At home, similarly radical 320Ts were constructed by Schnitzer, but these tested the worth of BMW moving into 1.5-litre Grand Prix as they had 1.4-litre turbo motors. In 1978 the formula was refined to the point where Harald Ertl won the German Championship outright with 410bhp and 9,400rpm within a winged 3-series racer.

Into the Eighties BMW continued to be the benchmark in European saloon car racing, albeit their success growing ever harder to achieve when Group A regulations were enforced in 1982. As the era of turbocharged and large capacity production-based cars – allegedly built at the rate of not less than 5,000 per annum – swept in, BMW were caught with the 528i as its sole homologated defence against incoming Rover V8s and Jaguar V12s – both from TWR – turbocharged Volvos and the 1986 Ford Sierra Cosworth. Something had to be done.

At first BMW fell back on the coupe tradition, fielding the 3.5-litre 635 CSi, but were prevented from utilizing its potent

24v sibling, the M635 CSi, by production numbers. Both 528i and 635 CSi were durable enough to win European long-distance races and championship titles, but neither had been created for the track. A purpose-built machine was needed and the M3 was the result.

Service specialist Wolfgang Peter Flohr managed Motorsport from January 1, 1985, and was supported by the inevitable Paul Rosche and Thomas Ammerschläger, who was responsible for production car and Group A racing development. In the late Eighties, Flohr was replaced by another loyal company man, this time drawn from the marketing department. Karl-Heinz Kalbfell became Managing Director of BMW Motorsport on October 1, 1988 and continued to direct their operations into 1992.

Kalbfell was supported on the BMW Motorsport executive board by Heinz Kolleuberg (Finance) and engines engineering legend Paul 'camshaft' Rosche. The BMW Motorsport payroll went from approximately 100 in 1985 to 400 by December 1987; in November 1991 the figure given was 460 employees. The majority of the increase was at

The 320i, in radically modified Group 5 form, under construction by BMW Motorsport in 1976. Note the front-mounted Formula 2 engine and basic steel skeleton beneath the glassfibre panels.

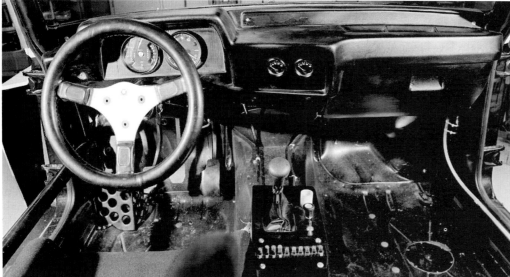

Desirable seat for sale. BMW Motorsport turned the racing Group 5 320i into a viable selling proposition with fine detail workmanship, superb handling and durable running gear.

Current Motorsport driver-manager Marc Surer tests his home team 320i at Hockenheim prior to the 1977 season.

Garching, where they took over and expanded the BMW Motorsport business of building very special cars on a professional basis.

Garching also supply equally thorough competition packages, providing everything necessary to assemble a competitive M3 (Group A or N and subsequent equivalents), although it is left to the customer to decide the engine specialist. At some £90,000 apiece in 1991 (£140,000 with a Motorsport engine and power train), these kits were not cheap, but they were effective and allowed some marvellously close competition to be seen.

The commercial sense of BMW Motorsport and its competition M3 was confirmed by company press officer Friedbert Holz. He confirmed to me in June 1991 that around 300 M3 racing cars/kits had been supplied to that date. In November 1991 a further breakdown was supplied by BMW Racing Team Manager Karsten Engel, which revealed that Motorsport GmbH had supplied so many cars that 250 M3s were 'racing regularly all over the world'. Further inquiries established the number of Group A kits

supplied by BMW as 270, with a further 60 supplied in Group N trim, to make a total of 330 BMW M3 racing packages supplied from Munich.

From the start it was obvious that the M3 BMWs were not going to be mere class-winning cars: they would challenge for outright victories in the World, European and national title races. This was despite the World Championship presence of viciously quick (from 360 to 480bhp in their first season) turbocharged Ford Sierra Cosworths from Eggenberger, and the rumbling presence of 5.8-litre GM Holden V8s.

Pirellis were the initial tyre selection for factory-backed BMWs, and were also popular in Britain at Prodrive. Japanese Yokohamas became the quickest choice during the World Championship season. 'Yokos' were the preference of the works-backed Schnitzer and Bigazzi teams into the early Nineties, and thus shared in a majority of BMW success. In Britain, Vic Lee Motorsport (VLM) bought their first car from Bigazzi and inherited the Yokohama habit, winning with Jeff Allam and securing the outright British title in 1991 for Will Hoy.

Extended aerodynamic appendages for the 3-series Group 5 racer are displayed by the factory-entered Junior Team 320i of Manfred Winkelhock. Tragically, he died following an accident with a Porsche Group C racer in 1985, but brother Joachim continued to race BMWs in the Nineties.

At the end of its 1987 debut season, the M3 had won the driver's section of the first and last World Touring Car Championship. However, it was a series so wracked by bitter regulation controversies that it was dropped by the international authorities immediately! It was a series in which the majority of the top 10 were disqualified in the final results of the first race (BMW for non-regulation bodywork), whilst the factory-backed Fords were not even allowed to run after changing engine management systems. Ford went on and won the parallel series for manufacturers.

Italian Roberto Ravaglia grasped four outright wins with the Schnitzer-prepared M3 in one of *the* giant-killing feats of modern motorsport. It was a triumph for Schnitzer's team work and the abilities of compatriot driver Emanuele Pirro, who accompanied Roberto 'Spaghetti' on all his winning runs and became a Formula 1 regular of the early Nineties.

BMW's other success at World Championship level was to prove a one-off result, but since it was their first win in the World Rally Championship for 14 seasons it was totally unexpected. Against fierce Ford and Lancia opposition,

British-based Prodrive prepared the Tour of Corsica-winning M3 for Bernard Beguin/JJ Lenne. Many other event and national championship-winning M3s would emerge from the premises in Oxfordshire in the years before Subaru became a more important rallying customer.

Additional spoils for BMW in that first M3 season were the European Championship, which went to the late Winfried 'Winni' Vogt in the Team Linder M3. Honours were equally shared amongst the top preparation specialists in the BMW fold, for Belgian Eric van de Poele had initiated the Zakspeed move from Ford to BMW with the greatest success that a German preparation company can wish for: the German Touring Car Championship title. The comparatively simple M3 formula also brought BMW the FIA Group A Trophy for makes in the European Hillclimb Championship, plus the national titles of Australia, France, Finland, Holland and Portugal.

Racing cars change specification from hour to hour, track to track, but BMW did produce an average M3 specification for the 1987 editions that is worth examining. A computer-

The 1977 Junior Team squad gang up on a privateer entry at the Nurburgring. Such close racing often led to tears and the factory cars were not always fielded under the Junior Team logo ...

... Motorsport deciding to enter a BMW-Gentleman-Team in an attempt to curb the excesses of their young chargers, employing contracted drivers of the calibre of Ronnie Peterson and Hans-Joachim Stuck.

calculated rollcage had been tested in scale model trim and manufactured by Matter. Made from 28 metres of lightweight steels welded within a factory M3, I was quoted a gain in torsional and bending rigidity over a standard 3-series by a factor triple that of the standard M3.

Initially the Group A M3 competed at 960kg rather than the production 1,200kg. The roofline touched 1,370mm in production, 1,330mm for Group A racing – the 40mm/1.57in saving also helping aerodynamics. A larger safety tank made from Kevlar and nylon-reinforced synthetic rubbers – with foam lining to protect the 'bag tank' fuel reservoir – was adopted, to a total of 110 litres/24.2 imperial gallons.

The wheelbase was altered by the adoption of racing hardware, climbing from the usual 2,562mm to 2,565.5mm, representing an insignificant 3.5mm matter beside the extra inches and millimetres generated by BBS replacement wheels and Pirelli, Yokohama or Dunlop racing rubber. For competition, the rim and overall diameters were permitted a maximum of a 2in increase, so BMW generally adopted a 9 x 17in 3-piece alloy with a magnesium centre and 245/610

rubber. Some teams were equipped with 16in wheels, which meant the tyre sections shrank to 235/590-16. Others used both 16 and 17in diameters, with the smaller size at the front to promote turn-in ability.

Bilstein aluminium tube front struts encased low-pressure gas damping, and were encircled by markedly uprated coil spring rates. The lower suspension arms for the struts were also in forged aluminium and cross-braced. New hubs and cast-magnesium uprights lay behind centre-lock wheel attachment. The hubs carried enlarged (332mm diameter x 32mm thick) vented disc brakes and facilitated single-nut pit stop speed for wheel changes.

These discs were served by four-piston calipers, and were originally supplied largely by Brembo in Italy. More teams changed to AP Racing in Britain during 1988, and their later six-piston calipers made them a regular components supplier to the fastest M3 equipes by 1991. ABS anti-lock braking was developed during the winter of 1990/91 by a co-operative effort between BMW Motorsport and Alfred Teves GmbH, to contest the German Championship in 1991. Steve Soper

The rakish turbo-look rear wing and front wing splitter were fitted to this Rudiger Falz Group 5 320 for the 1978 World Championship race at Brands Hatch, the drivers being Manfred Winkelhock and TWR boss Tom Walkinshaw.

The 19in Goodyear rear tyres, rear window safety stays and driver's door window net reveal that this is the American turbo-specification car at work. It was making its 1977 debut at Road Atlanta, where David Hobbs performed magnificently to sweep the 320T from the back of the grid to finish fourth.

Racing 3-series in the E30 body was not confined to the M3. The BMW Junior Team's Markus Oestreich tackled the 1986 European Touring Car Championship with Alpina power in this 325i.

The first of the British Prodrive BMWs, using a factory-supplied Matter shell, taking shape at the then new team base at Bicester. Prodrive were outstandingly successful in both races and rallies.

spoke for many of them when he told me, at the close of 1991, of lap speed gains measured in seconds for wet conditions. Incidentally, BMW were pioneers in the use of ABS braking for competition, right back to the 1973 CSLs, but such early experiments were not a success.

Power steering was deleted and faster steering rack ratios of 17:1 and 14.7:1 were recognized in place of the production M3 19.6:1. Rose joints and adjustable rollbars completed the competition picture at the front.

For the back end, semi-trailing arms had to be retained, but the arms themselves were extensively reinforced and provision was made for immediate – via spanner – camber and castor adjustment to tune the car to each track. As at the front, adjustable spring plates were also employed to vary vehicle ride height. There was a jointed and adjustable rollbar and central wheelnut hubs to carry bigger brakes: vented units of 280 x 20.7mm served by four-piston calipers.

The slant four-cylinder naturally built on its DOHC 16-valve layout to create a substantial power bonus, but the layout of production exhaust manifolding and the restrictions

of Group A regulations – standard-size valves, standard inlet manifolds – initially kept power beneath the old Formula 2 levels. M3 was slightly overbored (from 93.4mm to 94mm) to reach 2,331.8cc for racing rather than the showroom 2,302cc.

By running a Motronic engine management system that had been further developed by the BMW-Bosch alliance, BMW Motorsport were able to operate a 12:1 CR in place of the usual 10.5:1. Power was always quoted by the Munich press department as increased by 50% over standard. This meant 300bhp at 8,000rpm, which represented some 128.6bhp a litre.

The factory S14-coded motors were originally restricted to 8,500rpm and about 300bhp in Group A racing trim, but later German Championship units were allowed slide throttles and other non-Gp A tweaks that saw them revving close to 10,000rpm and making over 320bhp. Finally, 365bhp at 8,750rpm was reported for the 1991 regulations of Germany. By then the 2,493cc (95.5 x 87mm) M3 unit was electronically managed by a BMW Motorsport ECU, and

First of the factory-fresh Group A M3s awaiting the start of the 1987 season outside the Preussenstrasse base.

had a bhp per litre figure of 146.4.

Maximum torque for 2.3-litres was far from fabulous in that it was delivered only at a sky-high 7,000rpm. Yet the Group A M3 boasted some 20% bonus over standard, at 270Nm (198.5lb/ft) rather than 230Nm. The final 2.5s yielded 290Nm (210lb/ft), but still needed 7–8,000rpm to release maximum pulling power.

The factory gearbox choice was a five-speed Getrag with close ratios, stacked from 2.337 to a direct fifth, and a choice of final drives that encompassed 3.15 to 5.28:1. The factory picked a 4.41 to demonstrate a 0–62mph time of 4.6 seconds – the standard figure was nearly 7 seconds – and reported speeds up to 280km/h (174mph) that first season, although those were naturally recorded on the taller 3.25:1 final drive.

How did the M3 progress over the 1987 specification outlined above? First of all it is important to understand that British and German specification M3s diverged sharply after a 2-litre class was introduced to the UK, this capacity becoming the overall limit for the UK series in the Nineties. German and most other markets carried on racing the 2.3

Belgian Eric van de Poele and Zakspeed were new to BMW in 1987, but secured the vital German Championship title at their first attempt.

Seen at the 1987 Spa-Francorchamps 24-hours event, Winnie Vogt (the driver on the left) and Ludwig Linder (centre in civvies) were 3-series racing pioneers, Linder preparation and Vogt finesse securing the 1987 European title for the BMW M3. Also in this discussion are BMW loyalists Altfrid Heger (right) and the tall Christian Danner, then a BMW-backed Formula 1 driver.

and subsequent (1990) 2.5-litre evolutionary M3s. It is also worth remembering that British regulations originally banned ABS and that BMW could not use the later evolutionary aerodynamics, so there were substantial technical differences between superficially similar BMWs.

Back with the original M3, between 1987 and 1989 the 2,332cc engine capacity was deployed with the only real progress possible on those basic racing fronts: aerodynamics, tyres, power and gearing. The four-piston brakes remained at 332mm/278mm diameters, but wheel diameter could be increased to 18in – still wearing a 9in ledge – as a result of the annual evolution models.

M3 Evolutions also brought with them extended spoilers (1988) and an increasing number of the lightweight panels that had seen the factory M3s outlawed at Monza in 1987. According to factory records there were the logical three Evolution models (1987, 1988, 1989), and their basics have

been described in the preceding road car chapter.

The biggest change in race engineering principles during the 1988–89 seasons was the occasional adoption of the Prodrive six-speed gearbox, but German touring car runners just as frequently reverted to the five-speed, and an alternative Getrag six-speed was more widely used in Germany.

In 1989 the World and European Touring Car Championships were dead, but the German home international title hunt meant that BMW grafted to find a winning edge. Still utilizing a 12:1 CR, BMW Motorsport changed most key elements on the motor. The slide throttle air admission – as opposed to the Group A use of standard intakes – allowed a small power bonus, but the real search in 1989 was for higher rpm. A stronger crankcase, lightened camshafts and pistons, plus a BMW, as opposed to Motronic, Electronic Control Unit (ECU) were allied to double injectors to boost rpm and mixture flow.

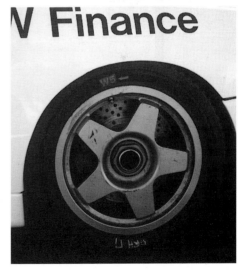

The 1989 face of the Prodrive 2.3-litre M3 is shown alongside its Kevlar composite air intake system for an engine restricted to around 300bhp by the tighter Group A regulations of that period. Other details include the massive cross-drilled front and rear brakes with AP calipers, five-spoke alloy wheels and the coaxial coil springs wrapped around the rear shock absorbers.

The process was effective. At the beginning of 1989, the drivers were allowed 8,800rpm, early summer brought 9,200 and the year ended with 9,800rpm at their disposal. Despite this, the official power peak was 8,500rpm and 320bhp, plus fractionally augmented (5Nm) pulling power, rated at 275Nm/202lb/ft of torque at the usual 7,000rpm.

The 1989 M3 was forced to race at 1,040kg/2,288lb, which was approximately 100kg/220lb heavier than the engineers could provide as a racing weight. The wide choice of differentials remained, but 0–62mph was still quoted as around 4.6 seconds, with top speed elevated to 300km/h (186mph).

What was the cost of such M3 speed? German independent sources quoted an on-the-grid cost of the equivalent of £77,200 in the late Eighties. A senior Prodrive executive quoted me £600,000 as the cost of running a pair of M3s in the 1991 UK Championship. By 1992 the 'going rate' in Britain was £800,000 apiece to Prodrive and VLM.

For German conditions, the 2.5-litre stretch of the M3 engine, unveiled in December 1990, was logical for racing purposes given the Mercedes opposition. Homologation was on March 1, 1990, production of the necessary 500 having begun in January '90. M3 Sport Evolution was intended primarily to defend BMW's slightly unexpected 1990 German victory over the 2.5-litre Mercedes. BMW faced Opel, playing their unsuccessful 24v 3-litre Omega/Carlton hand. Audi had near 500bhp in their weighty V8 saloon, so power was at a premium *chez* BMW.

The racing M3 Evolution started aerodynamic development in July 1989. The 1990 Evolution featured the manually adjustable front and rear spoiler extensions of the road car to vary downforce, as well as the use of ground effect venturi at the front end. Further lightweight panels and detail aerodynamic updates extended to reprofiling the traditional front radiator grille and sealing off front-end openings. Racing weight was 1,040kg in Germany, which was 160kg less than the road car.

In detail the 2.5-litre stretch meant the racers could use a 95.5mm bore (production was 95mm dead) with the standard 2.5-litre 87mm stroke to achieve 2,493cc in place of 2,467cc. There was the traditional 12:1 CR and further reworked

BMW-ECU electronic management, which allowed another 10bhp (a total of 330 at 8,500rpm in 1990) and a 15Nm boost in torque, to a seasonal average of 290Nm/213lb/ft, peaking at 7,500rpm.

The engineers were worried at the beginning of the year that this ultimate four-cylinder stretch would leave them 1,000rpm down on the 1989 'screamer', and they set an initial target of 9,200rpm. Some 9,500rpm was safe by the end of the season, which was an achievement for this large-bore 'four'.

The extra 2.5-litre M3 horsepower was vital as the Mercedes Evolution 190E 2.5-16 had even more radical aerodynamics than the BMW and 333bhp to propel the same race weight minimum of 1,040kg. BMW engineers were still confident that the car could be raced at 940kg, but that was never allowed on home turf because Mercedes would not run below 1,040kg.

Despite the modest horsepower and torque bonus, no major performance advances (0–62mph in 4.6 seconds, 186mph maximum) were reported; the aerodynamic and power advantages most apparent to the drivers were in the extra muscle between 50 and 150mph. Roberto Ravaglia, the most successful of all M3 drivers, with four international driver's titles to his credit by 1990, commented, 'the old motor had its power at 8,000rpm, the new 2.5-litre is beautiful at 7,000rpm. It is the best M3 I have driven.' The statistics from the Nurburgring GP circuit backed up that judgment emphatically: the 1987 M3's best upon debut was *eight* seconds slower than the 1990 best lap!

Contributing to that dramatic rise in lap speed were the replacement aerodynamics – particularly the venturi under the engine bay – and the routine use of 18in wheel diameters and Yokohama tyres. By 1991 some teams in Italy (including CibiEmme) were certainly using 9 x 19in diameter rear wheels regularly, usually in association with 18in diameter fronts and Pirelli tyres. In 1992 Johnny Cecotto's works M3 successfully used Michelin.

Detail chassis changes were headed by the availability of six-piston brakes, and BMW Motorsport specified an increase in vented disc diameters to 350mm/13.8in front and 11.8in rears. Yet the major technical advance for 1991 was

One of the most rewarding seats in saloon racing; a look inside the 1991 racing M3. This is a very competitive Bigazzi example with six-speed gearbox and ABS-monitored anti-lock braking.

Johnny Cecotto in 1990 at the wheel of a then new Schnitzer 2.5-litre M3 with rear spoiler to generate downforce. By 1992 Cecotto was the only driver to be run directly from a works-financed base (beside the Nurburgring), and his was the only M3 to run on Michelin tyres rather than the usually dominant Yokohamas.

the adoption of the anti-lock (ABS) braking system referred to earlier.

BMW did not win the 1990 or 1991 German titles, but the M3 scored some superb results in sprint and long-distance races. The 2.5-litre featured enough technical progress to ensure that arch rivals Mercedes were frequently defeated in the home series. Back in the Eighties Ford had fielded the Sierra Cosworth and BMW had the M3, both for 1987. The first and last World Championship was a struggle between two contestants of opposed ideologies. Fittingly, both won a 1987 World title, and BMW repeated their driver success in 1988 before the European series was abolished. The M3's lack of turbocharged power was offset by chassis agility and sheer weight of BMW M3 numbers. All these were telling factors versus the embryo Eggenberger Sierra team.

Ford then beat BMW outright by a touch of Evolution homologation known as the Sierra Cosworth RS500. It had

an enlarged turbocharger to be developed to exceed 500bhp. BMW and their simpler fuel-injected 16v could do no more than detail the 2.3-litres, exceeding 300bhp only under favourable circumstances or German national regulations.

The 1988 Evolution M3 had 220bhp for just 500 road customers, but it was for lighter body panels and extended aerodynamic spoilers that competitors valued the car.

Although the RS500 Ford was an outright winner from its mid-1987 season introduction, the M3 has continued to garner racing and rallying victories across Europe, and has raced with distinction in Australia and New Zealand. In Germany the M3 has remained competitive over five seasons, and was being readied for a sixth when this was written. In Germany, until 1993, the organizers handicapped winners on a weight and power basis to provide close racing.

The second (1988) season for BMW and their factory-supported teams was headlined by the successful Schnitzer campaign to secure the European Touring Car Championship for drivers. This was the last time that the title was offered – new descendants, plus a European Grand Prix-supporting formula, are being discussed as we go into the early Nineties – and it was fitting that an M3 won the last Euro edition. BMW drivers had won the title, or the class contested, 16 times since 1965, and the M3 took both 1987/88 honours via Winni Vogt and Roberto Ravaglia.

The 1988 German home international series was not the happy hunting ground for the M3 that it had been in 1987, but the M3 still acquitted itself well versus Champions Eggenberger Ford, whose RS500 was strangled back on turbocharger air supply for 1989 in the cause of fiercer track action.

Outside Germany the M3 enjoyed a successful 1988 season, scooping up the British (Frank Sytner), French (Jean Pierre Malcher), Dutch (Arthur van Dedem), FIA Asian-Pacific (Kiwi Trevor Crowe) and Swedish (Lennart Bohlin) Championships. Even the Portuguese touring car racing title went the way of the M3.

Prodrive excelled themselves on BMW's behalf, for they not only stood behind Frank Sytner's UK victory, but also snatched the Belgian *Rally* Championship. The same Prodrive crew – Patrick Snijers/Dany Colebunders – also finished as the runners-up in the European Rally Championship itself. BMW

were on the brink of a unique saloon car double in collecting European racing *and* rallying titles.

In the 1989 season BMW bounced back in Germany, for the M3 beat the best from Mercedes – even though the 190E now bore 2.5 litres – to add the 1989 title to their 1987 home Championship victory. Eggenberger Ford and their air-restricted RS500s were strangled to 360bhp in 1989 and withdrew from this enormously wealthy and well-attended series from 1990 onward. Now Audi joined the German series with their V8 four-door saloon in 1990. Like the BMW M3, the biggest quattro came home with the title in its debut season, but Ingolstadt also mugged the opposition again in 1991, wrenching a second title from the deeply unhappy opposition. Audi withdrew in mid-1992.

Back in the Eighties – aside from their German racing home win in 1989 – the BMW season was notable for a unique rallying double: the 2.3-litre M3 won both the French (Francois Chatriot/Michel Perin) and Belgian (Marc Duez/Alain Lopes) titles. Predictably Prodrive were behind this prestigious coup, but to prove it was no fluke the rally championships of Holland (John Bosch), Spain and Yugoslavia also fell to M3 drivers.

Schnitzer naturally retained their M3 racing links with Roberto Ravaglia throughout the 1987-91 seasons. Roberto was destined to add an Italian home championship to his

Successfully overturning the Prodrive BMW competition establishment in Britain, Will Hoy and Vic Lee Motorsport ran this 2-litre M3 to the 1991 British Championship title.

The Italian Bigazzi equipe always fielded immaculate racing M3s. Here Armin Hahne desperately tries to fend off his 1990/91 team-mate Steve Soper; both had previously driven for TWR Rover.

Winning profile. The 1991 M3 still represented the epitome of the racing saloon car, continuing to set standards that would be hard for its six-cylinder successor to eclipse.

1989 German title. Roberto's tally also included two European (1986/88) and one World Championship (1987) – all but one title secured at the wheel of an M3.

The BMW M3 – in 2.3-litre guise for some branches of the sport such as rallying, 2-litres for the British Touring Car Championship and 2.5-litre Evolution in German and other international Group A contests – continued to be a versatile winner. In 1990 Johnny Cecotto/Fabien Giroix/Markus Oesterreich headed a BMW M3 1-2 at the 24 Hours of Spa, the toughest event on the saloon car calendar. It was an event won on numerous occasions by BMW and Schnitzer, but on this occasion the 'sprint' car spent only seven and half minutes of the 24 hours in the pits.

Other notable 1990 M3 achievements were the acquisition of the Italian, Dutch, Finnish, Swiss and Belgian national championships, with a fine 1-2 result in Italy for M Team Schnitzer drivers Ravaglia and Emanuele Pirro. Runner-up positions were scored in the national title hunts of Britain and Germany. European titles did not mean much by this stage, but BMW had Frenchman Francis Dosieres down for the European hillclimb trophy in Group A.

Prodrive continued to prove the worth of the M3 in rallying, with a national double. They added the French national title to their bag with the efforts of Francois Chatriot/Michel Perin.

In 1991 and in the wake of former Ford specialist, Zakspeed's, departure for Mercedes-Benz, the BMW factory line-up included: Johnny Cecotto, Dane Kris Nissen and Joachim Winkelhock for Schnitzer; Bigazzi retained Steve Soper/Armin Hahne; and the freshly created MM-Diebels Team were awarded former BMW-backed GP aspirant Christian Danner. Linder were served by the rapid but unlucky former F3000 driver Altfrid Heger.

After 14 races, the M3 was once again embattled in the thick of German Championship honours, but it was not to be. Steve Soper for Bigazzi and Johnny Cecotto (Schnitzer) fought an Audi V8 quattro of Frank Biela. Despite the experience of Klaus Ludwig in the best of the factory-backed

Steve Soper with the 1992 extended-wing specification M3 was able to win both the German Championship races at the Norisring qualifying event in July. By then the title battles were a straight fight between BMW and Mercedes factory drivers, Audi having withdrawn from the contest. This would also be the last BMW-backed season with the 3-series, the most successful racing saloon in recent European history.

AMG Mercedes, the series resolved into a five-way fight, which eventually went to the Audi of Frank Biela.

As this went to press, Steve Soper had just won for the first time in the 1992 German season with the 2.5-litre M3 Evolution Sport in its last season. Mercedes were at last on the ascendant, with drivers like former World Champion Keke Rosberg in the ever wilder 2.5 190e-Evo II, whilst in Britain the '318iS' was beginning to show some form under regulations that offer lower racing weights for front-drive Vauxhalls, Toyotas, Nissans and Mazdas.

CHAPTER 8

Buying a used 3-series

The choice, the examination, the symptoms

Advice was taken from many sources to compile the information in this section, which concentrates on the first two generations of 3-series.

In the case of the original 3-series (E21) it must be remembered that I am essentially talking about a 1976–82 RHD span, so the youngest examples today should routinely have 100,000 miles behind them and be a decade old. Therefore I am not going to find examples through the BMW dealer network that have the benefit of the best warranty in the business. For that kind of reassurance sub-60,000 mile/three-year-old machines of the later E30 outline must be regarded.

That means I am discussing original machines that may have already been bought as bargain-basement 'runners', with the need to renew every aspect. Then there are the well maintained examples that have been conscientiously serviced and kept by two or three owners, or I could be discussing an immaculate concours competitor that is better presented than it was on first sale.

Either way, I believe, the '3' represents extraordinary value, better than the '02' which has become so fashionable of late. BMW GB positively encourage the sale of older parts and there are clubs which are interested in a practical way in keeping well-used examples not just safely roadworthy, but raceworthy as well, if that is the inclination. Addresses are given at the conclusion of the section.

If you are buying an E21, I suggest it is essential either that a thorough examination is carried out, or that whoever is going to service it comes along to view. Viewing should include raising the car on the ramp, because the older examples demand a full underbody inspection. The cars are not complex; simply regard one as a conscientiously fabricated Ford of the rear-drive era! MacPherson struts, trailing arms IRS, SOHC or DOHC four-cylinders - even the rarer 4x4 of the second generation - are not inherently more complex than a Sierra. In fact turbocharged RS Sierras are considerably more complex.

In addition to the basic safety and sensibility checks – tracking, brakes, any hire purchase outstanding, any obvious crash damage – there are specific weaknesses in the earlier '3s' which I have discovered, with the guidance of London-based Churchill Bennitt's Stuart Bennitt.

The primary problem is one shared with all elderly monocoque-construction cars: ensuring that rust has not taken a hold and weakened the inherent strength of the structure. Stuart commented, 'I would concentrate on two rear areas, the shock absorber top turrets and the underbody subframe-to-chassis mounts. This inspection is near impossible without a ramp because the spare wheel intrusion can hide the problems. You must examine under the back seats – patches of rust may yield perforations when prodded with a screwdriver – and the boot floor may well prove just as bad. That means the need for expensive floor replacement sheet metal work.

'The front body is not so much of a problem in that one can replace/plate chassis legs at reasonable cost, but do regard the presence of underbody treatment – and the seal of wings to flitch plates – as vital. We would all prefer to see the factory crinkly finish top the underbody, but we see far too many of the older cars that have rusted through because body repairs were done on the principle of a nice shiny paint job on the outside, and no treatment to the inside. Water gets in and you have terminal rust in just a couple of years.'

Elsewhere I found that most BMWs of the pre-ABS generation tended to hit other road users from behind. It means that there is a practical difference between the E21 and later E30 because the presence of plastic parts on the later generation allows that little fundamental damage is caused by a light traffic accident, whereas if factory – or a conscientious – standard of coachwork is not adhered to, the older cars will require metal work and suffer subsequent occurrence of rust.

Leaving the body, Stuart Bennitt commented upon the mechanical experience they have garnered with regular customers over the 100,000-mile mark – and his own E21 320i four-cylinder, which has surpassed 200,000 miles on the original engine – saying, 'they really are very, *very* strong. We prefer the four-cylinders on the durability side; my car had only one clutch change and all the rear-end components went through untroubled. We did change a gearbox, but only because I wanted a five-speed installed – an easy swap, provided you use a 316 propshaft. Incidentally, the five-speed made an enormous difference to the 320i in motorway use; it was quieter, and we got over 27mpg regularly, even at such high mileage.

'From that car, and other customers, we learned that wheel bearings will probably need changing at 100,000 miles (the factory supplier, Skefco, can be approached direct at a cost saving over BMW dealers – J.W.). The shock absorbers are not the longest-lived items. If you can still locate them, Fichtel and Sachs inserts work the best, and they used to offer both a Sport and Standard rebound/bump setting.'

Not rated by our specialists in the original E21 body were the six-cylinder models. I was reminded that the 320-6 was a troublesome beast in its earliest carburated form, when it was particularly hard to get the carburation set up accurately. The result was that many ran excessively rich. I had one such car at *Motor Sport* magazine in the Seventies, and it was enormously expensive to service because of the hours devoted to the carburation.

This could be a case of incorrect float chamber levels, but many will be 'fixed' by altering ancillaries like the tickover, leaving the basic problem to ruin bores and inflict 'severe engine war', in the words of one adviser. Churchill Bennitt reported that the Solex carburation was modified so that 'the 1979/80 cars were satisfactory.'

The E21 323i was a performer, but it was so willing that many were flogged to death whilst cold, so that bores, piston rings and valve guides could be dying in a used example. There are enough with properly rebuilt engines, no smoke and no rattles, to enable you to avoid the walking wounded. A service history is particularly relevant in this respect because assurance is needed that the camshaft belt drive has been changed at the manufacturer's specified intervals.

Ancillaries that can cause unexpectedly high levels of replacement cost and irritation from the first series of BMWs include the heater temperature and control cables, 'which always seem to cost twice what you expected. It is the same for the heater tap,' said one adviser. Churchill Bennitt also highlighted the failure – or extremely noisy operation – of the fuel pump, as 'more of a chore than you would think. Because the pump is in an exposed position, it will be rusted in place. Mounting brackets and metal pipes are not immediately obtainable as they are out of stock at a dealership these days. Four or five hours labour can be spent on what should be a simple job, plus the hassle of getting replacement bits.'

Looking at the E30 Stuart Bennitt summarized, 'The bodies are 80 to 90% better than the original series, and the wider use of plastics avoids some of the panel beating problems highlighted earlier. However, the E30 does suffer other ills that can be infuriating to customers.' I understand the electrical components are the worst culprits; the service interval indicator – 'for people who are not interested in cars,' said one industry observer – often goes on the blink, or the vital dials, which feed the indicator information. The boards were originally a £100-plus item, but a redesigned electrical board of increased efficiency saved about half that cost from – approximately – the 1984 model year onward.

Another weak link in E30 electronics was the fuel pump

relay. The symptoms were obvious enough – the 3-series engine stopped suddenly, but would often restart half an hour later, leading AA breakdown men to question one's sanity. Stuart Bennitt stated, 'the problem can appear on any fuel-injection 3-series, but the relay system was improved in later production E30s. The relay itself cost about £40 in 1992, but it's still a recurrent problem. With the later cars you may get it to restart immediately, when it will run without fault for five minutes, or five days. Either way, the relay needs replacing.'

Another common electrical defect is not the fault of BMW, but the bodgers who install too many in-car entertainment systems. 'We have found that any projection behind, from the radio/stereo unit, can chafe its way into the main wiring loom within the facia. We have had several examples of this, sometimes signalled by the sidelight circuit failing,' comments Stuart Bennitt.

Of the E30-mounted M40 engines (316i and 318i), there was not the same respect for the unit from the secondhand specialist as for its four-cylinder forerunners. As I suspected from the number of internal changes made to this motor by the factory – and its close cousin, the 16v DOHC M42 – there were service problems. Primarily in the M40 'fours' were cam drive belts snapping, but the M40 'fours' also showed an appetite for engine oil that could swallow a sump's scanty contents. A low oil-reserve warning light – such as that on the 325i – was recommended, along with use of synthetic oils. With purist condemnation, one company jibed, 'you get a lot of rep types in these cars, and they just never check anything, especially the dipstick.'

Another non-enthusiast problem was the calibration of the 318i automatic transmission model's fuel injection. It really was hard to unpark first thing in the morning, failing to run evenly when the power steering was twirled, and then waking up to give a good burst of 'unintended acceleration'. It is understood that the Motronic was recalibrated to overcome the initially lean mixture that was used for emissions reasons.

On manual transmission 316s I was advised that fast changes between third and fourth should be checked in any test drive, 'to make sure the clutch is not dragging. It is a weak point on this model, with a life around 40 to 50,000

miles, and you should ensure there is no trace of slip.'

Of the vastly improved – by comparison with 323i – 325i, Stuart Bennitt felt, 'it's a wonderful car, and currently an absolute bargain on a C or D-plate (August 1985 to July 1987 – J.W.). They go like the wind, and we have several customers who have proved they keep on going at 70 to 80,000 miles. Our only long-term mechanical warning would be simply to ensure that the timing belt for the camshaft is changed every 40–50,000 miles. We often find that this point also marks the impending demise of the water pump, so we often end up changing that as well.'

Whilst the braking and steering performance should be self-evident through visual examination of the brakes and any evidence of pulling under road test, the transmission may exhibit more subtle symptoms of distress: any reluctance to select second gear should be treated with deep suspicion, as a replacement gearbox/rebuild is a an expense that some of my colleagues suffered with lower mileage cars.

The cause could simply be a dragging clutch (as for 316), or one that has suffered at the foot of the dreaded lone pedal rider. Remember, there is enough choice around so that only the best mechanically fit car should be accepted supported by a comprehensive service history – even if it is not from a dealership in later years.

To help me with buying a lower-mileage (under 20,000 miles) E30 3-series Jeremy Mallett, Buying Director of Frank Sytner, gave me the benefit of 15 years of such experience, of buying not just BMWs, but up to 700 examples of prestige marques every year.

I asked what he looked for when one drove up at his kerbside, or when he had to travel several hundred miles to view and make a snap decision. 'If I do not like what I see in any way, I can afford to be fussier than the average BMW dealership buyer because we have other marque interests and plenty of choice. In the case of the 3-series, there are plenty of good used examples about, so – again – you can afford to walk away from one that just does not seem to be quite right.'

I asked for the Sytner/Mallett list of priorities, and they came across as these: firstly to be as close to new as possible, and of commensurate condition. Exceptionally low mileage – in the hundreds is not the rarity it may seem – and very original paint are my first priorities. If the car has not got original paint – which I deduce from looking all over to make sure panels are colour-matched – I want to know why.

'Then I ask to see evidence of at least a BMW dealer, or other quality coachwork, repair. Thus I will also examine fit and finish to see if it conforms to the factory standards of our showrooms, and look out for any evidence of oversprays, ripply panels, orange bloom or welding that is not to factory standards. In a similar manner, I'll look to see if the bulkheads have been correctly sprayed, and I will go to the extent of looking for bolt heads which lack spray as evidence of any short cuts taken in repair.

'The tyres of a young car can tell you a lot about how it has been driven, and if there are any tracking problems – perhaps from a kerbside bump, or more major repairs that have not been properly finished – that have allowed the rubber to wear unevenly. I don't find that 'clocking' is a major problem on prestige cars since they made the odometers more tamper-proof, particularly with the digital readouts of the current 3-series,' concluded our contact.

Useful addresses
The following contacts were useful in gathering information for this book, and for providing advice on operating – and uprating – BMWs:

BMW CAR CLUB
(includes specialist registers & racing series)
PO BOX 328
Andover
Hants SR10 1YN
Tel: 0264 337883
Contact: John Kinch

BMW CLUB EUROPA EV
Petuelring 130
D8000 Munich 40
Germany
Tel: (010 49 89) 3508281
Contact: Wolfgang Marx

BMW (GB) Ltd
Ellesfield Avenue
Bracknell
Berks RG12 4TA
Tel: 0344 426565

Churchill Bennitt Ltd
405 New Kings Road
London SW6
Tel: 071 736 7675
Contact: Stuart Bennitt

Dreamwheelers
(UK Concessionaires, Racing Dynamics)
Chepstow Place
Harrold
Bedford MK34 7BX
Tel: 0234 720068
Contact: Eve Wheeler

Magard
(UK importers for Bilstein, BBS and Eibach)
372 East Park Rd
Leicester LE5 5AY
Tel: 0533 730831

Prodrive
(official UK importers for AC Schnitzer)
Acorn Way
Banbury
Oxfordshire OX16 7XS
Tel: 0295 273355

Sytner of Nottingham Ltd
(Alpina UK Concessionaires)
165 Huntingdon St
Nottingham NG1 3NH
Tel: 0602 582831

APPENDIX A

Technical specifications: the collector's choice

From the myriad permutations of 3-series offered over the 1975–91 span, I have made a selection of models that should particularly interest collectors. As for 95% of the data in this book, the final authority is the factory specification.

ORIGINAL 3-SERIES (E21)
BMW 320i – produced 1975 to 1979

Style: A 2-door saloon that was sometimes identified as 320i/4 to differentiate it from the later 6-cylinders, which were simply badged '320'. The 'i' is vital, for fuel injection provides not only an extra 16bhp over its contemporary 320 4-cylinder, but is also easier to service and has far better economy. In Britain the 320i/4 was not available until 1976, and the production span given above reflects the fact that other markets took the 4-cylinder long after the majority – including Britain – had switched to the 320/6 replacement.

Engine: M10-coded inline 4-cylinder, iron block and alloy SOHC (chain drive) 8-valve cylinder head. 89 x 80mm, 1,990cc, CR 8:1. Bosch K-Jetronic fuel injection. 125bhp at 5,700rpm. Maximum torque, 127lb/ft at 4,500rpm.

Transmission: Front engine, rear drive. Hydraulically operated single-plate clutch, 4-speed gearbox. Axle ratio: 3.64:1. Gear ratios: 1st, 3.76; 2nd, 2.02; 3rd, 1.32; 4th, 1:00.

Suspension, steering and brakes: lfs, coil springs, MacPherson struts, lower wishbones, 23.5mm anti-rollbar and hydraulic strut damper inserts. Irs, coil springs, trailing arms at a 20deg swept angle, telescopic dampers and 16mm anti-rollbar. ZF rack-and-pinion steering (21:1 ratio), 4 turns lock-to-lock on manual models: optional power assistance on 6-cylinders only. Mastervac 9in servo assistance of 255mm/10.04in front discs (solid) and 258mm/10.16in rear drums.

Wheels and tyres: Steel 5.5J x 13in with 185/70 HR as standard.

Dimensions: Length 4,355mm/171.5in; wheelbase, 2,563mm/100.9in; width, 1,610mm/63.4in; height, 1,380mm/54.3in; front track, 1,387mm/54.6in; rear track, 1,396mm/55in. Unladen kerb weight (ex- factory) 1,080kg/2,376lb.

Number of this model manufactured: 98,899.

UK retail price: In 1976 the 320i cost £5,237.

BMW 323i – produced 1977 to 1982

Style: 2-door saloon primarily identified by separated dual exhausts and badge reflecting 2.3-litre motor. Optional factory front and rear spoilers. Running gear also available in Baur Cabriolet from 1980.

Engine: M60-coded inline 6-cylinders with iron block and alloy SOHC (belt drive), 12-valve cylinder head. 80 x 76.8mm, 2,315cc. CR 9.5:1. Bosch K-Jetronic fuel injection. 143bhp at 6,000rpm. Maximum torque, 140lb/ft at 4,500rpm.

Transmission: Front engine, rear drive. Hydraulically operated single-plate clutch. 4-speed manual or 3-speed ZF automatic until 1981 (UK) when 5-speed manual became standard equipment. Axle ratio 3.45:1 – a multiple-plate ZF limited-slip differential was optionally offered. Gear ratios for original 4-speed were shared with 320i (given above). The 5 speeds were: 1st, 3.681; 2nd, 2.002; 3rd, 1.329; 4th, 1:00; 5th, 0.805. An option was a close-ratio 'Sport' box. This had the following ratios: 1st, 3.764; 2nd, 2.325; 3rd, 1.612; 4th, 1.229; 5th, 1:00.

Suspension steering and brakes: Ifs, Macpherson struts, coil springs, hydraulic damper inserts, lower wishbones, 23.5mm anti-rollbar. Irs, trailing arms swept at 20deg, coil springs, hydraulic telescopic dampers, 17mm anti-rollbar. ZF rack-and-pinion steering, geared 19:0:1, 4 turns lock-to-lock. Mastervac + HP pump 9in servo-assistance of vented front discs, 255mm/10.04in, solid rear discs, 258mm/10.16in.

Wheels and tyres: Standard in steel, 5.5J x 13in with 185/70 HR.

Dimensions: Length, 4,355mm/171.5in; wheelbase, 2,563mm/100.9in; width, 1,610mm/63.4in; height, 1,380mm/ 54.3in; front track, 1,346mm/54.8in; rear track, 1,399mm/55.1in. Unladen kerb weight: 1,150kg/2,530lb.

Number of this model manufactured: 137,107.

UK retail price: £6,249 in April 1978.

SECOND GENERATION (E30)
BMW 318iS – produced 1989 to December 1990

Style: 2-door body, unique front and rear spoilers and lowered ride height identify 16-valve 318 derivative. Aerodynamic drag factor 0.35Cd.

Engine: M42-coded inline 4-cylinder with iron block and alloy DOHC (duplex roller chain drive), 16 valves. 84 x 81mm, 1,796cc. CR 10:1. Bosch DME electronically managed injection and ignition (MP 1.7). Peak power, 136bhp at 6,000rpm. Maximum torque, 127lb/ft at 4,600rpm.

Transmission: Front engine, rear drive. Hydraulic, single-plate, clutch and 5-speed gearbox. Axle ratio, 4.10:1. Gear ratios: 1st, 3.72; 2nd, 2.02; 3rd, 1.32; 4th, 1:00, 5th, 0.80.

Suspension, steering and brakes: M Technic-modified version of MacPherson-strut front and trailing-arm (15deg trailing angle) coil-sprung independent rear suspension, lowered by 15mm/0.60in, twin sleeve gas dampers. Front (20mm) and rear (14.5mm) anti-rollbars. Power-assisted ZF rack-and-pinion steering, 21.41 variable ratio. Mastervac 10in servo assistance of shared 325i vented front discs, 260mm/10.25in. Solid rear discs, 258mm/10.16in. ABS optional in the UK.

Wheels and tyres: Standard on steel 5.5J x 14in, 195/65 R. Factory cross-spoked alloy wheel options included 7J x 15in with 205/55 R-15 V, or 6.5J x 14 with original 195-section tyres.

Dimensions: Length, 4,325mm/170.3in; wheelbase, 2,570mm/101.2in; width, 1,645mm/64.8in; height, 1,360mm/ 53.5in; front track, 1,407mm/55.4in; rear track, 1,415mm/55.7in. Unladen kerb weight: 1,125kg/2,475lb.

Number of this model manufactured: 38,613.

UK retail price: £14,750 in December 1989.

BMW 325i – produced 1985 to 1992

Style: One of the most versatile powertrains BMW ever produced, the 2.5-litre engine was found in the 2- and 4-door saloons, convertible 2-doors and 5-door Touring, the latter and the convertible still being in production in 1992. There was also a 4x4 version (325iX), of which slightly under 30,000 were made in LHD form only.

For RHD collectors the UK-only 325i Sport in 2-door guise is recommended, of which 3,928 were registered during 1986–90, unfortunately with differing body packages, the most efficient being the 1989 to 1990 layout. LHD markets can duplicate much of the specification by using later M Technic aero package (unique front and rear spoilers, side sill extensions and deepened rear apron), close-ratio 5-speed gearbox and BBS cross-spoked wheels.

Engine: M20-coded inline 6-cylinder with iron block and alloy SOHC, 12-valve, cylinder head. CR 8.8:1. Bosch DME electronic ignition and injection management. Peak power, 171bhp (170 in catalytic convertor trim) at 5,800rpm. Maximum torque, 167lb/ft at 4,000rpm.

Transmission: Front engine, rear drive for all but 4x4 325iX, which used Ferguson-patented permanent all-wheel drive, epicyclic power split, with two-thirds rear bias and two viscous couplings. Axle ratio, 3.64 but Sport came with 3.91 final drive and standard ZF limited-slip differential. Rear-drive models had choice of 4-speed ZF automatic transmission (with Sport/Economy driving modes available from 1986 in UK), or hydraulic single-plate clutch and (Sport specification) close-ratio 5-speed gearbox. Sport gear ratios were: 1st, 3.76; 2nd, 2.33; 3rd, 1.61; 4th, 1.23; 5th, 1:00.

Suspension, steering and brakes: Usual BMW MacPherson-strut front, trailing-arm (15deg swept trailing angle) with coil springs and standard 18.5/12mm front and rear anti-rollbars. Sport had M Technic 15mm lowered ride heights, uprated gas dampers and replacement coil springs plus 20/14.5mm anti-rollbars. Power-assisted ZF variable-ratio 21.41 steering ratio. Mastervac 10in servo, 260mm/10.25in vented front discs, solid 258mm/10.16in rear discs.

Wheels and tyres: Standard 325i, steel wheels of 5.5J x 14in with 195/65 VR rubber. Sport, initially on cross-spoke alloy 6.5J x 14in wheels, but most (September 1986 on) had at least 7J x 15in with 205/55 VR tyres.

Dimensions: Sport as 318iS, standard cars had overall height of 1,380mm instead of 1,360mm. Unladen kerb weight, standard 325i two-door, 1,180kg/2,596lb.

UK retail prices: Sport (1986) £14,095 with 5-speed manual gearbox.

Numbers made/sold: BMW made 112,368 two-door 325i. BMW GB sold 3,928 Sport-branded 325i models, 1,236 of the more de sirable 1989 edition, 812 in the final (1990) season in the same specification.

BMW M3 – produced 1985 to 1989 (original series)

Style: Steel and unique plastics two-door body. Identified by extended wheelarches, unique spoilers and side skirts, raised bootline and re-raked back glass. Lowest E30 aerodynamic drag coefficient: Cd 0.33. The original M3 is listed; subsequent Evolutions on this theme are listed in the relevant chapter. Rare Motorsport M3 convertible used M3 powertrain, soft-top with electric operation.

Engine: S14-coded inline iron-block four-cylinder, aluminium DOHC (chain-drive), 16 valves. CR 10.5:1. Bosch ML Motronic injection/ignition. 93.4 x 84mm (2,302cc). Maximum power, 200bhp (195bhp with catalyst) @ 6,750rpm and 1,76lb/ft (1,69lb/ft, with Cat) torque @ 4,750rpm.

Transmission: Front engine, rear drive. 5-speed manual gearbox only with Borg-Warner synchromesh. Axle ratio: 3.25:1 and ZF limited-slip differential. Gear ratios: 1st, 3.72; 2nd, 2.40; 3rd, 1.77; 4th, 1.26; 5th, 1.00.

Suspension, steering and brakes: Uprated MacPherson-strut/15deg trailing arms, replacement BMW Motorsport geometry, Boge single-tube, gas-pressurized gas dampers, coil springs. Power-assisted rack-and-pinion steering, 19.6:1 ratio. Ex-5-series (vented front) brake discs and standard ABS, power-assisted, 284mm/11.18in front and 9.84in rear discs.

Wheels and tyres: Alloy BBS 7J x 15in; Uniroyal Rallye 340 or Pirelli P700, both with 205/55 VR.

Dimensions: Length, 4,360mm/171.7in; wheelbase, 2,562mm/100.9in; width, 1,675mm/65.9in; height, 1,365mm/53.7in; front track, 1,412mm/55.6in; rear track, 1,424mm/56.1in. Kerb Weight: 1,200kg/2,640lb.

UK retail price: £23,550 in April 1987. LHD only.

Number made of all M3 types, 1985 to 1990: 17,184.

APPENDIX B

Production figures by model and year

The figures given are from German production records retained by BMW GB Ltd. Note that the first 3-series came only in 2-door form and was coded E21. The second edition added a 4-door (saloon) to the basic 2- and 5-door (Touring) derivatives and was coded E30.

The M40 and M60 designations refer to engine types, M40 being the current small 4-cylinder (M42 in 16v form) and M60 or 20 the smaller inline 6-cylinder.

Most RHD production served the British market, but Japan, Australia, South Africa and others have also taken RHD, although the Japanese often prefer LHD for status reasons.

'Grey' imports of local South African-assembly BMWs are a recurrent Type Approval problem in the UK. From 1977 onward KD (Knock Down local assembly kits) were sent regularly to markets like Thailand, Uruguay, Indonesia and Malaysia. There was a pause until February 1983 before KD supplies of the revised E30 were exported.

At the close of production on most E30 3-series cars (December 1990), BMW had made 2,121,360 complete 3-series and shipped a reported 114,175 KD packages of 3-series. BMW currently sells the 3-series in over 100 markets worldwide.

Years refer to a German mass-production line start and finish, not UK sales date, unless specified.

Production totals

E21 (first 3-series)

1975	43,349
1976	130,821
1977	166,758
1978	183,377
1979	188,809
1980	206,326
1981	228,832
1982	182,010
1983	33,757
E21 total:	1,364,039*

(*Production figures quoted at the beginning of this book, which show small discrepancies with those tabulated here, were totals issued by BMW at the time of the launch of the third-generation 3-series.)

E21 Production by type

BMW 315

1980	2
1981	33,115
1982	47,112
1983	27,069
1980–83 total:	107,838

BMW 316

1975	10,629
1976	42,166
1977	52,834
1978	53,513
1979	45,914
1980	54,794
1981	44,019
1982	28,727
1983	4,438
1975–83 total:	337,034

BMW 318

1975	10,446
1976	14,618
1977	20,369
1978	20,897
1979	16,388
1980	10,491
1975–80 total:	93,209

BMW 318i

1979	9,901
1980	43,264
1981	71,739
1982	66,358
1983	1,302
1979–83 total:	192,564

BMW 320/4 (M10)

1975	20,423
1976	53,560
1977	42,459
1978	1,159
1979	804
1975–79 total:	118,399

BMW 320i/4-cyl

1975	1,851
1976	20,477
1977	32,322
1978	26,775
1979	17,474
1975–79 total:	98,899

BMW 320/M60 6-cyl

1977	18,203
1978	61,402
1979	65,369
1980	59,383
1981	44,882
1982	21,206
1977–82 total:	270,445

BMW 323i/M60 6-cyl

1977	37
1978	18,467
1979	31,123
1980	36,424
1981	33,205
1982	17,851
1977–83 total:	137,107

E30 (second 3-series)

1982	15,580
1983	218,201
1984	285,134
1985	297,886
1986	329,460
1987	316,075
1988	269,074
1989	257,307
1990	246,818
E30 total:	2,235,535*

(*See note above)

E30, production analysis by model to December 1990.

1989–90	318iS	38,613
1982–90	320i/2dr	198,279
1982–90	320i/4dr	181,680
1982–90	323i/2dr	64,076
1983–90	323i/4dr	26,700
1985–90	325i/2dr	112,368
1985–90	325i/4dr	82,873
1985–90	325iX 4x4	29,553
1983–88	325e 2 & 4dr	189,287
1986–90	M3 saloons	17,184
1988–91	M3 Cabrio	785
1986–90	320i Cabrio	25,620
1985–90	325i Cabrio	72,586

Note that some E30 variants of Touring and Cabriolet continued in production into 1991 alongside E36 new generation cars. From pilot production of 11 vehicles in 1985 to December 1990, 101,332 examples of all Cabriolet types were manufactured by BMW (Baur examples excluded). Similarly, 16 pre-production machines in 1987 presaged a run of 61,569 Touring-bodied 5-door variants.

GRAND TOTALS

1975–83: E21, first series	Total: 1,364,039
1975–85: E21/E30 combined 3-series (at 10 years)	Total: 2,143,743
1982–90: E30 2-doors built	Total: 1,108,972
1982–90: E30 4-doors "	Total: 1,056,563
1975–90 E21/E30 all 3-series to production end	
Grand Total	3,529,574[†]

[†] Totals based on factory's individual model analysis.

UK sales records
(from 1980 UK Concessionaires takeover onward)
3-series versus overall BMW (GB) total sales

	3-series	BMW UK total
1980	6,463	13,450
1981	10,330	17,088
1982	13,776	22,977
1983	14,214	25,178
1984	16,258	25,785
1985	20,793	33,448
1986	24,125	35,896
1987	24,883	N/A
1988	26,441	42,761
1989	29,072	48,910
1990	25,119	43,004
1991[‡]	25,699	38,707

[‡] The year that RHD E36 cars arrived to replace E30.

In 1991 the old model sold almost all the pre-planned 8,800 (actually 8,723 units), and the newcomer managed 16,976 in the most difficult car market the UK had witnessed. Most popular of the old models in the final UK sales year was the 316i (22.9% of registrations) whilst the best seller amongst the more restricted E36 replacements was the 318i (39.76%).

UK analysis of post-1980 collectable model sales

	M3	M3 Cabrio	M3 Evo
1987		55	
1988	58		
1989	62	19	
1990	36	13	38
TOTALS	211	32	38

These are the official totals of approved imports via BMW (GB). Expect at least as many original M3 saloons to be present in UK via unofficial/personal imports.

Six UK sales selections
E30 models of 323i & 325i, sales comparison 1983–90

	323i	325i
1983	2,095	
1984	1,858	
1985	2,093	
1986	87	5,038
1987	81	5,592
1988	–	5,964
1989	–	6,597
1990	–	4,203
1991	–	1,019
TOTALS	4,119	28,413

	325i Sport	Auto
1986	352	30
1987	1,320	106
1988	208	29
1989	1,236	199
1990	812	110

No 325i Sport was catalogued in 1988 due to switch over in body kit to Motorsport GmbH item for 1989.

	320 SE/2dr	Auto
1988	518	167
1989	828	200
1990	654	186

	320 SE/4dr	Auto
1988	416	202
1989	580	247
1990	565	240

Total 320/SE
	3,561	1,242

All 320/SE models
4,803

	325i SE/2dr	Auto
1988	729	240
1989	409	193
1990	225	120

	325i SE/4dr	Auto
1988	551	293
1989	660	303
1990	388	216

TOTAL 325i/SE
	2,962	1,365

All 325i SE models
4,327

Therefore, 9,130 SE-branded BMW 3-series were sold in the UK between 1988-90. This was out of a total 80,579 BMW 3-series sales in those years, or approximately 11.3%.

APPENDIX C

Engine designations and specifications

I have supplied original factory engine type prefix codes to help identify correct engine/vehicle combinations. This demands further explanation because this knowledge can be vital when buying secondhand. For the 3-series it is relevant to note that I could not chart every engine installed in detail. I have done my best to include all the major power units, ignoring whether they were available in Britain or not.

The initial 1.6/1.8/2-litre 4-cylinders all belonged to the M10 family; their competition cousins – from 1.5-litre Formula 1 to the 2-litre racing 320i projects – carried M12/ prefixes. Individual factory competition types were then identified with a number beyond the M / symbol, the most famous being M12/7 for the most successful Formula 2 type (as fitted to the Group 5 320i) and M12/13 (for the Grand Prix turbo type).

In date order, the M10s were augmented by the advent of the first small 6-cylinders. From 1977 into the early Eighties these were always referred to as M60, which covered a carburated 2-litre for 320 and the fuel-injection 2.3-litre of 323i. M60 then evolved into M20, which was an all fuel injection range of 6-cylinders, typified by the 12-valve E30 types of 320i and 325i. That coding was also applicable to the similarly belt-driven SOHC layout of the 2.7-litre 'eta sixes' as found in 325e, or its 525e contemporary. The diesel ignition cousins, normally aspirated or turbocharged, ran under the M21 designation and displaced 2.4 litres. The current 24-valve inline 6-cylinders for coupes and saloons badged 320i and 325i have the factory coding M50. The M10 family was replaced by the M40 4-cylinders, presently used for the 316i and 318i. The M3 unit was coded S14 in all its earlier 2.3-litre guises.

BMW do not always honour their series/capacity badging system, (ie: 320 = 3-series of 2.0-litres), because a 315 was actually 1,573cc in the first generation whilst the 316 at introduction of the second generation had the 1,766cc engine normally badged as 318, yet the 1,766cc with fuel injection was also badged 318i!

E21, first generation, 3-series primary engines

	316	318	320/4	320/6	323i/6
Motor Code	M10	M10	M10	M60	M60
Cylinders	4-inline	4-inline	4-inline	6-inline	6-inline
Head	SOHC	SOHC	SOHC	SOHC	SOHC
Cam drive	Chain	Chain	Chain	Belt	Belt
Bore x stroke	84x71mm	89x71mm	89x80mm	80x66mm	80x76.8mm
Capacity	1,573cc	1,766cc	1,990cc	1,990cc	2,315cc
Compression	8.3:1	8.3:1	8:1	9.2:1	9.5:1
Induction	Solex	Solex	Solex	Solex	Bosch
Carb/inj	—— All downdraught, compound, carburettor ——				inj
Type	—— All DIDTA 32/32 ——			4A1/TN	K-Jetronic
Crank bearings	5	5	5	7	7
Coolant, litres	7	7	7	12	12
Oil capacity L	3.75	3.75	3.75	4.0	4.0
Power, bhp	90	98	109	122	143
@ rpm	6,000	5,800	5,500	6,000	6,000
Torque, lb/ft	90	105	127	118	140
@ rpm	4,000	4,000	3,700	4,000	4,500
Bhp per litre	51	59.5	53.3	61.3	61.7

E21, Engine variants, road and track

	315	320i	Works 320i Group 5	Works 320T Group 5
Motor Code	M10	M10	M12/7	M12/9
Cylinders	4-inline	4-inline	4-inline	4-inline
Head	SOHC	SOHC	DOHC	DOHC
Cam drive	Chain	Chain	Gear	Gear
Bore x stroke	84x71mm	89x80mm	89.2x80mm	89.2x80mm
Capacity	1,573cc	1,990cc	1,999cc	1,999cc
Compression	9.5:1	9.3:1	11:2:1	7.5:1, or less
Induction	Pierburg	Bosch	Kugelfischer	Kugel+Garrett
Carb/inj	Carb	Injection	Injection	Turbo inj
Type	1b2	K-Jetronic	Mechanical	Intercooled
Lubrication	—— Wet sump ——		—— Dry sump ——	
Power, bhp	75	125	305	550–600
@ rpm	5,800	5,700	9,250	9,000
Torque, lb/ft	81	127	166	354
@ rpm	3,200	4,500	8,000	7,000
Bhp per litre	47.7	62.8	152.6	275.1–300.2

E30, second generation, 1982 LHD introduction engines

	316	318i	320i	323i
Motor code	M10	M10	M20	M20
Cylinders	4-inline	4-inline	6-inline	6-inline
Head	SOHC	SOHC	SOHC	SOHC
Cam drive	Chain	Chain	Belt	Belt
Bore x stroke	89x71mm	89x71mm	80x66mm	80x76.8mm
Capacity	1,766cc	1,766cc	1,990cc	2,316cc
Compression	9.5:1	10:1	9.8:1	9.8:1
Induction	Pierburg	Bosch	Bosch	Bosch
Carb/inj	Carb	Inj	Inj	Inj
Type	2B4	K-Jetronic	L-Jetronic	L-Jetronic
Oil capacity L	3.75	3.75	4.0	4.0
Power,bhp	90	105	125	139
@ rpm	5,500	5,800	5,800	5,300
Torque, lb/ft	101	105	123	148
@ rpm	4,000	4,500	4,000	4,000
Bhp per litre	51	59.5	62.8	60

E30 engine variants, UK 1990 model year
(Certain versions were still available in 1992 in Touring and Convertible models)

	316i	318i	3i8iS	320i	325i
Motor code	M40	M40	M42	M60	M60
Cylinders	4-inline	4-inline	4-inline	6-inline	6-inline
Head	SOHC	SOHC	DOHC	SOHC	SOHC
Cam drive	Belt	Belt	Chain	Belt	Belt
Bore x stroke	84x72mm	84x81mm	84x81mm	80x66mm	84x75mm
Capacity	1,596cc	1,796cc	1,796cc	1,990cc	2,494cc
Compression	9:1	8.8:1	10:1	8.8:1	8.8:1
Injection/	Digital Motor Electronics DME +			Both DME	
Ignition	(Bosch-BMW DME system)		M1.7	managed	
Oil capacity L	3.75	3.75	4.8	4.0	4.0
Power, bhp	102	115	136	129	171
@ rpm	5,500	5,500	6,000	6,000	5,800
Torque, lb/ft	105	122	127	128	167
@ rpm	4,250	4,250	4,600	4,000	4,000
Bhp per litre	63.9	64	75.7	64.8	68.6

E30, LHD 'eta' petrol and diesel developments, 1983 to 1988

	325e	**324d**	**324Tdi**
Motor code	M20	M21	M21
Cylinders	6-inline	6-inline	6-inline
Head	SOHC	SOHC	SOHC
Cam drive	Belt	Belt	Belt
Bore x stroke	84x81mm	80x81mm	80x81mm
Capacity	2,693cc	2,443cc	2,443cc
Compression	9:1	22:1	22:1
Induction	Bosch Motronic	Diesel pump injection	Diesel pump inj + turbo
Crank bearings	7	7	7
Oil capacity	4.25	5.25	5.25
Power, bhp	122	86	115
@ rpm	4,250	4,600	4,800
Torque, lb/ft	169	113	162
@ rpm	3,250	2,500	2,400
Bhp per litre	45.3	35.2	47.1

APPENDIX D

Performance figures for BMW 3-series

BMW, like most German manufacturers, are conservative in their performance claims, although average fuel consumption claims can be optimistic, and it is better to rely on 'Urban' consumption statistics when independent statistics are not available.

Taking the figures 'generation by generation' I find that the original series really only had enough straight-line performance to compare with its '02' predecessors in 323i guise, and then it was at the cost of sub-20mpg consumption. The closest 323i performance/fuel consumption comparison of the period was probably the 3-litre Capri, but both offer little more 'go' than a Nineties hot hatchback whilst consuming much more fuel. The 4-cylinders of the original series offer a better fuel consumption/performance balance, and the 320i also received

plaudits for its 200,000-mile durability during research for this *Collectors Guide.*

Of the second (E30) edition, the performance interest will naturally centre on the M3 and its various Evolutionary descendants, but it should be noticed how quick the 325i was compared with some M3 derivatives and it can be understood why so many opted for its 6-cylinder charms in RHD Britain, whereas the M3 was locked into LHD. I can only apologize for my failure to locate a reliable set of ultimate figures from the 238bhp/2.5-litre M3.

I am glad to acknowledge the courtesy and co-operation I received in publishing these statistics from the weekly British magazine, *Autocar & Motor,* and Editor-in-Chief Bob Murray. All the figures quoted were obtained using that magazine's internationally respected test procedures and are subject to copyright.

Top speeds quoted are those defined as 'best' by *Autocar & Motor*. Fuel consumption figures include the test track so that worse consumption is unlikely to be obtained. Weights are those quoted as 'kerb'.

BMW 3-series, Generation 1 (E21), 1975 to 1982

	316	320-4	320i-4	320-6	323i
Quoted bhp	90	109	125	122	143
Maximum, mph	102	109	114	114	126
0–30mph, sec	3.8	3.1	3.2	3.3	2.6
0–40mph	6.3	5.0	5.3	5.3	4.3
0–50mph	8.8	6.9	7.3	7.3	6.2
0–60mph	12.9	10.2	9.6	9.8	8.3
0–70mph	18.1	13.6	13.6	13.9	11.8
0–80mph	24.4	18.3	17.6	18.5	15.7
0–90mph	37.1	25.7	23.1	24.6	20.2
0–100mph	–	36.8	33.2	37.3	28.1
0–110mph	–	–	–	–	41.6
Standing ¼ mile/ 400 metres, sec	19.0	17.3	17.3	17.4	16.7
50–70mph, top	13.3	8.5	10.1	13.7	9.3
Overall mpg	23.2	21.2	25.0	24.5	19.7
Kerb weight, kg	1,036	1,036	1,051	1,090	1190
Date published	1/76	9/75	9/76	11/77	5/78

BMW 3-series, Generation 2 (E30), 1983 to 1990

	316i 4-dr	318i 2-dr	320i 2-dr	325i 2-dr	325i Touring 5-dr
Quoted bhp	102	115	125	171	170
Maximum, mph	114	116	116	132	132
0–30mph, sec	3.1	3.0	2.7	2.6	2.9
0–40mph	4.8	4.6	4.4	3.9	3.9
0–50mph	7.1	6.6	6.2	5.3	5.7
0–60mph	10.1	9.3	8.0	7.4	7.6
0–70mph	13.8	12.4	11.4	9.6	9.9
0–80mph	18.5	16.9	14.6	12.1	12.7
0–90mph	25.3	22.4	18.6	15.8	16.4
0–100mph	38.6	31.9	25.2	19.9	20.7
0–110mph	–	–	36.5	25.7	26.4
0–120mph	–	–	–	37.3	–
¼-mile, sec	17.4	16.9	16.4	15.4	15.9
50–70mph 5th, sec	16.0	12.7	15.7	10.2	10.1
Overall mpg	25.3	27.4	26.0	24.6	24.1
Quoted kerb weight, kg	1,109	1,085	1,103	1,048	1,258
Date published	3/89	12/87	2/83	10/85	5/88

The UK 325i Sport, including CR gearbox, LSD and 7 x 15in wheels, recorded 0–60mph in 6.8sec, 15.7sec for the ¼-mile, 0–100mph in 18.8sec and 22.4mpg in a brief test.

	325i Convertible	M3 Convert	M3 Saloon	M3 Evolution 1
Quoted bhp	171	200	200	220
Maximum, mph	135	146	140	148
0–30mph, sec	2.7	2.1	2.8	2.5
0–40mph	4.2	2.9	3.9	3.6
0–50mph	5.8	4.7	5.5	5.1
0–60mph	8.1	6.0	7.1	6.6
0–70mph	10.7	8.0	9.5	8.8
0–80mph	13.4	10.7	11.9	11.0
0–90mph	17.6	12.0	15.2	13.9
0–100mph	22.3	16.6	19.0	17.8
0–110mph	28.2	22.5	23.7	21.9
0–120mph	38.9	28.3	29.8	–
¼-mile, sec	16.1	15.8	15.7	15.2
50–70mph 5th, secs	11.6	9.5	9.4	9.8
Overall mpg	26.5	22.2	20.3	26.0
Quoted kerb weight, kg	1,169	1,411	1,252	1,274
Date published	9/86	2/89	4/87	9/88

Berlitz®

Gern

phrase book & dictionary

C000017519

Berlitz Publishing

New York London Singapore

Contacting the Editors
Every effort has been made to provide accurate information in this publication, but changes are inevitable. The publisher cannot be responsible for any resulting loss, inconvenience or injury. We would appreciate it if readers would call our attention to any errors or outdated information. We also welcome your suggestions; if you come across a relevant expression not in our phrase book, please contact us at: **comments@berlitzpublishing.com**

All Rights Reserved
© 2018 Apa Digital (CH) AG and Apa Publications (UK) Ltd.
Berlitz Trademark Reg. U.S. Patent Office and other countries. Marca Registrada. Used under license from Berlitz Investment Corporation.

Thirteenth Printing: March 2018
Printed in China

Editor: Helen Fanthorpe
Translation: updated by Wordbank
Cover Design: Rebeka Davies
Interior Design: Beverley Speight
Picture Researcher: Tom Smyth
Cover Photos: all images iStock and Shutterstock

Interior Photos: Kevin Cummins 51; Glyn Genin/APA 68, 72, 82, 85, 88, 118; Greg Gladman/APA 134; iStockphoto 14, 58, 129, 133, 144, 146, 149, 156, 168; Britta Jaschinski/APA 39, 97, 102; Lucy Johnston/APA 17, 172; Jon Santa-Cruz/APA 12, 28, 60, 71, 74, 79, 94, 104, 108, 111, 117, 123, 136, 139, 140, 143; Slovenia info 127, 130

Distribution

UK, Ireland and Europe
Apa Publications (UK) Ltd
sales@insightguides.com
United States and Canada
Ingram Publisher Services
ips@ingramcontent.com
Australia and New Zealand
Woodslane
info@woodslane.com.au
Southeast Asia
Apa Publications (SN) Pte
singaporeoffice@insightguides.com

Worldwide
Apa Publications (UK) Ltd
sales@insightguides.com

Special Sales, Content Licensing, and CoPublishing
Discounts available for bulk quantities. We can create special editions, personalized jackets, and corporate imprints. sales@insightguides.com; www.insightguides.biz

Contents

Food & Drink

People

Leisure Time

Special Requirements

In an Emergency

Dictionary

Pronunciation

This section is designed to make you familiar with the sounds of German, using our simplified phonetic transcription. You'll find the pronunciation of the German letters explained below, together with their 'imitated' equivalents. This system is used throughout the phrase book; simply read the pronunciation as if it were English, noting any special rules below.

The German alphabet is the same as English, with the addition of the letter **ß**. Some vowels appear with an **Umlaut**: **ä**, **ü** and **ö**. Of note, German recently underwent a spelling reform. The letter **ß** is now shown as **ss** after a short vowel, but is unchanged after a long vowel or diphthong. In print and dated material, you may still see the **ß**; e.g., formerly **Kuß**, now **Kuss**.

Stress has been indicated in the phonetic transcription: the underlined letters should be pronounced with more stress, e.g., *Adresse, ah-drehs-uh.*

Consonants

Letter	Approximate Pronunciation	Symbol	Example	Pronunciation
b	1. at the end of a word or between a vowel and a consonant, like p in up	**p**	**ab**	*ahp*
	2. elsewhere, as in English	**b**	**bis**	*bihs*
c	1. before e, i, ä and ö, like ts in hits	**ts**	**Celsius**	*tsehl·see·oos*
	2. elsewhere, like c in cat	**k**	**Café**	*kah·feh*
ch	1. like k in kit	**k**	**Wachs**	*vahks*
	2. after vowels, like ch in Scottish loch	**kh**	**doch**	*dohkh*

Letter	Approximate Pronunciation	Symbol	Example	Pronunciation
d	1. at the end of the word or before a consonant, like t in eat	**t**	**Rad**	*raht*
	2. elsewhere, like d in do	**d**	**danke**	*dahn·kuh*
g	1. at the end of a word, sounds like k	**k**	**fertig**	*fehr·teek*
	2. like g in go	**g**	**gehen**	*geh·uhn*
j	like y in yes	**y**	**ja**	*yah*
qu	like k + v	**kv**	**Quark**	*kvahrk*
r	pronounced in the back of the mouth	**r**	**warum**	*vah·room*
s	1. before or between vowels, like z in zoo	**z**	**sie**	*zee*
	2. before p and t, like sh in shut	**sh**	**Sport**	*shpohrt*
	3. elsewhere, like s in sit	**s**	**es ist**	*ehs ihst*
ß	like s in sit	**s**	**groß**	*grohs*
sch	like sh in shut	**sh**	**schnell**	*shnehl*
tsch	like ch in chip	**ch**	**deutsch**	*doych*
tz	like ts in hits	**ts**	**Platz**	*plahts*
v	1. like f in for	**f**	**vier**	*feer*
	2. in foreign words, like v in voice	**v**	**Vase**	*vah·seh*
w	like v in voice	**v**	**wie**	*vee*
z	like ts in hits	**ts**	**zeigen**	*tsie·gehn*

Letters f, h, k, l, m, n, p, t and x are pronounced as in English.

Vowels

Letter	Approximate Pronunciation	Symbol	Example	Pronunciation
a	like a in father	**ah**	**Tag**	*tahk*
ä	1. like e in let	**eh**	**Lärm**	*lehrm*
	2. like a in late	**ay**	**spät**	*shpayt*
e	1. like e in let	**eh**	**schnell**	*shnehl*
	2. at the end of a word, if the syllable is not stressed, like u in us	**uh**	**bitte**	*biht·tuh*
i	1. like i in hit, before a doubled consonant	**ih**	**billig**	*bih·leek*
	2. otherwise, like ee in meet	**ee**	**ihm**	*eem*
o	like o in home	**oh**	**voll**	*fohl*
ö	like er in fern	**er**	**schön**	*shern*
u	like oo in boot	**oo**	**Nuss**	*noos*
ü	like ew in new	**ew**	**über**	*ew·behr*
y	like ew in new	**ew**	**typisch**	*tew·peesh*

Combined Vowels

Letter	Approximate Pronunciation	Symbol	Example	Pronunciation
ai, ay, ei, ey	like ie in tie	**ie**	**nein**	*nien*
ao, au	like ow in now	**ow**	**auf**	*owf*
äu, eu, oy	like oy in boy oy	**oy**	**neu**	*noy*

How to use this Book

Sometimes you see two alternatives separated by a slash. Choose the one that's right for your situation.

ESSENTIAL

When does the bank open/close?

Wann öffnet/schließt die Bank? *vahn erf•nuht/ shleest dee bahnk*

I'd like to change dollars/pounds into euros.

Ich möchte Dollar/Pfund in Euro wechseln. *eekh mehrkh•tuh doh•lahr/pfoont ihn oy•roh vehkh•zuhln*

I'd like to cash traveler's checks [cheques].

Ich möchte Reiseschecks einlösen. *eekh mehrkh•tuh rie•zuh•shehks ien•ler•zuhn*

Words you may see are shown in YOU MAY SEE boxes.

YOU MAY SEE...

ZOLL	customs
ZOLLFREIE WAREN	duty-free goods
ZOLLPFLICHTIGE WAREN	goods to declare

Any of the words or phrases listed can be plugged into the sentence below.

Tickets

When's...to Berlin?

Wann geht ... nach Berlin? *vahn geht ... nahkh behr•leen*

the (first) bus

der (erste) Bus *dehr (ehr•stuh) boos*

the (next) flight

der (nächste) Flug *dehr (nehks•tuh) floog*

the (last) train

der (letzte) Zug *dehr (lehts•tuh) tsoog*

German phrases appear in purple.

Read the simplified pronunciation as if it were English. For more on pronunciation, see page 7.

The Dating Game

Can I join you?

Kann ich mitkommen?
kahn eekh miht•koh•muhn

You're very attractive.

Sie sind sehr attraktiv.
zee zihnt zehr aht•rahk•teef

For Communications, see page 49.

Related phrases can be found by going to the page number indicated.

When addressing anyone but a very close friend, it is polite to use a title: **Herr** (Mr.), **Frau** (Miss/Ms./Mrs.), or **Herr Dr.** (Dr.) and to speak to him or her using **Sie**, the formal form of 'you', until you are asked to use the familiar **Du**.

Information boxes contain relevant country, culture and language tips.

Expressions you may hear are shown in You May Hear boxes.

When different gender forms apply, the masculine form is followed by *m*; feminine by *f*

YOU MAY HEAR...

Kann er *m*/sie *f* zurückrufen? *khan ehr/zee tsoo•rewkh•roof•uhn*

Can he/she call you back?

Was ist Ihre Nummer? *vahs ihst eehr•uh noom•ehr*

What's your number?

Color-coded side bars identify each section of the book.

Survival

ESSENTIAL

I'm on vacation [holiday].	**Ich mache Urlaub.** eekh _mahkh_•uh _oor_•lowb
I'm on business.	**Ich bin auf Geschäftsreise.** eekh bihn owf guh•_shehfts_•rie•zuh
I'm going to…	**Ich reise nach …** eekh _rie_•zuh nahkh …
I'm staying at the…Hotel.	**Ich übernachte im Hotel …** eekh ew•buhr•_nahkh_•tuh ihm hoh•_tehl_ …

YOU MAY HEAR…

Ihren Reisepass, bitte. _eer_•uhn _rie_•zuh•pahs _biht_•tuh	Your passport, please.
Was ist der Grund Ihrer Reise? vahs ihst dehr groont _ihr_•uhr _rie_•zuh	What's the purpose of your visit?
Wo übernachten Sie? voh ew•behr•_nahkh_•tuhn zee	Where are you staying?
Wie lange bleiben Sie? vee _lahng_•uh _blie_•buhn zee	How long are you staying?
Mit wem reisen Sie? miht vehm _rie_•zuhn zee	Who are you traveling with?

Border Control

I'm just passing through.	**Ich bin auf der Durchreise.** *eekh been owf dehr doorkh•rie•zuh*
I'd like to declare…	**Ich möchte … verzollen.** *eekh merkh•tuh … fehr•tsoh•luhn*
I have nothing to declare.	**Ich habe nichts zu verzollen.** *eekh hah•buh neekhts tsoo fehr•tsoh•luhn*

YOU MAY HEAR…

Haben Sie etwas zu verzollen? *hah•buhn zee eht•vahs tsoo fehr•tsoh•luhn*
Do you have anything to declare?

Darauf müssen Sie Zoll zahlen. *dahr•owf mew•suhn zee tsol tsah•luhn*
You must pay duty on this.

Öffnen Sie diese Tasche. *erf•nuhn zee dee•zuh tah•shuh*
Open this bag.

YOU MAY SEE...

ZOLL	customs
ZOLLFREIE WAREN	duty-free goods
ZOLLPFLICHTIGE WAREN	goods to declare
NICHTS ZU VERZOLLEN	nothing to declare
PASSKONTROLLE	passport control
POLIZEI	police

Money

ESSENTIAL

Where's...?
  the ATM
  the bank
  the currency
  exchange office
When does the
bank open/close?
I'd like to change
dollars/pounds
into euros.
I'd like to cash
traveler's checks
[cheques].

Wo ist ...? *voh ihst ...*
der Bankautomat *dehr <u>bahnk</u>·ow·toh·maht*
die Bank *dee bahnk*
die Wechselstube *dee <u>vehkh</u>·zuhl·shtoo·buh*

Wann öffnet/schließt die Bank? *vahn <u>erf</u>·nuht/
shleest dee bahnk*
Ich möchte Dollar/Pfund in Euro wechseln.
*eekh <u>mehrkh</u>·tuh <u>doh</u>·lahr/pfoont ihn
<u>oy</u>·roh <u>vehkh</u>·zuhln*
Ich möchte Reiseschecks einlösen. *eekh
<u>mehrkh</u>·tuh <u>rie</u>·zuh·shehks ien·<u>ler</u>·zuhn*

At the Bank

I'd like to change money/get a cash advance.	**Ich möchte Geld wechseln.** *eekh mehrkh·tuh gehlt vehkh·zuhln*
What's the exchange rate/fee?	**Was ist der Wechselkurs/die Gebühr?** *vahs ihst dehr vehkh·zuhl·koors/dee guh·bewr*
I think there's a mistake.	**Ich glaube, hier stimmt etwas nicht.** *eekh glow·buh heer shtihmt eht·vahs neekht*
I lost my traveler's cheques.	**Ich habe meine Reiseschecks verloren.** *eekh hah·buh mie·nuh rie·zuh·shecks fehr·loh·ruhn*
My card was stolen/doesn't work.	**Meine Karte wurde gestohlen/funktioniert nicht.** *mie·nuh kahr·tuh voor·duh guh·shtoh·luhn/ foonk·tzyoh·neert neekht*
My card was lost.	**Ich habe meine Karte verloren.** *eek hah·buh mie·nuh kahr·tuh fehr·loh·ruhn*
The ATM ate my card.	**Der Bankautomat hat meine Karte eingezogen.** *dehr bahnk·ow·toh·maht haht mie·nuh kahr·tuh ien·geh·tsoh·ghun*

YOU MAY SEE...

KARTE HIER EINFÜHREN	insert card here
ABBRECHEN	cancel
LÖSCHEN	clear
EINGEBEN	enter
PIN-NUMMER	PIN
ABHEBUNG	withdrawal
VOM GIROKONTO	from checking [current] account
VOM SPARKONTO	from savings account
QUITTUNG	receipt

The best rates for exchanging money will be found at banks. You can also change money at travel agencies, currency exchange offices and hotels, though the rate may not be as good. Traveler's checks are accepted at most banks (though banks are not required to accept them) and currency exchange offices, but a variable fee will be charged. Cash can be obtained from **Bankautomaten** (ATMs) with many international bank and credit cards. ATMs are multilingual, so English-language instructions can be selected. Remember to bring your passport when you want to change money.

For Numbers, see page 165.

YOU MAY SEE...

German currency is the **Euro €**, divided into 100 **Cent**.
Coins: 1, 2, 5, 10, 20, 50 **Cent**; €1, 2
Notes: €5, 10, 20, 50, 100, 200, 500

Getting Around

ESSENTIAL

How do I get to town?	**Wie komme ich in die Stadt?** *vee koh·muh eekh ihn dee shtaht*
Where's . . . ?	**Wo ist . . . ?** *voh ihst . . .*
the airport	**der Flughafen** *dehr flook·hah·fuhn*
the train [railway] station	**der Bahnhof** *dehr bahn·hohf*
the bus station	**die Bushaltestelle** *dee boos·hahl·tuh·shteh·luh*
the subway [underground] station	**die U-Bahn-Haltestelle** *dee oo·bahn·hahl·tuh·shteh·luh*
Is it far from here?	**Wie weit ist es?** *vee viet ihst ehs*
Where do I buy a ticket?	**Wo kann ich eine Fahrkarte kaufen?** *voh kahn eekh ie·nuh fahr·kahr·tuh kow·fuhn*
A one-way/ return ticket to. . .	**Ein Einzelticket/Eine Fahrkarte für Hin- und Rückfahrt nach . . .** *ien ien·tsehl·tee·kuht/ ie·nuh fahr·kahr·tuh fewr hihn oond rewk·fahrt nahkh. . .*
How much?	**Wie viel kostet es?** *vee feel kohs·tuht ehs*
Which gate/line?	**Welches Gate/Linie?** *vehl·khehs geht/leen·yah*
Which platform?	**Welcher Bahnsteig?** *vehl·khehr bahn·shtieg*
Where can I get a taxi?	**Wo finde ich ein Taxi?** *voh fihn·duh eekh ien tahk·see*
Take me to this address, please.	**Bitte fahren Sie mich zu dieser Adresse.** *biht·tuh fah·ruhn zee meekh tsoo dee·zehr ah·dreh·suh*
Can I have a map, please?	**Können Sie mir bitte einen Stadtplan geben?** *ker·nuhn zee mihr biht·tuh ien·uhn shtaht·plahn geh·behn*

Tickets

When's...to Berlin?	**Wann geht ... nach Berlin?** *vahn geht ... nahkh behr-_leen_*
the (first) bus	**der (erste) Bus** *dehr (_ehr_-stuh) boos*
the (next) flight	**der (nächste) Flug** *dehr (_nehks_-tuh) floog*
the (last) train	**der (letzte) Zug** *dehr (_lehts_-tuh) tsoog*
Where do I buy...?	**Wo kaufe ich ...?** *voh _kow_-fuh eekh ...*
One/two airline ticket(s), please.	**Ein/Zwei Ticket(s), bitte.** *ien/tsvie tee-kuht(s) _biht_-tuh*
One/two (bus/train/ subway) ticket(s), please.	**Ein/Zwei Fahrkarte(n), bitte.** *ien/tsvie _fahr_-kahr-tuh(n) _biht_-tuh*
For today/tomorrow.	**Für heute/morgen.** *fewr _hoy_-tuh/_mohr_-guhn*
A...(airline) ticket.	**Ein ... Ticket.** *ien ... _tee_-kuht*
one-way	**einfaches** *_ien_-fah-khuhs*
return trip	**Hin- und Rückflug-** *hihn oont _rewk_-floog*
first class	**Erste-Klasse-** *_ehr_-stuh-_klah_-suh*
business class	**Business-Class-** *_bihz_-nehs-klahs*
economy class	**Economy-Class-** *eh-_koh_-noh-mee-klahs*
A...(bus/train/ subway) ticket.	**Eine ...** *_ie_-nuh ...*
one-way	**Einzelfahrkarte** *_ien_-zuhl-fahr-karh-tuh*
return trip	**Hin- und Rückfahrkarte** *hihn oont _rewk_-fahr-kahr-tuh*
first class	**Erste-Klasse-Fahrkarte** *_ehr_-stuh-_klah_-suh-fahr-karh-tuh*
How much?	**Wie viel kostet es?** *vee feel _kohs_-tuht ehs*
Can I buy a ticket on the bus/train?	**Kann ich im Bus/Zug eine Fahrkarte kaufen?** *kahn eekh ihm boos/tsoog _ie_-nuh _fahr_-kahr-tuh _kow_-fuhn*
I have an airline/ a train e-ticket.	**Ich habe ein E-Ticket/Online-Ticket.** *eekh _hah_-buh ien _ay_-tee-keht/_ohn_-lien-_tee_-keht*

Is there a discount for...?	**Gibt es eine Ermäßigung für ...?** *gihpt ehs ie·nuh ehr·meh·see·goong fewr ...*
children	**Kinder** *kihn·dehr*
students	**Studenten** *shtoo·dehn·tuhn*
senior citizens	**Rentner** *rehnt·nehr*
tourists	**Touristen** *too·rih·stuhn*
The express/local bus/train, please.	**Den Express-/Nahverkehrs-Bus/Zug, bitte.** *dehn ehks·prehs·/nah·fuhr·kehrs·boos/tsoog biht·tuh*
Do I have to stamp the ticket before boarding?	**Muss ich das Ticket vor dem Einsteigen entwerten?** *moos eekh dahs tihk·khet fohr dehm ayn·shtayg·uhn ehnt·vehr·thun*
How long is this ticket valid?	**Wie lange ist das Ticket gültig?** *vee lahng·uh ihst dahs tihk·khet gewl·teekh*
Can I return on the same ticket?	**Kann ich mit demselben Ticket zurückfahren?** *kahn eekh miht dehm·sehl·bhun tihk·khet tsoo·rewkh·fah·ruhn*
I'd like to... my reservation.	**Ich möchte meine Reservierung ...** *eekh merkh·tuh mie·nuh reh·zehr·vee·roong ...*
cancel	**stornieren** *shtohr·nee·ruhn*
change	**ändern** *ehn·dehrn*
confirm	**bestätigen** *beh·shtay·tee·guhn*

For Days, see page 167.
For Time, see page 166.

Plane

Airport Transfer

How much is a taxi to the airport?	**Was kostet ein Taxi zum Flughafen?** *vahs kohs·tuht ien tahk·see tsoom flook·hah·fuhn*
To...Airport, please.	**Zum Flughafen ..., bitte.** *tsoom flook·hah·fuhn ... biht·tuh*

My airline is…	**Meine Fluggesellschaft ist …**
	mie•nuh floo•geh•zehl•shahft ihst …
My flight leaves at…	**Mein Flug geht um …** _mien floog geht oom …_
I'm in a rush.	**Ich habe es eilig.** _eekh hah•buh ehs ie•leek_
Can you take an alternate route?	**Können Sie eine andere Strecke fahren?**
	ker•nuhn zee ie•nuh ahn•deh•ruh shtreh•kuh fah•ruhn
Can you drive faster/slower?	**Können Sie schneller/langsamer fahren?**
	ker•nuhn zee shneh•lehr/lahng•sah•mehr fah•ruhn

YOU MAY HEAR…

Mit welcher Fluggesellschaft fliegen Sie?	Which airline are you flying?
meet vehlkh•ehr floog•geh•sehl•shahft flee•gehn zee	
Inland oder international? _ihn•lahnt oh•dehr ihn•tuhr•nah•syoh•nahl_	Domestic or international?
Welcher Terminal? _vehlkh•ehr tehr•mee•nahl_	What terminal?

YOU MAY SEE…

ANKUNFT	arrivals
ABFLUG	departures
GEPÄCKAUSGABE	baggage claim
INLANDSFLÜGE	domestic flights
INTERNATIONALE FLÜGE	international flights
CHECK-IN	check-in
E-TICKET CHECK-IN	e-ticket check-in
ABFLUG-GATES	departure gates

Checking In

Where's check-in?	**Wo ist das Check-in?**	*voh ihst dahs <u>tshehk</u>·in*
My name is…	**Mein Name ist …**	*mien <u>nahm</u>·uh ihst …*
I'm going to…	**Ich reise nach …**	*eekh <u>riez</u>·uh nahkh …*
I have…	**Ich habe …**	*eekh <u>hahb</u>·uh …*
one suitcase	**einen Koffer**	*<u>ien</u>·uhn <u>kohf</u>·fehr*
two suitcases	**zwei Koffer**	*tsvie <u>kohf</u>·fehr*
one piece of hand luggage	**ein Handgepäckstück**	*ien <u>hahnd</u>·guh·pehk·shtewk*
How much luggage is allowed?	**Wie viel Gepäck ist erlaubt?**	*vee feel guh·<u>pehk</u> ihst ehr·<u>lowbt</u>*
Is that pounds or kilos?	**Sind das Pfund oder Kilo?**	*zihnt dahs pfoont <u>oh</u>·duhr <u>kee</u>·loh*
Which terminal?	**Welcher Terminal?**	*<u>vehlkh</u>·ehr tehr·mee·<u>nahl</u>*
Which gate?	**Welches Gate?**	*<u>vehlkh</u>·uhs geht*
I'd like a window/ an aisle seat.	**Ich möchte gern einen Fensterplatz/ Platz am Gang.**	*eekh <u>merkht</u>·uh gehrn <u>ien</u>·uhn <u>fehnst</u>·ehr·plahts/plahts ahm gahng*
When do we leave/arrive?	**Wann ist der Abflug/die Ankunft?**	*vahn ihst dehr <u>ahp</u>·floog/dee <u>ahn</u>·kuhnft*
Is the flight delayed?	**Hat der Flug Verspätung?**	*haht dehr floog fehr·<u>shpeh</u>·toong*
How late?	**Wie viel?**	*vee feel*

Luggage

Where is/are…?	**Wo ist/sind …?**	*voh ihst/zihnt …*
the luggage trolleys	**die Gepäckwagen**	*dee guh·<u>pehk</u>·vah·guhn*
the luggage lockers	**die Gepäckschließfächer**	*dee guh·<u>pehk</u>·shlees·fehkh·ehr*

YOU MAY HEAR...

Der Nächste, bitte! *dehr nehkhst•uh biht•tuh*	Next, please!
Ihren Reisepass/Ihr Ticket, bitte. *eehr•uhn riez•uh•pahs/eehr tih•kuht biht•tuh*	Your passport/ticket, please.
Geben Sie Gepäck auf? *gehb•ehn zee guh•pehk owf*	Are you checking in any luggage?
Das ist zu groß für Handgepäck. *dahs ihst tsoo grohs fuehr hahnd•guh•pehk*	That's too large for a carry-on [piece of hand luggage].
Haben Sie diese Taschen selbst gepackt? *hah•buhn zee dees•uh tahsh•uhn sehlbst guh•pahkt*	Did you pack these bags yourself?
Hat Ihnen jemand etwas mitgegeben? *haht eehn•uhn yeh•mahnd eht•vahs miht•guh•geh•buhn*	Did anyone give you anything to carry?
Leeren Sie Ihre Taschen. *lehr•uhn zee eehr•uh tahsh•uhn*	Empty your pockets.
Ziehen Sie Ihre Schuhe aus. *tsee•uhn zee eehr•uh shoo•uh ows*	Take off your shoes.
Wir beginnen jetzt mit dem Einsteigen ... *weer beh•gihn•nuhn yehtst miht dehm ayn•shtayg•uhn ...*	We are now boarding...

23

the baggage claim	**die Gepäckausgabe** *dee guh•pehk•ows•gahb•uh*
My luggage has been lost/stolen.	**Mein Gepäck ist weg/wurde gestohlen.** *mien guh•pehk ihst vehk/voor•duh guh•shtohl•uhn*
My suitcase is damaged.	**Mein Koffer wurde beschädigt.** *mien kohf•fehr voord•uh buh•shehd•eekht*

Finding your Way

Where is/are...?	**Wo ist/sind ...?** *voh ihst/zihnt ...*
the currency exchange	**die Wechselstube** *dee vehkh·zuhl·shtoo·buh*
the car hire	**die Autovermietung** *dee ow·toh·fehr·meet·oong*
the exit	**der Ausgang** *dehr ows·gahng*
the taxis	**die Taxis** *dee tahks·ees*
Is there a...into town?	**Gibt es ... in die Stadt?** *gihbt ehs ... ihn dee shtadt*
bus	**einen Bus** *ien·uhn boos*
train	**einen Zug** *ien·uhn tsoog*
subway [underground]	**eine U-Bahn** *ien·uh oo·bahn*

For Asking Directions, see page 34.

Train

Where's the train [railway] station?	**Wo ist der Bahnhof?** *voh ihst dehr bahn·hohf*
How far is it?	**Wie weit ist es?** *vee viet ihst ehs*
Where is/are...?	**Wo ist/sind ...?** *voh ihst/zihnt ...*
the ticket office	**der Fahrkartenschalter** *dehr fahr·kahrt·uhn·shahl·tehr*
the information desk	**die Information** *dee ihn·fohrm·ah·syohn*
the luggage lockers	**die Gepäckschließfächer** *dee guh·pehk·shlees·fehkh·ehr*
the platforms	**die Bahnsteige** *dee bahn·shtieg·uh*
Can I have a schedule [timetable]?	**Kann ich einen Fahrplan haben?** *kahn eehk ien·uhn fahr·plahn hah·buhn*
How long is the trip?	**Wie lange dauert die Fahrt?** *vee lahng·uh dow·ehrt dee fahrt*

Is it a direct train?	**Ist das eine direkte Zugverbindung?**
	ihst dahs <u>ien</u>•uh dee•<u>rehkt</u> tsoog•ver•<u>bind</u>•ungh
Do I have to	**Muss ich umsteigen?** *moos eekh*
change trains?	<u>oom</u>•<u>shtieg</u>•uhn
Is the train on time?	**Ist der Zug pünktlich?** *ihst dehr tsoog <u>pewnkt</u>•leekh*

For Asking Directions, see page 34.

For Tickets, see page 19.

YOU MAY SEE…

BAHNSTEIGE	platforms
INFORMATION	information
RESERVIERUNGEN	reservations
WARTERAUM	waiting room
ANKUNFT	arrivals
ABFAHRT	departures

German trains are fast, comfortable and reliable. Train travel
in Germany is a highly recommended alternative to driving. The
Deutsche Bahn AG is the national railway of Germany. It offers
many domestic and international routes. Tickets can be purchased at
the station or through a travel agent. Buy your tickets in advance to get
the cheapest fare and to guarantee seating. Many reduced-fare options
are available; visit the **Deutsche Bahn AG** website or speak to a travel
agent for more information.

Departures

Which track [platform] to...?	**Von welchem Bahnsteig fährt der Zug nach ...?** *fohn vehlkh-ehm bahn-shtieg fehrt dehr tsoog nahkh ...*
Is this the track [platform]/train to...?	**Ist das der Bahnsteig/Zug nach ...?** *ihst dahs dehr bahn-shtieg/tsoog nahkh ...*
Where is platform...?	**Wo ist Bahnsteig ...?** *voh ihst bahn-shtieg ...*
Where do I change for...?	**Wo steige ich um nach ...?** *voh shtieg-uh eekh oom nahkh ...*

On Board

Can I sit here?	**Kann ich mich hier hinsetzen?** *kahn eekh meekh heer hihn-seht-suhn*
Can I open the window?	**Kann ich das Fenster öffnen?** *kahn eekh dahs fehn-stehr erf-nuhn*
Is this seat available?	**Ist der Platz frei?** *ihst dehr plahts frie*
That's my seat.	**Das ist mein Platz.** *dahs ihst mien plahts*
Here's my reservation.	**Hier ist meine Reservierung.** *heer ihst mien-uh reh-sehr-veer-roong*

YOU MAY HEAR...

Bitte einsteigen! *biht-tuh ien-shtieg-uhn*	All aboard!
Die Fahrkarten, bitte. *dee fahr-kahr-tuhn biht-tuh*	Tickets, please.
Sie müssen in ... umsteigen. *zee mews-uhn ihn ... oom-shtieg-uhn*	You have to change at...
Nächster Halt ... Hauptbahnhof. *nehkh-stehr hahlt ... howpt-bahn-hohf*	Next stop...

Bus

Where's the bus station?	**Wo ist die Bushaltestelle?** *voh ihst dee boos•hahlt•uh•shtehl•uh*
How far is it?	**Wie weit ist es?** *vee viet ihst ehs*
How do I get to...?	**Wie komme ich nach ...?** *vee kohm•uh eekh nahk...*
Is this the bus to...?	**Ist das der Bus nach ...?** *ihst dahs dehr boos nahkh...*
Can you tell me when to get off?	**Können Sie mir sagen, wann ich aussteigen muss?** *kerhn•uhn zee meer zahg•uhn vahn eekh ows•shtieg•uhn moos*
Do I have to change buses?	**Muss ich umsteigen?** *moos eekh oom•shtieg•uhn*
Stop here, please!	**Bitte halten Sie hier!** *biht•tuh hahlt•uhn zee heer*

For Tickets, see page 19.

Bus and tram stops are marked by a green **H** for **Haltestelle** (stop). Larger cities, such as Berlin, Munich and Hamburg, offer 24-hour service. Service is limited on holidays and weekends. In large German cities, the same ticket or pass can be used for the bus, subway, tram and above-ground train systems. Purchase tickets from the machines at bus stops or subway/tram stations. Check with a local travel agency or tourist information office about special discount tickets and offers.

YOU MAY SEE...

BUSHALTESTELLE	bus stop
STOPP-TASTE	request stop
EINGANG/AUSGANG	enter/exit
FAHRSCHEIN ENTWERTEN	validate your ticket

Linie	Ziel	Abfahrt in
M46	U Britz-Süd	4 min
M29	U Hermannplatz	8 min
M19	U Mehringdamm	10 min
M46	U Britz-Süd	11 min
M29	U Hermannplatz	

U-Bahnhof Wittenbergplatz

BVG

YOU MAY SEE...

FAHRTZIEL	destination
EINZELFAHRT	one-trip ticket
TAGESKARTE	day pass
GRUPPENKARTE	group pass
WOCHENKARTE	weekly pass

U-Bahn

Where's the U-Bahn [underground] station?	**Wo ist die U-Bahn-Haltestelle?** *voh ihst dee oo•bahn•halt•uh•shtehl•uh*
A map, please.	**Eine Übersichtskarte, bitte.** *ien•nuh ew•behr•zehkhts•kahr•tuh biht•tuh*
Which line for...?	**Welche Linie fährt nach ...?** *vehlkh•uh lihn•ee•uh fehrt nahkh ...*
Which direction?	**Welche Richtung?** *vehlkh•uh reekh•toong*
Do I have to transfer [change]?	**Muss ich umsteigen?** *moos eekh oom•shtieg•uhn*
Is this the U-Bahn [train] to...?	**Ist das die U-Bahn nach ...?** *ihst dahs dee oo•bahn nahkh ...*

How many stops to...?	**Wie viele Haltestellen sind es bis ...?**
	vee feel-uh halt-uh-shtehl-uhn zihnt ehs bihs ...
Where are we?	**Wo sind wir?** *voh zihnt veer*

For Tickets, see page 19.

All main cities in Germany have an **U-Bahn** (underground/ subway), an **S-Bahn** (light rail system, above and below ground) or both. In most cities, the same ticket can be used for the **U-Bahn**, **S-Bahn** and bus and tram lines. Operating times vary for each city, but most operate from 4:00 a.m to midnight or 1:00 a.m. during the week, with some routes offering 24-hour service on weekends. Most stations feature ticket machines; some may be in English.

Boat & Ferry

When is the ferry to...?	**Wann geht die Fähre nach ...?** *vahn geht dee fehr-uh nahkh ...*
Can I take my car?	**Kann ich mein Auto mitnehmen?** *kahn eekh mien ow-toh miht-nehm-uhn*
What time is the next sailing?	**Wann fährt das nächste Schiff ab?** *vahn fehrt dahs nehkh-ste shihf ahb*
Can I book a seat/cabin?	**Kann ich einen Sitzplatz/eine Kabine reservieren?** *kahn eekh ien-uhn sihts-plahts/ ien-uh kah-bee-nuh reh-sehr-veer-uhn*

YOU MAY SEE...

| RETTUNGSBOOT | life boat |
| SCHWIMMWESTE | life jacket |

How long is the crossing?	**Wie lange dauert die Überfahrt?**
	vee <u>lahng</u>•uh <u>dow</u>•ehrt dee <u>ew</u>•behr•fahrt

For Tickets, see page 19.

Ferry service across the Baltic Sea is available between Germany and Denmark, Sweden, Finland and Norway, or across the North Sea to the U.K. Ferry service is also available across Lake Constance to Austria and Switzerland. Boat trips are a fun way to explore the many rivers and lakes throughout Germany. Ferry and boat trips can be arranged by contacting your travel agent or searching the internet.

Taxi

Where can I get a taxi?	**Wo finde ich ein Taxi?** *voh <u>fihnd</u>•uh eekh ien <u>tahk</u>•see*
Can you send a taxi?	**Können Sie ein Taxi schicken?** *kern•nuhn zee ein tahk•see shihk•uhn*

YOU MAY HEAR...

Wohin? *voh•<u>hihn</u>*

Where to?

Wie ist die Adresse? *wee ihst dee ah•<u>drehs</u>•uh*

What's the address?

Es wird ein Nachtzuschlag/ Flughafenzuschlag berechnet. *ehs veerd ien <u>nahkht</u>•tsoo•shlahg/ <u>floog</u>•hahf•uhn•tsoo•shlahg buh•<u>rehkh</u>•nuht*

There's a nighttime/ airport surcharge.

You can catch a taxi at taxi stands, by calling to arrange for pick up, or by flagging down a passing available taxi. Taxi stands can be found at train stations, airports, large hotels and other popular areas in the city, such as shopping areas, parks and tourist destinations. Taxi service numbers can be found in the phone book or by asking your hotel concierge. All taxis are metered and will charge a base rate plus a rate per kilometer traveled. To tip the driver, round the fare up to the next euro or two, depending on the service.

Do you have the number for a taxi?	**Haben Sie die Telefonnummer für ein Taxi?** *hah·buhn zee dee tehl·uh·fohn·noom·ehr fewr ien tahk·see*
I'd like a taxi now/ for tomorrow at...	**Ich brauche jetzt/für morgen um ... ein Taxi.** *eekh browkh·uh yehtst/fewr mohrg·uhn oom ... ien tahk·see*
Pick me up at...	**Holen Sie mich um ... ab.** *hohl·uhn zee meekh oom ... ahp*
I'm going...	**Ich möchte ...** *eekh merkh·tuh ...*
to this address	**zu dieser Adresse** *tsoo deez·ehr ah·drehs·suh*
to the airport	**zum Flughafen** *tsoom floog·hah·fuhn*
to the train station	**zum Bahnhof** *tsoom bahn·hohf*
I'm late.	**Ich bin spät dran.** *eekh bihn shpayt drahn*
Can you drive faster/slower?	**Können Sie schneller/langsamer fahren?** *kern·nuhn zee shnehl·ehr/lahng·sahm·ehr fahr·uhn*
Stop here.	**Halten Sie hier an.** *hahl·tuhn zee heer ahn*
Wait here.	**Warten Sie hier.** *vahrt·uhn zee heer*
How much?	**Wie viel kostet es?** *vee feel kohs·tuht ehs*

You said it would cost...	**Sie sagten, es würde ... kosten.** *zee zahg·tuhn ehs vewrd·uh ... kohs·tuhn*
Keep the change.	**Stimmt so.** *shtihmt zoh*
The receipt, please.	**Die Quittung, bitte.** *dee kviht·oong biht·tuh*

Bicycle & Motorbike

I'd like to hire...	**Ich möchte gern ... mieten.** *eekh merkh·tuh gehrn ... meet·uhn*
a bicycle	**ein Fahrrad** *ien fahr·raht*
a moped	**ein Moped** *ien moh·pehd*
a motorbike	**ein Motorrad** *ien moh·tohr·raht*
How much per day/week?	**Wie viel pro Tag/Woche?** *vee feel proh tahk/vohkh·uh*
Can I have a helmet/lock?	**Kann ich einen Helm/ein Schloss haben?** *kahn eekh ien·uhn hehlm/ien shlohs hah·buhn*

Car Hire

Where's the car hire?	**Wo ist die Autovermietung?** *voh ihst dee ow·toh·fehr·miet·oong*
I'd like...	**Ich möchte ...** *eekh merkh·tuh ...*
a cheap/small car	**ein billiges/kleines Auto** *ien bihl·lee·guhs/klien·uhs ow·toh*
an automatic/ a manual car	**ein Auto mit Automatikschaltung/ Gangschaltung** *ien ow·toh miht ow·toh·mah·teek·shahl·toong/gahng·shahl·toong*
air conditioning	**ein Auto mit Klimaanlage** *ien ow·toh miht klee·mah·ahn·lah·guh*
a car seat	**einen Kindersitz** *ien·uhn kihnd·ehr·zihts*
How much...?	**Wie viel kostet es ...?** *vee feel kohs·tuht ehs ...*
per day/week	**pro Tag/Woche** *proh tahk/vohkh·uh*
per kilometer	**pro Kilometer** *proh kee·loh·meh·tehr*

for unlimited mileage	**mit unbegrenzter Kilometerzahl**
	miht oon·buh·grehnts·tuhr kee·loh·meh·tehr·tsahl
with insurance	**mit Versicherung** *miht fehr·zeekh·ehr·oong*
Are there any discounts?	**Gibt es irgendwelche Ermäßigungen?**
	gihpt ehs eer·guhnd·vehlkh·uh ehr·meh·see·goong·uhn

YOU MAY HEAR...

Haben Sie einen internationalen Führerschein? *hah·buhn zee ien·uhn* *ihnt·ehr·nah·syoh·nahl·uhn fewhr·uhr·shien*	Do you have an international driver's license?
Ihren Reisepass, bitte. *eehr·uhn riez·uh·pahs biht·tuh*	Your passport, please.
Möchten Sie eine Versicherung? *merkht·uhn zee ien·uh fehr·seekh·ehr·roong*	Do you want insurance?
Ich benötige eine Anzahlung. *eekh buh·nert·ee·guh ien·uh ahn·tsah·loong*	I'll need a deposit.
Bitte unterschreiben Sie hier. *biht·tuh oont·ehr·shrieb·uhn zee heer*	Sign here, please.

Fuel Station

Where's the fuel station?	**Wo ist die Tankstelle?** *voh ihst dee tahnk·shtehl·luh*
Fill it up, please.	**Bitte volltanken.** *biht·tuh fohl·tahnk·uhn*
. . .euros, please.	**. . . Euro, bitte. . . .** *oy·roh biht·tuh*
I'll pay in cash/by credit card.	**Ich bezahle bar/mit Kreditkarte.** *eekh beht·sahl·uh bahr/miht kreh·deet·kahr·tuh*

YOU MAY SEE...

BENZIN	gas [petrol]
BLEIFREI	unleaded
NORMAL	regular
SUPER	super
DIESEL	diesel

Asking Directions

Is this the way to…?	**Ist das der Weg nach …?**
	ihst dahs dehr vehg nahkh …
How far is it to…?	**Wie weit ist es bis …?** *vee viet ihst ehs bihs …*

YOU MAY HEAR...

geradeaus *geh·rahd·uh·ows*	straight ahead
links *leenks*	left
rechts *rehkhts*	right
an der/um die Ecke *ahn dehr/oom dee eh·kuh*	on/around the corner
gegenüber *geh·guhn·ew·behr*	opposite
hinter *hihnt·ehr*	behind
neben *nehb·uhn*	next to
nach *nahkh*	after
nördlich/südlich *nerd·leekh/zewd·leekh*	north/south
östlich/westlich *erst·leekh/vehst·leekh*	east/west
an der Ampel *ahn dehr ahmp·ehl*	at the traffic light
an der Kreuzung *ahn dehr kroytz·oong*	at the intersection

Where's…?	**Wo ist …?** *voh ihst …*	
Street	**die … Straße** *dee … _shtrahs_•suh*	
this address	**diese Adresse** *_deez_•uh ah•_drehs_•uh*	
the highway [motorway]	**die Autobahn** *_dee_•uh _ow_•toh•bahn*	
Can you show me on the map?	**Können Sie mir das auf der Karte zeigen?** *_kern_•nuhn zee meer dahs owf dehr _kahrt_•uh _tsieg_•uhn*	
I'm lost.	**Ich habe mich verfahren.** *eekh _hahb_•uh meekh fehr•_fahr_•uhn*	

YOU MAY SEE…

(50)	**HÖCHSTGESCHWINDIGKEIT**	maximum speed limit
	ÜBERHOLVERBOT	no passing
	VERBOT FÜR FAHRZEUGE ALLER ART	all vehicles prohibited
	EINBAHNSTRASSE	one-way street
	KEINE DURCHFAHRT	no entry
STOP	**STOPP**	stop
	VORFAHRT GEWÄHREN	yield

Parking

Can I park here?	**Kann ich hier parken?** *kahn eekh heer pahrk•uhn*
Where's ...?	**Wo ist ...?** *voh ihst ...*
the parking garage	**das Parkhaus** *dahs pahrk•hows*
the parking lot [car park]	**der Parkplatz** *dehr pahrk•plahts*
the parking meter	**die Parkuhr** *dee pahrk•oor*
How much...?	**Wie viel kostet es ...?** *vee feel kohs•tuht ehs ...*
per hour	**pro Stunde** *proh shtoond•uh*
per day	**pro Tag** *proh tahk*
for overnight	**über Nacht** *ew•behr nahkht*

Parking on the street is common in Germany; look for the sign showing a white letter 'P' on a blue background. You may see additional parking instructions located under the sign.

The parking sign with the meter symbol indicates that you can park there for the amount of time shown (in hours - for example, **2 Std.** means 2 hours). Ask your rental car company for a parking disc when you pick up your car. Once parked, turn the dial to indicate the time you parked and put the disc on your dashboard where it is visible.

If you see a **mit Parkschein** sign you must buy a parking ticket from a nearby machine and place it on your dashboard where it is visible. Parking lots and garages are other parking options. Most lots and garages use a self-pay system. When entering, obtain the time-stamped ticket from the machine. Use the machine near the pedestrian entrance to pay for parking; insert your ticket into the machine, pay the amount it displays and then remove the validated ticket. Proceed to your car and insert that ticket into the machine at the exit.

Breakdown & Repair

Where's the garage?	**Wo ist die Autowerkstatt?**
	voh ihst dee ow·toh·vehrk·shtaht
My car broke down/	**Mein Auto ist kaputt/springt nicht an.**
won't start.	*mien ow·toh ihst kah·poot/shprihngt neekht ahn*
Can you fix it	**Können Sie es (heute) reparieren?**
(today)?	*kern·nuhn zee ehs (hoy·tuh) reh·pah·reer·uhn*
When will it be ready?	**Wann wird es fertig sein?**
	vahn wirt ehs fehr·teekh zien
How much?	**Wie viel kostet es?** *vee feel kohs·tuht ehs*
I have a puncture/	**Ich habe eine Reifenpanne.** *eekh hah·buh*
flat tyre (tire).	*ien·uh rie·fehn·pahn·nuh*

Accidents

There was an	**Es hat einen Unfall gegeben.** *ehs haht*
accident.	*ien·uhn oon·fahl guh·geh·buhn*
Call an ambulance/	**Rufen Sie einen Krankenwagen/die Polizei.**
the police.	*roof·uhn zee ien·uhn krahnk·uhn·vahg·uhn/*
	dee poh·lee·tsie

Places to Stay

ESSENTIAL

Can you recommend	**Können Sie ein Hotel empfehlen?**
a hotel?	*ker·nuhn zee ien hoh·tehl ehm·pfeh·luhn*
I have a reservation.	**Ich habe eine Reservierung.** *eekh hahb·uh*
	ien·uh rehz·ehr·veer·oong
My name is…	**Mein Name ist …** *mien nahm·uh ihst …*

38

Do you have a room…?	**Haben Sie ein Zimmer …?** _hah_•buhn zee ien _tsihm_•mehr …
for one person/ two people	**für eine Person/zwei Personen** _fewr ien_•uh pehr•_sohn_/tsvie pehr•_sohn_•uhn
with a bathroom	**mit Bad** _miht bahd_
with air conditioning	**mit Klimaanlage** miht _kleem_•uh•ahn•lahg•uh
For…	**Für …** _fewr …_
tonight	**heute Nacht** _hoy_•tuh nahkht
two nights	**zwei Nächte** tsvie _nehkht_•uh
one week	**eine Woche** _ien_•uh _vohkh_•uh
How much?	**Wie viel kostet es?** vee feel _kohs_•tuht ehs
Is there anything cheaper?	**Gibt es etwas Billigeres?** gihpt ehs _eht_•vahs _bihl_•lee•geh•ruhs
When's check-out?	**Wann ist der Check-out?** vahn ihst dehr _tshehk_•owt
Can I leave this in the safe?	**Kann ich das im Safe lassen?** kahn eekh dahs ihm sehf _lahs_•suhn
Can I leave my bags?	**Kann ich meine Taschen hierlassen?** kahn eekh _mien_•uh _tahsh_•uhn _heer_•lahs•suhn
Can I have my bill/a receipt?	**Kann ich meine Rechnung/eine Quittung haben?** kahn eekh _mien_•uh _rehkh_•noong/ _ien_•uh _kveet_•oong _hah_•buhn
I'll pay in cash/by credit card.	**Ich bezahle bar/mit Kreditkarte.** eekh beht•_sahl_•uh bahr/miht kreh•_deet_•kahr•tuh

Somewhere to Stay

| Can you recommend…? | **Können Sie … empfehlen?** _kern_•uhn zee … ehm•_pfeh_•luhn |
| a hotel | **ein Hotel** ien hoh•_tehl_ |

If you didn't reserve accommodation before your trip, visit the local **Touristeninformationsbüro** (tourist information office) for recommendations on places to stay.

a hostel	**eine Jugendherberge** *ien•uh yoog•uhnd•hehr•behr•guh*
a campsite	**einen Campingplatz** *ien•uhn kahmp•eeng•plahts*
a bed and breakfast	**eine Pension** *ien•uh pehn•syohn*
What is near it?	**Was ist in der Nähe davon?** *vahs ihst ihn dehr neh•uh dah•fohn*
How do I get there?	**Wie komme ich dorthin?** *vee kohm•uh eekh dohrt•hihn*

At the Hotel

I have a reservation.	**Ich habe eine Reservierung.** *eekh hahb•uh ien•uh rehz•ehr•veer•oong*
My name is...	**Mein Name ist ...** *mien nahm•uh ihst ...*
Do you have a room...?	**Haben Sie ein Zimmer ...?** *hah•buhn zee ien tsihm•mehr ...*

Travelers have numerous accommodation options in Germany, from budget to luxury. A **Pension** (bed and breakfast) provides opportunities to experience life in a German home. **Jugendherbergen** (youth hostels) are also available, catering to travelers of all ages. **Urlaub auf dem Bauernhof** (farm stay) is a great way to see the countryside and enjoy rural Germany. In some areas, you may be able to find **Modernisierte Schlossunterkünfte**, old castles that have been converted into beautiful accommodations. **Ferienwohnungen** (vacation apartments) and **Ferienhäuser** (holiday homes) allow travelers to rent fully equipped apartments and villas throughout Germany. All options can be booked with travel agents, tour companies or on the internet.

with a bathroom [toilet]/shower	**mit Bad/Dusche**	miht bahd/<u>doo</u>•shuh
with air conditioning	**mit Klimaanlage**	miht <u>kleem</u>•uh•ahn•lah•guh
that's smoking/ non-smoking	**für Raucher/Nichtraucher**	fewr <u>rowkh</u>•ehr/ <u>neekht</u>•rowkh•ehr
For...	**Für ...**	fewr ...
tonight	**heute Nacht**	<u>hoyt</u>•uh nahkht
two nights	**zwei Nächte**	tsvie <u>nehkht</u>•uh
a week	**eine Woche**	<u>ien</u>•uh <u>vohkh</u>•uh
Do you have...?	**Haben Sie ...?**	<u>hah</u>•buhn zee ...
a computer	**einen Computer**	<u>ien</u>•uhn kohm•<u>pjoot</u>•ehr
an elevator [a lift]	**einen Fahrstuhl**	<u>ien</u>•uhn <u>fahr</u>•shtoohl
(wireless) internet service	**(wireless) Internetanschluss**	(<u>wier</u>•luhs) <u>ihnt</u>•ehr•neht•ahn•shloos

room service	**Zimmerservice** _tsihm_·mehr·sehr·vees
a pool	**einen Pool** _ien_·uhn pool
a gym	**einen Fitnessraum** _ien_·uhn _fiht_·nehs·rowm
I need...	**Ich brauche ...** eekh _browkh_·uh ...
an extra bed	**ein zusätzliches Bett**
	ien tsoo·_zehts_·leeks·uhs beht
a cot	**ein Kinderbett** ien _kihnd_·ehr·beht
a crib	**ein Gitterbett** ien _giht_·tehr·beht

For Numbers, see page 165.

YOU MAY HEAR...

Ihren Reisepass/Ihre Kreditkarte, bitte.	Your passport /credit
eehr·uhn _riez_·uh·pahs/_eehr_·uh	card, please.
kreh·_deet_·kahrt·uh _biht_·tuh	
Bitte füllen Sie dieses Formular aus.	Fill out this form,
biht·tuh _fewl_·uhn zee _deez_·uhs fohr·moo·_lahr_ ows	please.
Bitte unterschreiben Sie hier. _biht_·tuh	Sign here, please.
oon·tehr·_shrieb_·uhn zee heer	

Price

How much per night/week?	**Wie viel kostet es pro Nacht/Woche?**
	vee feel _kohs_·tuht ehs proh nahkht/_vohkh_·uh
Does that include breakfast/sales tax [VAT]?	**Beinhaltet der Preis ein Frühstück/ Mehrwertsteuer?** beh·_ien_·hahlt·uht dehr
	pries ien _frewh_·shtewkh/_mehr_·wehrt·shtoy·ehr
Are there any discounts?	**Gibt es irgendwelche Ermäßigungen?**
	gihpt ehs _eer_·guhnd·vehlkh·uh ehr·_meh_·see·goong·uhn

Preferences

Can I see the room?	**Kann ich das Zimmer sehen?**
	kahn eekh dahs tsihm·mehr zeh·uhn
I'd like a . . . room.	**Ich möchte ein . . . Zimmer.** *eekh merkh·tuh ien . . .*
	tsihm·muhr
better	**besseres** *behs·sehr·uhs*
bigger	**größeres** *grers·ehr·uhs*
cheaper	**billigeres** *bihl·lee·gehr·uhs*
quieter	**ruhigeres** *roo·ee·gehr·uhs*
I'll take it.	**Ich nehme es.** *eekh nehm·uh ehs*
No, I won't take it.	**Nein, ich nehme es nicht.**
	nien eekh nehm·uh ehs neekht

Questions

Where's . . . ?	**Wo ist . . . ?** *voh ihhst . . .*
the bar	**die Bar** *dee bahr*
the bathroom [toilet]	**die Toilette** *dee toy·leht*
the elevator [lift]	**der Fahrstuhl** *dehr fahr·shtoohl*
Can I have . . . ?	**Kann ich . . . haben?** *kahn eekh . . . hah·buhn*
a blanket	**eine Decke** *ien·uh dehk·uh*
an iron	**ein Bügeleisen** *ien bew·guh·liez·ehn*
the room key/the	**den Zimmerschlüssel/die Schlüsselkarte key card**
	dehn tsihm·mehr·shlews·uhl/dee shlews·ehl·kahrt·uh
a pillow	**ein Kissen** *ien kihs·suhn*
soap	**Seife** *zief·uh*
toilet paper	**Toilettenpapier** *toy·leht·tuhn·pah·peer*
a towel	**ein Handtuch** *ien hahnt·tookh*
Do you have an adapter for this?	**Haben Sie hierfür einen Adapter?** *hah·buhn*
	zee heer·fewr ien·uhn ah·dahp·tehr

How do I turn on the lights?	**Wie schalte ich das Licht an?** *vee shahlt·uh eekh dahs leekht ahn*
Can you wake me at…?	**Können Sie mich um … wecken?** *kern·nuhn zee meekh oom … vehk·uhn*
Can I leave this in the safe?	**Kann ich das im Safe lassen?** *kahn eekh dahs ihm sehf lahs·suhn*
Can I have my things from the safe?	**Kann ich meine Sachen aus dem Safe haben?** *kahn eekh mien·uh zahkh·uhn ows dehm sehf hah·buhn*
Is there mail [post]/ a message for me?	**Haben Sie Post/eine Nachricht für mich?** *hah·buhn zee pohst/ien·uh nahkh·reekht fewr meekh*
Do you have a laundry service?	**Bieten Sie einen Wäscheservice?** *bih·tuhn zee ien·uhn vehsh·eh·ser·vice*

Problems

| There's a problem. | **Es gibt ein Problem.** *ehs gihbt ien prohb·lehm* |
| I lost my key/my key card. | **Ich habe meinen Schlüssel/meine Schlüsselkarte verloren.** *eekh hahb·uh mien·uhn shlews·uhl/mien·uh shlews·ehl·kahrt·uh fehr·lohr·uhn* |

YOU MAY SEE…

DRÜCKEN/ZIEHEN	push/pull
TOILETTE	bathroom [toilet]
DUSCHE	shower
FAHRSTUHL	elevator [lift]
TREPPE	stairs
WÄSCHEREI	laundry
BITTE NICHT STÖREN	do not disturb
FEUERSCHUTZTÜR	fire door
NOTAUSGANG	(emergency) exit
WECKRUF	wake-up call

I'm locked out of the room.	**Ich habe mich ausgesperrt.** *eekh hahb·uh meekh ows·guh·shpehrt*
There's no hot water/toilet paper.	**Ich habe kein heißes Wasser/Toilettenpapier.** *eekh hahb·uh kien hies·suhs vahs·sehr/ toy·leht·uhn·pah·peer*
The room is dirty.	**Das Zimmer ist schmutzig.** *dahs tsihm·mehr ihst shmoot·seek*
There are bugs in the room.	**Im Zimmer sind Insekten.** *ihm tsihm·mehr zihnt ihn·sehkt·uhn*
The...doesn't work.	**... funktioniert nicht.** *... foonk·syoh·neert neekht*
Can you fix...?	**Können Sie ... reparieren?** *kern·nuhn zee ... reh·pah·reer·ruhn*
the air conditioning	**die Klimaanlage** *dee kleem·uh·ahn·lahg·uh*
the fan	**den Ventilator** *dehn vehn·tee·laht·ohr*
the heat [heating]	**die Heizung** *dee hiets·oong*
the light	**das Licht** *dahs leekht*
the TV	**den Fernseher** *dehn fehrn·seh·ehr*
the toilet	**die Toilette** *dee toy·leht·tuh*
I'd like another room.	**Ich möchte gern ein anderes Zimmer.** *eekh merkh·tuh gehrn ien ahn·dehr·uhs tsihm·mehr*

Checking Out

| Can I have an itemized bill/ a receipt? | **Kann ich eine aufgeschlüsselte Rechnung/ Quittung haben?** *kahn eekh ien·uh owf·guh·shlews·ehlt·uh rekh·noong/ kveet·oong hah·buhn* |

Voltage is 220, and plugs are two-pronged. You may need a converter and/or an adapter for your appliances.

When's check-out?	**Wann ist der Check-out?** *vahn ihst dehr <u>tshehk</u>•owt*
Can I leave my bags here until…?	**Kann ich mein Gepäck bis … hierlassen?** *kahn eekh mien geh•<u>pehk</u> bihs … <u>heer</u>•lahs•uhn*
I think there's a mistake.	**Ich glaube, hier stimmt etwas nicht.** *eekh <u>glowb</u>•uh heer shtihmt <u>eht</u>•vahs neekht*
I'll pay in cash/by credit card.	**Ich bezahle bar/mit Kreditkarte.** *eekh beht•<u>sahl</u>•uh bahr/miht kreh•<u>deet</u>•kahrt•uh*

45

At hotels, it is common to leave tips for services provided. If you are happy with the housekeeping service, leave a tip of € 1-2 per day for the housekeeper in your room when you leave. Tip porters and your concierge € 2-3 if they provide assistance.

Renting

I reserved an apartment/a room.	**Ich habe ein Apartment/ein Zimmer reserviert.** *eekh <u>hahb</u>•uh ien ah•<u>pahrt</u>•muhnt/ ien <u>tsihm</u>•mehr reh•sehr•<u>veert</u>*
My name is…	**Mein Name ist …** *mien <u>nahm</u>•uh ihst …*
Can I have the keys?	**Kann ich den Schlüssel haben?** *kahn eekh dehn <u>shlews</u>•suhl <u>hah</u>•buhn*
Are there…?	**Gibt es …?** *gihpt ehs …*
dishes	**Geschirr** *guh•<u>sheer</u>*
pillows	**Kissen** *<u>kihs</u>•suhn*
sheets	**Bettwäsche** *<u>beht</u>•vehsh•uh*
towels	**Handtücher** *<u>hahnt</u>•tewkh•ehr*
kitchen utensils	**Haushaltsgeräte** *<u>hows</u>•hahlts•guh•reht•uh*
When do I put out the bins/recycling?	**Wann stelle ich den Abfall/Müll raus?** *vahn <u>shtehl</u>•luh eekh dehn ahp•<u>fahl</u>/mewl rows*

...is broken.	**... funktioniert nicht.** .... *foonk•syoh•neert neekht*
How does...work?	**Wie funktioniert ...?** *vee foonk•syoh•neert* ...
the air conditioner	**die Klimaanlage** *dee kleem•uh•ahn•lahg•uh*
the dishwasher	**die Spülmaschine** *dee shpewl•mah•sheen•uh*
the freezer	**der Gefrierschrank** *dehr guh•freer•shrahnk*
the heating	**die Heizung** *dee hiet•soong*
the microwave	**die Mikrowelle** *dee mee•kroh•vehl•luh*
the refrigerator	**der Kühlschrank** *dehr kewhl•shrahnk*
the stove	**der Herd** *dehr hehrd*
the washing machine	**die Waschmaschine** *dee vahsh•mah•shee•nuh*

Domestic Items

I need...	**Ich brauche ...** *eekh browkh•uh* ...
an adapter	**einen Adapter** *ien•uhn ah•dahp•tehr*
aluminum [kitchen] foil	**Alufolie** *ah•loo•foh•lee•uh*
a bottle opener	**einen Flaschenöffner** *ien•uhn flahsh•uhn•erf•nehr*
a broom	**einen Besen** *ien•uhn behz•uhn*
a can opener	**einen Dosenöffner** *ien•uhn doh•suhn•erf•nehr*
cleaning supplies	**Reinigungsmittel** *rien•ee•goongs•miht•tuhl*
a corkscrew	**einen Korkenzieher** *ien•uhn kohrk•uhn•tsee•ehr*
detergent	**Waschmittel** *vahsh•miht•tuhl*
dishwashing liquid	**Geschirrspülmittel** *guh•sheer•shpewl•miht•tuhl*
bin bags	**Abfallsäcke** *ahb•fahl•seh•khuh*
a lightbulb	**eine Glühbirne** *ien•uh glewh•beer•nuh*
matches	**Streichhölzer** *shtriekh•herlt•sehr*
a mop	**einen Wischmopp** *ien•uhn vihsh•mohp*
napkins	**Servietten** *sehr•vyeht•tuhn*
paper towels	**Küchenrollen** *kewkh•uhn•rohl•luhn*

plastic wrap [cling film]	**Frischhaltefolie** _frihsh_·hahl·tuh·foh·lee·uh
a plunger	**eine Saugglocke** _ien_·uh _zowg_·lohk·uh
scissors	**eine Schere** _ien_·uh _shehr_·uh
a vacuum cleaner	**einen Staubsauger** _ien_·uhn _shtowb_·sowg·ehr

For In the Kitchen, see page 77.

For Oven Temperatures, see page 171.

At the Hostel

Is there a bed available?	**Haben Sie ein Bett frei?** _hah_·buhn zee ien beht frie
Can I have…?	**Kann ich … haben?** kahn eekh … _hah_·buhn
a single/double room	**ein Einzelzimmer/Doppelzimmer** _ien _ient_·sehl·tsihm·mehr/_dohp_·pehl·tsihm·muhr
a blanket	**eine Decke** _ien_·uh _dehk_·huh
a pillow	**ein Kissen** ien _kihs_·suhn
sheets	**Bettwäsche** _beht_·vehsh·uh
a towel	**ein Handtuch** ien _hahnt_·tookh

There are more than 500 hostels throughout Germany, in cities large and small and in rural locations. You may need a Hostelling International membership card to stay at these hostels, many of which belong to **Deutsches Jugendherbergswerk (DJV)**. Hostels are inexpensive accommodations that offer dormitory-style rooms and, sometimes, private or semi-private rooms. Some offer private bathrooms, though most have shared facilities. There is usually a self-service kitchen on site. Booking in advance is a good idea, especially in large cities during festivals or holidays. Reservations can be made over the phone or online. Visit the Hostelling International website for more information.

Do you have lockers?	**Haben Sie Schließfächer?** _hah_-buhn zee _shlees_-fehkh-ehr
When do you lock up?	**Wann schließen Sie ab?** vahn _shlees_-suhn zee ahp
Do I need a membership card?	**Brauche ich eine Mitgliedskarte?** _browkh_-uh eekh _ien_-uh _miht_-gleeds-kahrt-uh
Here's my international student card.	**Hier ist mein internationaler Studentenausweis.** heer ihst mien ihn-tehr-nah-syoh-_nahl_-ehr shtoo-_dehnt_-uhn-ows-vies

Going Camping

Can I camp here?	**Kann ich hier campen?** kahn eekh heer _kahmp_-uhn
Where's the campsite?	**Wo ist der Campingplatz?** voh ihst dehr _kahmp_-eeng-plahts
What is the charge per day/week?	**Was kostet es pro Tag/Woche?** vahs _kohst_-uht ehs proh tahk/_vohkh_-uh
Are there...?	**Gibt es ...?** gihpt ehs ...
cooking facilities	**Kochmöglichkeiten** _kohkh_-merg-leekh-kiet-uhn
electric outlets	**Steckdosen** _shtehkh_-dohz-uhn
laundry facilities	**Waschmaschine** _vahsh_-maksch-een-uh
showers	**Duschen** _doosh_-uhn
tents for hire	**Mietzelte** _meet_-tsehl-tuh
Where can I empty the chemical toilet?	**Wo kann ich die Campingtoilette leeren?** voh kahn eekh dee _kahmp_-eeng-toy-leh-tuh _lehr_-uhn

For Domestic Items, see page 46.

For In the Kitchen, see page 77.

YOU MAY SEE...

TRINKWASSER	drinking water
ZELTEN VERBOTEN	no camping
OFFENES FEUER VERBOTEN	no fires

Communications

ESSENTIAL

Where's an internet cafe?	**Wo gibt es ein Internetcafé?** *voh gihpt ehs ien ihnt·ehr·neht·kah·feh*
Can I access the internet/check e-mail?	**Kann ich das Internet benutzen/meine E-Mails lesen?** *kahn eekh dahs ihnt·ehr·neht beh·noot·suhn/mien·uh ee·miels lehz·uhn*
How much per (half) hour?	**Wie viel kostet eine (halbe) Stunde?** *vee feel kohst·uht ien·uh (hahlb·uh) shtoond·uh*
How do I log on?	**Wie melde ich mich an?** *vee mehld·uh eekh meekh ahn*
A phone card, please.	**Eine Telefonkarte, bitte.** *ien·uh tehl·uh·fohn·kahrt·uh biht·tuh*
Can I have your phone number?	**Kann ich Ihre Telefonnummer haben?** *kahn eekh eehr·uh tehl·uh·fohn·noom·ehr hah·buhn*
Here's my number/e-mail.	**Hier ist meine Telefonnummer/E-Mail.** *heer ihst mien·uh tehl·uh·fohn·noom·ehr/ee·miel*
Call me.	**Rufen Sie mich an.** *roo·fuhn zee meekh ahn*
E-mail me.	**Mailen Sie mir.** *miel·uhn zee meer*
Hello. This is…	**Hallo. Hier ist …** *hah·loh heer ihst …*
Can I speak to…?	**Kann ich mit … sprechen?** *kahn eekh miht … shprehkh·uhn*
Can you repeat that, please?	**Könnten Sie das bitte wiederholen?** *kern·tuhn zee dahs biht·tuh veed·ehr·hohl·uhn*
I'll call back later.	**Ich rufe später zurück.** *eekh roof·uh shpeht·ehr tsoo·rewkh*
Bye.	**Auf Wiederhören.** *owf veed·ehr·her·ruhn*

| Where's the post office? | **Wo ist die Post?** *voh ihst dee pohst* |
| I'd like to send this to… | **Ich möchte das nach … schicken.** *eekh merkh·tuh dahs nahkh … shihk·uhn* |

Online

Where's an internet cafe?	**Wo gibt es ein Internetcafé?** *voh gihpt ehs ien ihnt·ehr·neht·kah·feh*
Does it have wireless internet?	**Gibt es dort wireless Internet?** *gihpt ehs dohrt wier·luhs ihnt·ehr·neht*
What is the WiFi password?	**Wie lautet das WLAN-Passwort?** *vee low·teht dahs veh·lahn·pahs·vohrt*
Is the WiFi free?	**Ist der WLAN-Zugang gratis?** *ihst dehr veh·lahn·tsoo·gahng grah·tihs*
Do you have bluetooth?	**Haben Sie Bluetooth?** *hah·buhn zee bloo·tooth*
How do I turn the computer on/off?	**Wie schalte ich den Computer an/aus?** *vee shahlt·uh eekh dehn kohm·pjoot·ehr ahn/ows*
Can I…?	**Kann ich …?** *kahn eekh …*
access the internet	**das Internet benutzen** *dahs ihnt·ehr·neht beh·noot·suhn*
check e-mail	**E-Mails lesen** *ee·miels lehz·uhn*
print	**drucken** *drook·uhn*
plug in/charge my laptop/iPhone/iPad/BlackBerry?	**meinen Laptop/mein iPhone/iPad/BlackBerry aufladen?** *kahn eekh mien·uhn lap·top/mien iphone/ipad/blackberry owf·lahd·uhn*
access Skype?	**Skype verwenden?** *skype fuhr· vehn· dehn*
use any computer	**einen Computer benutzen** *ien·uhn kohm·pjoot·ehr beh·noot·suhn*
How much per (half) hour?	**Wie viel kostet eine (halbe) Stunde?** *vee feel kohst·uht ien·uh (hahlb·uh) shtoond·uh*

How...?	**Wie ...?** *vee ...*
do I connect	**stelle ich eine Verbindung her**
	shteh•luh eekh ien•uh fuhr•bihnd•oong hehr
do I disconnect	**trenne ich eine Verbindung** *trehn•uh eekh*
	ien•uh fuhr•bihnd•oong
do I log on/off	**melde ich mich an/ab** *mehld•uh eekh meekh ahn/ahp*
do I type this	**gebe ich dieses Zeichen ein** *geh•buh eekh*
symbol	*deez•uhs tsiekh•ehn ien*
What's your e-mail?	**Wie ist Ihre E-Mail-Adresse?**
	vee ihst eehr•uh ee•miel•ah•drehs•uh
My e-mail is...	**Meine E-Mail-Adresse ist ...**
	mien•uh ee•miel•ah•drehs•uh ihst ...
Do you have	**Haben Sie einen Scanner?**
a scanner?	*hah•buhn zee ien•uhn scan•nuhr*

Social Media

Are you on	**Sind Sie bei Facebook/Twitter?** *(polite form)*
Facebook/Twitter?	*zihnt zee by face•book/twit•ter*
	Bist du bei Facebook/Twitter? *(informal form)*
	bihst doo by face•book/twit•ter

YOU MAY SEE...

SCHLIESSEN	close
LÖSCHEN	delete
E-MAIL	e-mail
BEENDEN	exit
HILFE	help
INSTANT MESSENGER	instant messenger
INTERNET	internet
ANMELDEN	login
NEUE NACHRICHT	new message
AN/AUS	on/off
ÖFFNEN	open
DRUCKEN	print
SPEICHERN	save
SENDEN	send
BENUTZERNAME/PASSWORT	username/password
WIRELESS INTERNET	wireless internet

What's your user name?	**Was ist Ihr Benutzername?** *(polite form)* *vahs ihst eehr beh•noots•uhr•nah•muh*
	Was ist dein Benutzername? *(informal form)* *vahs ihst dien beh•noots•uhr•nah•muh*
I'll follow you on Twitter.	**Ich werde Ihre Twitter-Einträge verfolgen.** *(polite form) eekh vehr•duh eer•he twit•ter•ien•treh•ghe fehr•folg•hun*
	Ich werde deine Twitter-Einträge verfolgen. *(informal form) eekh vehr•duh die•nuh twit•ter•ien•treh•ghe fehr•folg•hun*
Are you following...?	**Verfolgen Sie ...?** *(polite form) fehr•folg•hun zee ...*
	Verfolgst du ...? *(informal form) fehr•folgst doo ...*

I'll add you as a friend.	**Ich werde Sie als Freund/Freundin hinzufügen.** *(polite form)* eekh vehrd•uh zee ahls froynd/ froyn•dihn hihn•tsoo•few•guhn
	Ich werde dich als Freund/Freundin hinzufügen. *(informal form)* eekh vehrd•uh deekh ahls froynd/ froyn•dihn hihn•tsoo•few•guhn
I'll put the pictures on Facebook/Twitter.	**Ich werde die Fotos auf Facebook/Twitter hochladen.** eekh vehr•duh dee foh•tohs owf face•book/ twit•ter hokh•lah•duhn
I'll tag you in the pictures.	**Ich werde Sie auf den Fotos markieren.** *(polite form)* eekh vehr•duh zee owf dehn foh•tohs mahr•kih•ruhn
	Ich werde dich auf den Fotos markieren. *(informal form)* eekh vehr•duh deekh owf dehn foh•tohs mahr•kih•ruhn

Phone

A phone card, please	**Eine Telefonkarte, bitte.** *ien•uh tehl•eh•<u>fohn</u>•kahrt•uh <u>biht</u>•tuh*
A prepaid phone please	**Ein Prepaid-Handy, bitte.** *ien pree•paid han•dee biht•tuh*
An international phonecard for...	**Eine internationale Telefonkarte für ...** *ien•uh ihnt•ehr•nah•syoh•<u>nahl</u>•uh tehl•uh•<u>fohn</u>•kahrt•uh fewr ...*
Australia	**Australien** *ow•<u>shtrah</u>•lee•ehn*
Canada	**Kanada** <u>kah</u>•nah•dah
Ireland	**Irland** <u>eer</u>•lahnt
the U.K.	**Großbritannien** grohs•bree•<u>tahn</u>•ee•ehn
the U.S.	**die USA** dee <u>oo</u>•ehs•ah
How much?	**Wie viel kostet es?** vee feel <u>kohs</u>•tuht ehs

Where's the pay phone?	**Wo ist das Münztelefon?**
	voh ihst dahs mewnts•tehl•uh•fohn
What's the area code/country code for...?	**Was ist die Ortsvorwahl/Landesvorwahl für ...?**
	vahs ihst dee <u>ohrts</u>•fohr•vahl/
	<u>lahnd</u>•uhs•fohr•vahl fewr ...
What's the number for Information?	**Was ist die Nummer für die Auskunft?**
	vahs ihst dee <u>noom</u>•ehr fewr dee <u>ows</u>•kuhnft
I'd like the number for...	**Ich hätte gern die Nummer für ...**
	eekh <u>heht</u>•uh gehrn dee <u>noom</u>•ehr fewr ...

YOU MAY HEAR...

Ruff an? *roof ahn*	Who's calling?
Einen Moment, bitte.	Hold on, please.
<u>ien</u>•uhn moh•<u>mehnt</u> <u>biht</u>•tuh	
Ich verbinde Sie. *eekh fehr•<u>bihnd</u>•uh zee*	I'll put you through.
Er _m_ /Sie _f_ ist nicht da/spricht gerade.	He/She is not here/
ehr/zee ihst neekht dah/shpreekht	on another line.
geh•<u>rahd</u>•uh	
Möchten Sie eine Nachricht hinterlassen?	Would you like to
<u>merkh</u>•tuhn zee <u>ien</u>•uh <u>nahkh</u>•reekht	leave a message?
<u>hihnt</u>•ehr•lahs•suhn	
Bitte rufen Sie später/in zehn	Please call back
Minuten zurück. *<u>biht</u>•tuh <u>roof</u>•uhn zee*	later/in ten minutes.
<u>shpeht</u>•ehr/ihn tsehn mee•<u>noot</u>•uhn <u>tsoo</u>•rewkh	
Kann er _m_ /sie _f_ zurückrufen?	Can he/she call you
khan ehr/zee <u>tsoo</u>•rewkh•<u>roof</u>•uhn	back?
Was ist Ihre Nummer?	What's your number?
vahs ihst <u>eehr</u>•uh <u>noom</u>•ehr	

German public phones are mainly card operated. Phone cards in
various amounts can be purchased at newsstands, supermarkets
and other shops.
Important telephone numbers include:
Police 110
Fire 112
Ambulance 115
National Directory 11833
National Directory (in English) 11837
International Directory 11834
To call the U.S. or Canada from Germany, dial 001 + area code + phone
number. To call the U.K. from Germany, dial 0044 + area code (minus
the first 0) + phone number.

I'd like to call collect [reverse the charges].	**Ich möchte ein R-Gespräch führen.** *eekh merkh•tuh ien ehr•guh•shprehkh fewhr•uhn*
My phone doesn't work here.	**Mein Telefon funktioniert hier nicht.** *mien tehl•leh•fohn foonk•syoh•neert heer neekht*
What network are you on?	**Welches Netz nutzen Sie?** *vehl•khehs nehts noot•suhn zee*
Is it 3G?	**Ist es ein 3G-Netz?** *ihst ehs ien drie•geh•nehts*
I have run out of credit/minutes.	**Ich habe kein Guthaben mehr.** *eekh hah•buh kien goot•hah•buhn mehr*
Can I buy some credit?	**Kann ich eine Guthabenkarte kaufen?** *kahn eekh ie•nuh goot•hah•buhn•kahr•tuh kow•fuhn*
Do you have a phone charger?	**Haben Sie ein Handy-Ladegerät?** *hah•buhn zee ien han•dee•lah•duh•guh•reht*
Can I recharge this phone?	**Kann ich dieses Telefon wieder aufladen?** *kahn eekh deez•uhs tehl•uh•fohn veed•ehr owf•lahd•uhn*

Can I have your number, please?	**Können Sie mir bitte Ihre Nummer geben?** _kern·uhn zee meer biht·tuh eehr·uh noom·ehr gehb·uhn_
Here's my number.	**Hier ist meine Nummer.** _heer ihst mien·uh noom·ehr_
Please call me.	**Bitte rufen Sie mich an.** _biht·tuh roof·uhn zee meekh ahn_
Please text me.	**Bitte schicken Sie mir eine SMS.** _bit·tuh shihk·uhn zee meer ien·uh ehs·ehm·ehs_
I'll call you.	**Ich werde Sie anrufen.** _eekh vehrd·uh zee ahn·roof·uhn_
I'll text you.	**Ich werde Ihnen eine SMS schicken.** _eekh vehrd·uh eehn·uhn ien·uh ehs·ehm·ehs shihk·uhn_

Telephone Etiquette

Hello. This is...	**Hallo. Hier ist ...** _hahl·loh heer ihst ..._
Can I speak to...?	**Kann ich mit ... sprechen?** _kahn eekh miht ... shprehkh·uhn_
Extension...	**Durchwahl ...** _doorkh·vahl ..._
Speak louder/more slowly, please.	**Bitte sprechen Sie lauter/langsamer.** _biht·tuh shprehkh·uhn zee lowt·ehr/lahng·sahm·ehr_
Can you repeat that, please?	**Könnten Sie das bitte wiederholen?** _kern·tuhn zee dahs biht·tuh vee·dehr·hohl·uhn_
I'll call back later.	**Ich rufe später zurück.** _eekh roof·uh shpeht·ehr tsoo·rewkh_
Bye.	**Auf Wiederhören.** _owf veed·ehr·her·ruhn_

For Business Travel, see page 137.

Fax

Can I send/receive a fax here?	**Kann ich hier ein Fax senden/empfangen?** _kahn eekh heer ien fahks zehnd·uhn/ehm·pfahng·uhn_
What's the fax number?	**Was ist die Faxnummer?** _vahs ihst dee fahks·noom·ehr_
Please fax this to...	**Bitte faxen Sie das nach ...** _biht·tuh fahks·uhn zee dahs nahkh ..._

YOU MAY HEAR...

Bitte füllen Sie das Zollformular aus.
biht•tuh fewl•luhn zee dahs
tsohl•fohr•moo•lahr ows

Fill out the customs declaration form, please.

Wie viel ist es wert? *vee feel ihst ehs vehrt*

What's the value?

Was ist der Inhalt? *vahs ihst dehr ihn•hahlt*

What's inside?

Post

Where's the post office/mailbox?	**Wo ist die Post/der Briefkasten?** *voh ihst dee pohst/dehr breef•kahs•tuhn*
A stamp for this postcard/letter to..., please.	**Eine Briefmarke für diese Postkarte/ diesen Brief nach ... bitte.** *ien•uh breef•mahrk•uh fewr deez•uh pohst•kahrt•uh/ deez•uhn breef nahhk ... biht•tuh*
How much?	**Wie viel kostet das?** *vee feel kohs•tuht dahs*
Please send this package by airmail/express.	**Senden Sie dieses Paket bitte per Luftpost/Express.** *zehnd•uhn zee deez•uhs pah•keht biht•tuh pehr looft•pohst/ehks•prehs*
A receipt, please.	**Eine Quittung, bitte.** *ien•uh kveet•toong biht•tu*

In addition to mailing options, German post offices offer a variety of other services. Most provide banking services and allow you to deposit or withdraw money and apply for a credit card. On weekdays, post offices are usually open from 8:30 a.m. to 1:00 p.m., and again from 2:30 p.m. to 4:00 p.m. (in larger cities to 6:30 p.m.). On Saturdays they are open from 8:30 a.m. to 1:00 p.m.

Food & Drink

ESSENTIAL

Can you recommend a good restaurant/bar?	**Können Sie ein gutes Restaurant/eine gute Bar empfehlen?** _ker_·nuhn zee ien _goo_·tuhs reh·stow·_rahnt_/_ien_·uh _goo_·tuh bahr ehm·_pfeh_·luhn
Is there a traditional German/an inexpensive restaurant nearby?	**Gibt es in der Nähe ein typisch deutsches/preisgünstiges Restaurant?** gihpt ehs ihn dehr _neh_·uh ien _tew_·peesh _doy_·chuhs/_pries_·gewn·stee·guhs reh·stow·_rahnt_
A table for..., please.	**Bitte einen Tisch für ...** _biht_·tuh _ien_·uhn tihsh fewr ...
Can we sit...?	**Können wir ... sitzen?** _ker_·nuhn veer ... _ziht_·tsuhn
here/there	**hier/dort** heer/dohrt
outside	**draußen** _drow_·suhn
in a non-smoking area	**in einem Nichtraucherbereich** ihn _ien_·uhm neekht·_row_·khehr·beh·riehk
I'm waiting for someone.	**Ich warte auf jemanden.** eekh _vahr_·tuh owf _yeh_·mahnd·uhn
Where are the toilets?	**Wo ist die Toilette?** voh ihst dee toy·_leh_·tuh
A menu, please.	**Die Speisekarte, bitte.** dee _shpie_·zuh·kahr·tuh _biht_·tuh
What do you recommend?	**Was empfehlen Sie?** vahs ehm·_pfeh_·luhn zee
I'd like...	**Ich möchte ...** eekh _merkh_·tuh ...
Some more..., please.	**Etwas mehr ..., bitte.** _eht_·vahs mehr ... _biht_·tuh
Enjoy your meal!	**Guten Appetit!** _goo_·tuhn ah·puh·_teet_

The check [bill], please.	**Die Rechnung, bitte.** *dee rehkh·noonk biht·tuh*
Is service included?	**Ist die Bedienung im Preis enthalten?** *ihsht dee buh·dee·nung ihm pries ehnt·hahl·tuhn*
Can I pay by credit card/have a receipt?	**Kann ich mit Kreditkarte bezahlen/eine Quittung haben?** *kahn eekh miht kreh·deet·kahr·tuh beht·sahl·uhn/ien·uh kvee·toonk hah·buhn*
Thank you!	**Danke!** *dahn·kuh*

Where to Eat

Can you recommend...?	**Können Sie ... empfehlen?** *ker·nuhn zee ... ehm·pfeh·luhn*
a restaurant	**ein Restaurant** *ien reh·stow·rahnt*
a bar	**eine Bar** *ien·uh bahr*
a cafe	**ein Café** *ien kah·feh*
a fast-food place	**ein Schnellrestaurant** *ien shnehl·reh·stow·rahnt*
a snack bar	**einen Imbiss** *ien·uhn ihm·bees*
a cheap restaurant	**ein billiges Restaurant** *ien bihl·lee·guhs reh·stow·rahnt*

an expensive restaurant	**ein teures Restaurant** *ien toy•rehs reh•stow•rahnt*
a restaurant with a good view	**ein Restaurant mit schöner Aussicht** *ien reh•stow•rahnt miht sher•nuhr ows•seekht*
an authentic/ a non-touristy restaurant	**ein authentisches/ein nicht so touristisches Restaurant** *ien ow•tehn•tih•shuhs/ien neekht zoh tou•rihs•tih•shuhs reh•stow•rahnt*

Reservations & Preferences

I'd like to reserve a table...	**Ich möchte einen Tisch ... reservieren** *eekh merkh•tuh ien•uhn tihsh ... reh•zuh•veer•ehn*
for two	**für zwei Personen** *fewr tsvie pehr•zohn•uhn*
for this evening	**für heute Abend** *fewr hoy•tuh ah•behnt*
for tomorrow at...	**für morgen um ...** *fewr mohr•guhn oom ...*
A table for two, please.	**Bitte einen Tisch für zwei.** *biht•tuh ien•uhn tihsh fewr tsvie*

YOU MAY HEAR...

Haben Sie eine Reservierung? *hah•buhn zee ien•uh reh•zuh•veer•uhng*	Do you have a reservation?
Für wie viele Personen? *fewr vee fee•luh pehr•zohn•uhn*	For how many people?
Raucher oder Nichtraucher? *row•khuhr oh•duhr neekht•row•khuhr*	Smoking or non-smoking?
Möchten Sie jetzt bestellen? *merkh•tuhn zee yehtst buh•shteh•luhn*	Are you ready to order?
Was möchten Sie? *vahs merkh•tuhn zee*	What would you like?
Ich empfehle ... *eekh ehm•pfeh•luh ...*	I recommend...
Guten Appetit. *goo•tuhn ah•puh•teet*	Enjoy your meal.

We have a reservation.	**Wir haben eine Reservierung.** *veer hah·buhn ien·uh reh·zuh·veer·uhng*
My name is...	**Mein Name ist ...** *mien nahm·uh ihst ...*
Can we sit...?	**Können wir ... sitzen?** *ker·nuhn veer ... ziht·tsuhn*
here/there	**hier/dort** *heer/dohrt*
outside	**draußen** *drow·suhn*
in a non-smoking area	**in einem Nichtraucherbereich** *ihn ien·uhm neekht·row·khuhr·beh·riekh*
by the window	**am Fenster** *ahm fehn·stehr*
in the shade	**im Schatten** *ihm shaht·tehn*
in the sun	**in der Sonne** *ihn dehr sohn·nuh*
Where are the toilets?	**Wo ist die Toilette?** *voh ihst dee toy·leh·tuh*

How to Order

Waiter/Waitress!	**Bedienung!** *buh·dee·nounk*
We're ready to order.	**Wir möchten bitte bestellen.** *weer merkh·tuhn biht·tuh buh·shteh·luhn*
May I see the wine list, please?	**Die Weinkarte, bitte.** *dee vien·kahr·tuh biht·tuh*
I'd like...	**Ich möchte ...** *eekh merkh·tuh ...*
a bottle of...	**eine Flasche ...** *ien·uh flah·shuh ...*
a carafe of...	**eine Karaffe ...** *ien·uh kah·rah·fuh ...*
a glass of...	**ein Glas ...** *ien glahs ...*
The menu, please.	**Die Speisekarte, bitte.** *dee shpie·zuh·kahr·tuh biht·tuh*
Do you have...?	**Haben Sie ...?** *hah·buhn zee ...*
a menu in English	**eine Speisekarte in Englisch** *ien·uh shpie·zuh·kahr·tuh ihn ehn·gleesh*
a fixed-price menu	**ein Festpreismenü** *ien fehst·pries·meh·new*
a children's menu	**ein Kindermenü** *ien kihn·dehr·meh·new*
What do you recommend?	**Was empfehlen Sie?** *vahs ehm·pfeh·luhn zee*

What's this?	**Was ist das?** *vahs ihsht dahs*
What's in it?	**Was ist darin?** *vahs ihsht dah·rihn*
Is it spicy?	**Ist es scharf?** *ihsht ehs shahrf*
I'd like…	**Ich möchte gern …** *eekh merkh·tuh gehrn …*
More…, please.	**Mehr …, bitte.** *mehr … biht·tuh*
With/Without…	**Mit/Ohne …** *miht/oh·nuh …*
I can't eat…	**Ich vertrage kein/keine …**
	eekh fehr·trah·guh kien/kien·uh …
rare	**roh** *roh*
medium	**medium** *meh·dee·uhm*
well-done	**durchgebraten** *doorkh·geh·brah·tuhn*
Without…, please.	**Ohne …, bitte.** *oh·nuh … biht·tuh*
It's to go [take	**Bitte zum Mitnehmen.** *biht·tuh tsoom*
away], please.	*miht·neh·muhn*

For Drinks, see page 79.

For Negations, see page 161.

For Drinks, see page 79.

For Negations, see page 161.

YOU MAY SEE…

SPEISEKARTE	menu
TAGESMENÜ	menu of the day
SPEZIALITÄTEN	specials

Cooking Methods

baked	**gebacken** *guh·bahkh·uhn*
boiled	**gekocht** *guh·kohkht*
braised	**geschmort** *guh·shmohrt*
breaded	**paniert** *pah·neert*
creamed	**püriert** *pew·reert*
diced	**gewürfelt** *guh·vewr·fuhlt*

filleted	**filetiert** fee·luh·_teert_
fried	**gebraten** guh·_brah_·tuhn
grilled	**gegrillt** guh·_grihlt_
poached	**pochiert** _poh_·sheert
roasted	**geröstet** guh·_rer_·stuht
sautéed	**sautiert** _zow_·teert
smoked	**geräuchert** guh·_roy_·khuhrt
steamed	**gedünstet** guh·_dewn_·stuht
stewed	**geschmort** guh·_shmohrt_
stuffed	**gefüllt** guh·_fewlt_

Dietary Requirements

I'm...	**Ich bin ...** eekh bihn ...
diabetic	**Diabetiker** dee·ah·_beh_·tee·kehr
lactose intolerant	**laktoseintolerant** lahk·thoh·suh·een·tho·luh·rahnt
vegetarian	**Vegetarier** veh·guh·_tah_·ree·ehr
vegan	**Veganer** _veh_·gah·nehr
I'm allergic to...	**Ich bin allergisch auf ...** eekh bihn ah·_lehr_·geesh owf ...
I can't eat...	**Ich kann ... essen.** eekh kahn ... _eh_·zuhn
dairy products	**keine Milchprodukte** _kien_·uh _meelkh_·proh·dook·tuh
gluten	**kein Gluten** kien _gloo_·tuhn
nuts	**keine Nüsse** _kien_·uh _new_·suh
pork	**kein Schweinefleisch** kien _shvie_·nuh·fliesh
shellfish	**keine Schalentiere** _kien_·uh _shah_·luhn·tee·ruh
spicy foods	**keine scharf gewürzten Speisen** _kien_·uh shahrf guh·_vewrt_·stuhn _shpie_·zuhn
wheat	**kein Weizen** kien _vie_·tsuhn
Is it halal/kosher?	**Ist es halal/koscher?** ihsht ehs hah·_lahl_/_koh_·shuhr
Do you have...?	**Haben Sie...?** _hah_·buhn zee
skimmed milk	**Magermilch** mah·guhr·meelkh

| whole milk | **Vollmilch** *foll•meelkh* |
| soya milk | **Sojamilch** *soh•yah•meelkh* |

Dining with Children

Do you have children's portions?	**Haben Sie Kinderportionen?** *hah•buhn zee kihn•dehr•pohr•syoh•nuhn*
Can I have a highchair/ child's seat?	**Einen Kindersitz/Kinderstuhl, bitte.** *ien•uhn kihnd•ehr•zihtz/kihn•dehr•shtuhl biht•tuh*
Where can I feed/ change the baby?	**Wo kann ich das Baby füttern/wickeln?** *voh kahn eekh dahs beh•bee few•tuhrn/vihk•uhln*
Can you warm this?	**Können Sie das warm machen?** *ker•nuhn zee dahs vahrm mah•khuhn*

For Traveling with Children, see page 140.

How to Complain

When will our food be ready?	**Wie lange dauert es noch mit dem Essen?** *vee lahng•uh dow•ehrt ehs nohkh miht dehm eh•suhn*
We can't wait any longer.	**Wir können nicht mehr länger warten.** *veer ker•nuhn neekht mehr lehng•ehr vahr•tuhn*
We're leaving.	**Wir gehen jetzt.** *veer geh•ehn yehtst*
I didn't order this.	**Das habe ich nicht bestellt.** *dahs hah•buh eekh neekht buh•shtehlt*
I ordered...	**Ich habe ... bestellt.** *eekh hah•buh ... buh•shtehlt*
I can't eat this.	**Ich kann das nicht essen.** *eekh kahn dahs neekht eh•suhn*
This is too...	**Das ist zu ...** *dahs ihsht tsoo ...*
cold/hot	**kalt/heiß** *kahlt/hies*
salty/spicy	**salzig/scharf gewürzt** *sahl•tseek/shahrf guh•vewrts*
tough/bland	**zäh/fad** *tseh/fahd*
This isn't clean/ fresh.	**Das ist nicht sauber/frisch.** *dahs ihsht neekht zow•buhr/frihsh*

Service is included in German restaurants and bars, as is value added tax (VAT). However, it is still typical to leave a small tip; round to the nearest euro or two for a small bill or add 5-10%, rounding to a full euro, for a larger bill. Note that it is not typical to be given a check [bill]. The server will usually just tell you your total, and you will hand the money to the server, specifying how much change you need back (so the tip is included, not left on the table later).

Paying

The check [bill], please.	**Die Rechnung, bitte.** *dee rehkh·noonk biht·tuh*
Separate checks [bills], please.	**Getrennte Rechnungen, bitte.** *geh·trehn·tuh rehkh·noong·uhn biht·tuh*
It's all together.	**Alles zusammen.** *ah·luhs tsoo·zah·muhn*
Is service included?	**Ist die Bedienung im Preis enthalten?** *ihsht dee buh·dee·noonk ihm pries ehnt·hahl·tuhn*
What's this amount for?	**Wofür ist diese Summe?** *voh·fewr ihsht dee·zuh soo·muh*
I didn't have that. I had…	**Das hatte ich nicht. Ich hatte …** *dahs hah·tuh eekh neekht eekh hah·tuh …*
Can I…?	**Kann ich …?** *kahn eekh …*
pay with a credit card	**mit Kreditkarte bezahlen** *miht kreh·deet·kahr·tuh beht·sahl·uhn*
have a receipt	**eine Quittung haben** *ien·uh kvee·toonk hah·buhn*
have an itemized bill	**eine aufgeschlüsselte Rechnung haben** *ien·uh owf·guh·shlew·sehl·tuh rehkh·oong·uhn hah·buhn*
That was delicious!	**Das war lecker!** *dahs vahr leh·khehr*
I've already paid	**Ich habe schon bezahlt.** *eekh hah·buh shohn beht·sahlt*

Meals & Cooking

Breakfast

der Apfelsaft dehr _ah_•pfuhl•zahft	apple juice
der Aufschnitt dehr _owf_•shniht	cold cuts [charcuterie]
das Brot dahs broht	bread
das Brötchen dahs _brert_•khuhn	roll
die Butter dee _boo_•tehr	butter
das ... Ei dahs ... ie	...egg
hart/weich gekochte	hard-/soft-boiled
_hahrt/viekh guh•_kohkh_•tuh_	
der Joghurt dehr _yoh_•goort	yogurt
der Kaffee/Tee ... dehr kah•_feh_/tee ...	coffee/tea...
entkoffeiniert ehnt•_koh_•feh•een•eert	decaf
mit Milch miht mihlkh	with milk
mit Süßstoff miht _zews_•shtohf	with artificial sweetener
mit Zucker miht _tsoo_•khuhr	with sugar
schwarz shvahrts	black
der Käse dehr _kay_•zuh	cheese
der Kräutertee dehr _krow_•tehr•tee	herbal tea
die Marmelade dee mahr•muh•_lah_•duh	jam/jelly

Das Frühstück (breakfast) can range from a large meal, usually served buffet style, to a simple dish of bread, jam and butter. **Das Mittagessen** (lunch), typically a large and heavy meal, is normally served from 12:00 to 2:00 p.m. In larger cities, many Germans will have lunch at a beer garden or hall with cafeteria-style service. **Das Abendessen** (dinner) is served from 6:00 to 9:00 p.m. and is usually a light meal.

die Milch *dee mihlkh*	milk
der Muffin *dehr moo•fihn*	muffin
das Müsli *dahs mew•slee*	granola [muesli]
das Omelett *dahs ohm•luht*	omelet
der Orangensaft *dehr oh•rahng•uhn•zahft*	orange juice
der Pampelmusensaft *dehr pahm•puhl•moo•zuhn•zahft*	grapefruit juice
das Rührei *dahs rew•rie*	scrambled egg
der Saft *dehr zahft*	juice
der Schinken *dehr shihn•kuhn*	ham
das Spiegelei *dahs shpeeg•uh•lie*	fried egg
der Toast *dehr tohst*	toast
das Wasser *dahs vah•sehr*	water

Appetizers

die Appetithäppchen *dee ah•peh•teet•hehp•khehn*	finger sandwiches
die Aufschnittplatte *dee owf•shniht•plah•tuh*	cold cuts served with bread
der Bismarckhering *dehr bees•mahrk•heh•reeng*	marinated herring with onions
die Fleischpastete *dee fliesh•pah•steh•tuh*	meat pâté

die Gänseleberpastete *dee gehn·zehl·leh·behr·pah·steh·tuh*	goose liver pâté
die gefüllten Champignons *dee geh·fewl·tehn shahm·pee·nyohns*	stuffed mushrooms
der gemischte Salat *dehr geh·meesh·tuh sah·laht*	mixed salad
die Käseplatte *dee kay·zuh·plah·tuh*	cheese platter
das Knoblauchbrot *dahs knoh·blowkh·broht*	garlic bread
der Krabbencocktail *dehr krahb·behn·kohk·tayl*	shrimp cocktail
die russischen Eier *dee roo·see·shuh ier*	hard-boiled eggs with mayonnaise
der Räucherlachs *dehr roy·khurt·lahks*	smoked salmon
der Salat *dehr sah·laht*	salad
die Soleier *dee soh·lier*	eggs boiled in brine
der Tomatensalat *dehr toh·mah·tehn·sah·laht*	tomato salad
der Wurstsalat *dehr voorst·sah·laht*	cold cuts with onion and oil

Soup

die Backerbsensuppe *dee bahk·ehrb·sehn·zoo·puh*	broth with crisp, round noodles
die Bohnensuppe *dee boh·nuhn·zoo·puh*	bean soup
die Champignoncremesuppe *dee shahm·pee·nyohn·krehm·zoo·puh*	cream of mushroom soup
die Erbsensuppe *dee ehrb·zuhn·zoo·puh*	pea soup
die Fleischbrühe *dee fliesh·brew·uh*	bouillon
die Frittatensuppe *dee free·tah·tehn·zoo·puh*	broth with pancake strips
die Frühlingssuppe *dee frew·leeng·zoo·puh*	spring vegetable soup
die Gemüsesuppe *dee guh·mew·zuh·zoo·puh*	vegetable soup
die Gulaschsuppe *dee gool·ahsh·zoo·puh*	stewed beef in a spicy soup

die Hühnersuppe dee <u>hewn</u>•ehr•zoo•puh	chicken soup
die klare Gemüsebrühe dee <u>klah</u>•ruh geh•<u>mew</u>•zuh•brew•uh	vegetable broth
die Linsensuppe dee <u>leen</u>•zehn•zoo•puh	lentil soup
die Semmelknödelsuppe dee <u>zeh</u>•mehl•kner•dehl•zoo•puh	bread dumpling soup
die Tomatensuppe dee toh•<u>mah</u>•tuhn•zoo•puh	tomato soup
die Zwiebelsuppe dee <u>tsvee</u>•behl•zoo•puh	onion soup

Fish & Seafood

der Aal dehr ahl	eel
die Auster dee <u>ow</u>•stehr	oyster
die Brachse dee <u>brahk</u>•suh	bream
der Barsch dehr bahrsh	perch
der Brathering dehr <u>brah</u>•theh•reeng	fried sour herring
der Dorsch dehr dohrsh	cod
die Forelle dee foh•<u>reh</u>•luh	trout
die Garnele dee gahr•<u>neh</u>•luh	shrimp
der Heilbutt dehr <u>hiel</u>•boot	halibut
der Hering dehr <u>heh</u>•rihng	herring
der Hummer dehr <u>hoo</u>•mehr	lobster
der Krebs dehr krehbs	crab
der Lachs dehr lahks	salmon
die Makrele dee <u>mah</u>•kreh•luh	mackerel
die Muschel dee <u>moo</u>•shuhl	clam
der Oktopus dehr <u>ohk</u>•toh•poos	octopus
die Sardelle dee sahr•<u>deh</u>•luh	anchovy
die Sardine dee zahr•<u>dee</u>•nuh	sardine
die Scholle dee <u>shoh</u>•luh	flounder
der Schwertfisch dehr <u>shvehrt</u>•fihsh	swordfish
der Seebarsch dehr <u>zeh</u>•bahrsh	sea bass

die Seezunge *dee <u>zeh</u>·tsoong·uh*	sole
der Tintenfisch *dehr <u>tihn</u>·tuhn·fihsh*	squid
der Thunfisch *dehr <u>toon</u>·fihsh*	tuna

Meat & Poultry

die Berliner Buletten *dee behr·<u>lee</u>·nuh boo·<u>leh</u>·tehn*	fried meatballs, a specialty of Berlin
der Braten *dehr <u>brah</u>·tuhn*	roast
die Bratwurst *dee <u>braht</u>·voorst*	fried sausage
die Ente *dee <u>ehn</u>·tuh*	duck
das Filet *dahs <u>fee</u>·leh*	filet
der Fleischkäse *dehr <u>fliesh</u>·kay·zuh*	a kind of meatloaf
die Frikadelle *dee free·kah·<u>dehl</u>·luh*	fried meatballs
das Gulasch *dahs <u>gool</u>·ahsh*	stewed beef with spicy paprika gravy
der Hackbraten *dehr <u>hahk</u>·brah·tuhn*	meatloaf
das Hackfleisch *dahs <u>hahk</u>·fliesh*	ground meat
das Hühnchen *dahs <u>hewn</u>·khuhn*	chicken
das Spanferkel *dahs <u>shpahn</u>·fehr·kehl*	crunchy roasted suckling pig
das Kalbfleisch *dahs <u>kahlb</u>·fliesh*	veal
das Kaninchen *dahs kah·<u>nihn</u>·khehn*	rabbit

das Kotelett *dahs koht•leht* — pork chop

das Lamm *dahs lahm* — lamb

die Leber *dee leh•behr* — liver

die Niere *dee nee•ruh* — kidney

das Pökelfleisch *dahs pehr•kehl•fliesh* — pickled meat

der Rinderbraten *dehr reen•dehr•brah•tuhn* — roast beef

das Rindfleisch *dahs rihnt•fliesh* — beef

die Rouladen *dee roo•lah•dehn* — stuffed beef slices, rolled and braised in brown gravy

der Sauerbraten *dehr zow•ehr•brah•tuhn* — beef roast, marinated with herbs, in a rich sauce

der Schinken *dehr shihn•kuhn* — ham

der Schinkenspeck *dehr shihn•kuhn•shpehk* — bacon

das Schmorfleisch *dahs shmohr•fliesh* — stewed meat

das Schweinefleisch *dahs shvien•uh•fliesh* — pork

der Schweinebraten *dehr shvien•brah•tuhn* — roast pork

das Steak *dahs shtayhk* — steak

der Tafelspitz *dehr tah•fehl•shpeets* — Viennese-style boiled beef

der Truthahn *dehr troot•hahn* — turkey

das Wiener Schnitzel *dahs vee•nehr shniht•tzehl* — veal cutlet

die Wurst *dee voorst*	sausage
die Zunge *dee <u>tsoong</u>·uh*	tongue

Vegetables & Staples

die Artischocke *dee ahr·tee·<u>shoh</u>·kuh*	artichoke
die Aubergine *dee <u>ow</u>·behr·gee·neh*	eggplant [aubergine]
die Avocado *dee ah·voh·<u>kah</u>·doh*	avocado
die Bohnen *dee <u>boh</u>·nuhn*	beans
die grünen Bohnen *dee <u>grew</u>·nuhn <u>boh</u>·nuhn*	green beans
der Blumenkohl *dehr <u>bloo</u>·muhn·kohl*	cauliflower
der Brokkoli *dehr <u>broh</u>·koh·lee*	broccoli
die Erbse *dee <u>ehrb</u>·zuh*	pea
das gemischte Gemüse *dahs geh·<u>meesh</u>·tuh geh·<u>mew</u>·zuh*	mixed vegetables
das Gemüse *dahs geh·<u>mew</u>·zuh*	vegetable
die Gurke *dee <u>goor</u>·kuh*	cucumber
die Kartoffel *dee kahr·<u>toh</u>·fuhl*	potato
der Kartoffelbrei *dehr kahr·<u>toh</u>·fehl·brie*	mashed potato
der Knoblauch *dehr <u>knoh</u>·blowkh*	garlic
der Kohl *dehr kohl*	cabbage
der Krautsalat *dehr <u>krowt</u>·sah·laht*	coleslaw
der Mais *dehr mies*	corn
der Maiskolben *dehr <u>mies</u>·kohl·behn*	corn on the cob
die Möhre *dee <u>mer</u>·ruh*	carrot
die Olive *dee oh·<u>lee</u>·vuh*	olive
der rote/grüne Paprika *dehr <u>roh</u>·teh/ <u>grew</u>·neh pah·<u>pree</u>·kuh*	red/green pepper
die Pasta *dee <u>pah</u>·stah*	pasta
die Pellkartoffeln *dee <u>pehl</u>·kahr·toh·fehl·ehn*	boiled, unpeeled potatoes

der Pilz *dehr pihlts*	mushroom
der Reis *dehr ries*	rice
der Rettich *dehr <u>reh</u>•teekh*	radish
das Roggenbrot *dahs <u>roh</u>•gehn•broht*	rye bread
der Salat *dehr sah•<u>laht</u>*	lettuce
der Spargel *dehr <u>shpahr</u>•gehl*	asparagus
der Spinat *dehr shpee•<u>naht</u>*	spinach
die Tomate *dee toh•<u>mah</u>•teh*	tomato
die Zucchini *dee tsoo•<u>khee</u>•nee*	zucchini [courgette]
die Zwiebel *dee <u>tsvee</u>•buhl*	onion

Fruit

die Ananas *dee <u>ah</u>•nah•nahs*	pineapple
der Apfel *dehr <u>ahp</u>•fuhl*	apple
die Apfelsine *dee ah•pfehl•<u>zee</u>•nuh*	orange
die Banane *dee bah•<u>nah</u>•nuh*	banana
die Birne *dee <u>beer</u>•nuh*	pear
die Blaubeere *dee <u>blow</u>•beh•ruh*	blueberry
die Erdbeere *dee <u>ehrd</u>•beh•ruh*	strawberry
die Himbeere *dee <u>hihm</u>•beh•ruh*	raspberry
die Kirsche *dee <u>keer</u>•shuh*	cherry

die Limette *dee lee-meh-tuh*	lime
die Melone *dee meh-loh-nuh*	melon
das Obst *dahs ohpst*	fruit
die Pampelmuse *dee pahm-pehl-moo-zuh*	grapefruit
der Pfirsich *dehr pfeer-zeekh*	peach
die Pflaume *dee pflow-muh*	plum
die rote/schwarze Johannisbeere	red/black currant
dee roh-tuh/shvahr-tsuh yoh-hah-nihs-beh-ruh	
die Weintraube *dee vien-trow-buh*	grape
die Zitrone *dee tsee-troh-nuh*	lemon

Cheese

der Appenzeller *dehr ah-pehn-tseh-lehr*	hard cheese from Switzerland
der Blauschimmelkäse	blue cheese
dehr blow-shihm-mehl-kay-zuh	
der Emmentaler *dehr ehm-mehn-tah-lehr*	mild Swiss cheese
der Frischkäse *dehr freesh-kay-zuh*	cream cheese
der Handkäse *dehr hahnt-kay-zuh*	sharp, soft cheese
die Käseplatte *dee kay-zuh-plah-tuh*	cheese platter
der Schafskäse *dehr shahf-kay-zuh*	feta cheese
der Tilsiter *dehr teel-seet-ehr*	semi-soft Austrian cheese
der Ziegenkäse *dehr tsee-guhn-kay-zuh*	goat cheese

Dessert

der Apfelkuchen *dehr ah-pfuhl-kookh-uhn*	apple pie or tart
das Eis *dahs ies*	ice cream
der Käsekuchen *dehr kay-zuh-kookh-uhn*	cheesecake
der Krapfen *dehr krah-pfehn*	fritter
die Makrone *dee mah-kroh-nuh*	macaroon
das Marzipan *dahs mahr-tsee-pahn*	marzipan
der Obstsalat *dehr ohpst-sah-laht*	fruit salad

die Rote Grütze *dee roh·tuh grewt·zuh*	berry pudding
die Schwarzwälder Kirschtorte	Black Forest chocolate
dee schvahrts·vahl·dehr keersh·tohr·tuh	cake with cherries
die Torte *dee tohr·tuh*	cake

Sauces & Condiments

salt	**salz** *sahlts*
pepper	**pfeffer** *pfehf·fehr*
mustard	**senf** *sehnf*
ketchup	**ketchup** *ket·shahp*

At the Market

Where are the trolleys/baskets?	**Wo sind die Einkaufswagen/Einkaufskörbe?** *voh zihnt dee ien·kowfs·vah·guhn/ien·kowfs·kehr·buh*
Where is . . .?	**Wo ist . . .?** *voh ihsht . . .*
I'd like some of that/this.	**Ich möchte etwas von dem/diesem.** *eekh merkh·tuh eht·vahs fohn dehm/dee·zuhm*
Can I taste it?	**Kann ich es kosten?** *kahn eekh ehs kohs·tuhn*
I'd like . . .	**Ich möchte . . .** *eekh merkh·tuh . . .*
a kilo/ half-kilo of . . .	**ein Kilo/halbes Kilo . . .** *ien kee·loh/ hahl·buhs kee·loh . . .*
a liter of . . .	**einen Liter . . .** *ien·uhn lee·tehr . . .*
a piece of . . .	**ein Stück . . .** *ien shtewk . . .*
a slice of . . .	**eine Scheibe . . .** *ien·uh shie·buh . . .*
More/less	**Mehr/Weniger** *mehr/veh·nee·guhr*

Local markets that sell fresh produce and homemade goods can be found in most cities throughout Germany. The days and hours of operation vary widely. Your hotel concierge or a tourist information office can provide details.

How much?	**Wie viel kostet das?** *vee feel kohs·tuht dahs*	
Where do I pay?	**Wo bezahle ich?** *voh beht·sahl·uh eekh*	
A bag, please.	**Eine Tüte, bitte.** *ien·uh tew·tuh biht·tuh*	
I'm being helped.	**Ich werde schon bedient.** *eekh vehr·duh shohn buh·deent*	

For Conversion Tables, see page 170.

For Meals & Cooking, see page 67.

In the Kitchen

bottle opener	**der Flaschenöffner** *dehr flah·shuhn·erf·nehr*	
bowl	**die Schüssel** *dee shew·suhl*	
can opener	**der Dosenöffner** *dehr doh·zuhn·erf·nuhr*	
corkscrew	**der Korkenzieher** *dehr kohr·kuhn·tsee·uhr*	
cup	**die Tasse** *dee tah·suh*	
fork	**die Gabel** *dee gah·buhl*	
frying pan	**die Bratpfanne** *dee braht·pfah·nuh*	
glass	**das Glas** *dahs glahs*	
(steak) knife	**das (Steak-) Messer** *dahs (shtehk·) meh·sehr*	
measuring cup	**der Messbecher** *dehr mehs·beh·khuhr*	
measuring spoon	**der Messlöffel** *dehr mehs·ler·fuhl*	
napkin	**die Serviette** *dee sehr·vyeh·tuh*	
plate	**der Teller** *dehr teh·lehr*	

YOU MAY SEE...

MINDESTENS HALTBAR BIS ...	best before...
KALORIEN	calories
FETTARM	low fat
GEKÜHLT LAGERN	keep refrigerated
KANN SPUREN VON ... BEINHALTEN	may contain traces of...
MIKROWELLENGEEIGNET	microwaveable
FÜR VEGETARIER GEEIGNET	suitable for vegetarians

pot	**der Topf** dehr tohpf
spatula	**der Spatel** dehr shpah•tuhl
spoon	**der Löffel** dehr ler•fuhl

Measurements in Europe are metric – and that applies to the weight of food too. If you tend to think in pounds and ounces, it's worth brushing up on what the metric equivalent is before you go shopping for fruit and veg in markets and supermarkets. Five hundred grams, or half a kilo, is a common quantity to order, and that converts to just over a pound (17.65 ounces, to be precise).

Drinks

ESSENTIAL

The wine list/drink menu, please.	**Die Weinkarte/Getränkekarte, bitte.** *dee <u>vien</u>·kahr·tuh/geh·<u>trehnk</u>·uh·kahr·tuh <u>biht</u>·tuh*
What do you recommend?	**Was empfehlen Sie?** *vahs ehm·<u>pfeh</u>·luhn zee*
I'd like a bottle/ glass of red/ white wine.	**Ich möchte gern eine Flasche/ein Glas Rotwein/Weißwein.** *eekh <u>merkh</u>·tuh gehrn <u>ien</u>·uh <u>flah</u>·shuh/ien glahs <u>roht</u>·vien/<u>vies</u>·vien*
The house wine, please.	**Den Hauswein, bitte.** *dehn <u>hows</u>·vien <u>biht</u>·tuh*
Another bottle/glass, please.	**Noch eine Flasche/ein Glas, bitte.** *nohkh <u>ien</u>·uh <u>flah</u>·shuh/ien glahs <u>biht</u>·tuh*
I'd like a local beer.	**Ich möchte gern ein Bier aus der Region.** *eekh <u>merkh</u>·tuh gehrn ien beer ows dehr rehg·<u>yohn</u>*
Can I buy you a drink?	**Darf ich Ihnen einen ausgeben?** *dahrf eekh <u>eehn</u>·uhn <u>ows</u>·geh·buhn*
Cheers!	**Prost!** *prohst*

A coffee/tea, please.	**Einen Kaffee/Tee, bitte.**
	ien-uhn kah-feh/tee biht-tuh
Black.	**Schwarz.** *shvahrts*
With...	**Mit ...** *miht ...*
milk	**Milch** *mihlkh*
sugar	**Zucker** *tsoo-kehr*
artificial sweetener	**Süßstoff** *zews-shtohf*
..., please.	**..., bitte.** ... *biht-tuh*
A juice	**Einen Saft** *ien-uhn zahft*
A soda	**Eine Cola** *ien-uh koh-lah*
A still/sparkling water	**Ein stilles Wasser/Wasser mit Kohlensäure** *ien shtihl-uhs vah-sehr/ vah-sehr miht kohl-ehn-zoy-ruh*

Non-alcoholic Drinks

die Cola *dee koh-lah*	soda
der Kaffee *dehr kah-feh*	coffee
der Kakao *dehr kah-kah-ow*	hot chocolate
die Milch *dee mihlkh*	milk
der Saft *dehr zahft*	juice
der (Eis-)Tee *dehr (ies) tee*	(iced) tea
das stille Wasser/Wasser mit Kohlensäure *dahs shtihl-uh vah-sehr/ vah-sehr miht kohl-ehn-zoy-ruh*	still/sparkling water

YOU MAY HEAR...

Möchten Sie etwas trinken? _merkh•tuhn_
zee eht•vahs trihn•kuhn

Can I get you
a drink?

Mit Milch oder Zucker? _miht mihelkh_
oh•dehr tsoo•kehr

With milk or sugar?

Stilles Wasser oder mit Kohlensäure?
shtihl•uhs vah•sehr oh•dehr miht
koh•lehn•zoy•ruh

Still or sparkling
water?

Aperitifs, Cocktails & Liqueurs

der Gin _dehr djihn_	gin
der Rum _dehr room_	rum
der Scotch _dehr skohch_	scotch
der Tequila _dehr teh•kee•lah_	tequila
der Weinbrand _dehr vien•brahnt_	brandy
der Whisky _dehr vees•kee_	whisky
der Wodka _dehr voht•kah_	vodka

Kaffee (coffee) is popular in Germany and a fresh cup can
be found at a **Café** or **Kaffeehaus**. **Kräutertee** (herbal tea)
is another common beverage, and pharmacies, supermarkets and
health-food stores carry a variety of teas.

Beer

das Flaschenbier *dahs flah-shuhn-beer*	bottled beer
das Bier vom Fass *dahs beer fohm fahs*	draft beer
das Helle/Pilsner *dahs heh-luh/pihls-nehr*	lager/pilsner
die Halbe *dee hahlb-uh*	pint
das ... Bier *dahs ... beer*	...beer
dunkle/helle *doon-kluh/heh-luh*	dark/light
regionale/importierte	local/imported
reh-gyoh-nah-luh/eem-pohr-teer-tuh	
alkoholfreie *ahl-koh-hohl-frie-uh*	non-alcoholic

There are more than 1,000 breweries in Germany, producing more than 5,000 different brands of beer.
Styles include: **Altbier** (high hops content, similar to British ale), **Bockbier** (high malt content), **Hefeweizen** (pale, made from wheat), **Kölsch** (lager, brewed in Cologne), **Malzbier** (dark and sweet) and **Pilsener** (pale and strong). Popular German brands include: **Augustiner™**, **Beck's™**, **Jever™**, **Löwenbräu™** and **Spaten™**.

Wine

der Champagner *dehr shahm·pahn·yehr*		champagne
der Wein *dehr vien*		wine
der Dessertwein *dehr deh·sehrt·vien*		dessert wine
der Hauswein/Tischwein *dehr hows·vien/tihsh·vien*		house/table wine
der Rotwein/Weißwein *dehr roht·vien/vies·vien*		red/white wine
der trockene/liebliche Wein *dehr troh·keh·neh/lee·blee·kheh vien*		dry/sweet wine
der Schaumwein *dehr showm·vien*		sparkling wine

On the Menu

der Aal *dehr ahl*	eel
die Ananas *dee ahn·ah·nahs*	pineapple
der Aperitif *dehr ah·pehr·ee·teef*	aperitif
der Apfel *dehr ahp·fehl*	apple
die Apfelsine *dee ah·pfuhl·zee·nuh*	orange
der Apfelwein *dehr ah·pfuhl·vien*	cider (alcoholic)
die Aprikose *dee ah·pree·koh·zuh*	apricot
die Artischocke *dee ahr·tee·shoh·kuh*	artichoke
die Aubergine *dee ow·behr·gee·nuh*	eggplant [aubergine]
der Aufschnitt *dehr owf·shniht*	cold cuts [charcuterie]
die Auster *dee ows·tuhr*	oyster
die Avocado *dee ah·voh·kah·doh*	avocado
die Backpflaume *dee bahk·pflow·muh*	prune
der Bacon *dehr bah·kohn*	bacon
die Banane *dee bah·nah·nuh*	banana
der Barsch *dehr bahrsh*	bass

das Basilikum *dahs bah·zee·lee·koom*		basil
das Bier *dahs beer*		beer
die Birne *dee beer·nuh*		pear
die Blaubeere *dee blow·beh·ruh*		blueberry
der Blauschimmelkäse		blue cheese
dehr blow·shihm·mehl·kay·zuh		
der Blumenkohl *dehr bloo·muhn·kohl*		cauliflower
die Blutwurst *dee bloot·voorst*		blood sausage
die Bohne *dee boh·nuh*		bean
die Bouillon *dee boo·yohn*		broth
der Branntwein *dehr brahnt·vien*		brandy
der Braten *dehr brah·tuhn*		roast
die Brombeere *dee brohm·beh·ruh*		blackberry
das Brot *dahs broht*		bread
das Brötchen *dahs brert·khehn*		roll
die Brunnenkresse		watercress
dee broo·nuhn·kreh·zuh		
die (Hühnchen-) Brust		breast (of chicken)
dee (hewn·khehn-) broost		
die Butter *dee boo·tehr*		butter
die Buttermilch *dee boo·tehr·mihlkh*		buttermilk
die Cashewnuss *dee keh·shoo·noos*		cashew
der Chikorée *dehr chee·koh·reh*		chicory
die Chilischote *dee chee·lee·shoh·tuh*		chili pepper
die Cola *dee koh·lah*		soda
der Cracker *dehr kreh·kehr*		cracker
die Datteln *dee dah·tuhln*		dates
der Dessertwein *dehr deh·zehrt·vien*		dessert wine
der Dill *dehr dihl*		dill
der Donut *dehr doh·nuht*		doughnut
der Dorsch *dehr dohrsh*		cod

das Ei *dahs ie*	egg
das Eigelb *dahs ie•gehlb*	egg yolk
der Eierkuchen *dehr ier•koo•khuhn*	pancake
das Eis *dahs ies*	ice cream
der Eiswürfel *dehr ies•vewr•fehl*	ice (cube)
das Eiweiß *dahs ie•vies*	egg white
die Endivie *dee ehn•dee•vee•uh*	endive
die Ente *dee ehn•tuh*	duck
die Erbsen *dee ehrb•zuhn*	peas
die Erdbeere *dee ehrd•beh•ruh*	strawberry
die Erdnuss *dee ehrd•noos*	peanut
der Essig *dehr eh•zeek*	vinegar
das Estragon *dahs eh•strah•gohn*	tarragon
der Fasan *dehr fah•zahn*	pheasant
die Feige *dee fie•guh*	fig
der Fenchel *dehr fehn•khehl*	fennel
der Fisch *dehr fihsh*	fish
das Fleisch *dahs fliesh*	meat
die Fleischstücke *dee fliesh•shtew•kuh*	chopped meat
die Forelle *dee foh•reh•luh*	trout
die Gans *dee gahns*	goose

die Gänseleberpastete	goose liver pâté
dee gehn•zehl•leh•behr•pah•steh•tuh	
die Garnele *dee gahr•neh•luh*	shrimp
das Gebäck *dahs guh•behk*	pastry
das Geflügel *dahs guh•flew•gehl*	poultry
das Gemüse *dahs geh•mew•zuh*	vegetable
die Gewürze *dee guh•vewr•tsuh*	spices
die Gewürzgurke *dee guh•vewrts•goor•kuh*	pickle/gherkin
der Gin *dehr djihn*	gin
der Granatapfel *dehr grah•naht•ahp•fehl*	pomegranate
die grünen Bohnen *dee grew•nuhn boh•nuhn*	green beans
die Guave *dee gwah•veh*	guava
die Gurke *dee goor•kuh*	cucumber
die Hachse *dee hahk•suh*	shank
der Hamburger *dehr hahm•boor•gehr*	hamburger
der Hammel *dehr hah•mehl*	mutton
die Haselnuss *dee hah•zuhl•noos*	hazelnut
der Heilbutt *dehr hiel•boot*	halibut
die Henne *dee heh•nuh*	hen
der Hering *dehr heh•reeng*	herring
das Herz *dahs hehrts*	heart
die Himbeere *dee heem•beh•ruh*	raspberry
der Honig *dehr hoh•neek*	honey
der Hotdog *dehr hoht•dohg*	hot dog
das Hühnchen *dahs hewn•khehn*	chicken
der Hummer *dehr hoo•mehr*	lobster
der Hüttenkäse *dehr hew•tuhn•kay•zuh*	cottage cheese
der Imbiss *dehr ihm•buhs*	snack
der Ingwer *dehr eeng•vehr*	ginger
die Innereien *dee ihn•eh•rie•uhn*	organ meat [offal]
der Joghurt *dehr yoh•goort*	yogurt

der Kaffee *dehr kah•feh*	coffee
das Kalb *dahs kahlb*	veal
das Kaninchen *dahs kah•neen•khehn*	rabbit
die Kaper *dee kah•pehr*	caper
das Karamell *dahs kah•rah•mehl*	caramel
die Kartoffel *dee kahr•toh•fehl*	potato
die Kartoffelchips *dee kahr•toh•fehl•cheeps*	potato chips [crisps]
der Käse *dehr kay•zuh*	cheese
die Kastanie *dee kah•stahn•yuh*	chestnut
der Keks *dehr keks*	cookie [biscuit]
der Kerbel *dehr kehr•behl*	chervil
der Ketchup *dehr keh•chuhp*	ketchup
die Kichererbse *dee kee•khehr•ehrb•zuh*	chickpea
die Kirsche *dee keer•shuh*	cherry
die Kiwi *dee kee•vee*	kiwi
der Kloß *dehr klohs*	dumpling
der Knoblauch *dehr knoh•blowkh*	garlic
die Koblauchsauce *dee knoh•blowkh•zow•suh*	garlic sauce
der Kohl *dehr kohl*	cabbage
die Kokosnuss *dee koh•kohs•noos*	coconut
das Kompott *dahs kohm•poht*	stewed fruit
die Konfitüre *dee kohn•fee•tew•ruh*	jelly
der Koriander *dehr koh•ree•ahn•dehr*	cilantro [coriander]
die Kräuter *dee kroyt•uhr*	herbs
die Kraftbrühe *dee krahft•brew•uh*	consommé
der Krebs *dehr krehbs*	crab
das Krustentier *dahs kroos•tehn•tyehr*	shellfish
der Kuchen *dehr kookh•uhn*	pie
der Kümmel *dehr kew•mehl*	caraway
der Kürbis *dehr kewr•bees*	squash
die Kutteln *dee koo•tehln*	tripe

der Lachs *dehr lahks*	salmon
das Lamm *dahs lahm*	lamb
die Lauchzwiebel *dee lowkh•svee•buhl*	scallion [spring onion]
die Leber *dee leh•buhr*	liver
die Lende *dee lehn•duh*	loin
das Lendenfilet *dahs lehn•dehn•fee•leh*	sirloin
der Likör *dehr lee•ker*	liqueur
die Limette *dee lee•meh•tuh*	lime
die Limonade *dee lee•moh•nah•duh*	lemonade
die Linse *dee leen•zuh*	lentil
das Loorbeerblatt *dahs lohr•behr•blaht*	bay leaf
der Mais *dehr mies*	sweet corn
das Maismehl *dahs mies•mehl*	cornmeal
die Makkaroni *dee mah•kah•roh•nee*	macaroni
die Makrele *dee mah•krehl•uh*	mackerel
die Mandarine *dee mahn•dah•reen•uh*	tangerine
die Mandel *dee mahn•duhl*	almond
die Mango *dee mahn•goh*	mango
die Margarine *dee mahr•guh•ree•nuh*	margarine
die Marmelade *dee mahr•muh•lah•duh*	marmalade/jam
das Marzipan *dahs mahr•tsee•pahn*	marzipan

die Mayonnaise *dee mah•yoh•nay•zuh*	mayonnaise
die Meerbarbe *dee mehr•bahr•buh*	red mullet
die Meeresfrüchte *dee meh•rehs•frewkh•tuh*	seafood
die Melone *dee meh•loh•nuh*	melon
die Milch *dee mihlkh*	milk
das Milchmixgetränk *dahs mihlkh•mihks•geh•traynk*	milk shake
die Minze *dee mihn•tsuh*	mint
die Möhre *dee mer•ruh*	carrot
die Muschel *dee moo•shehl*	clam
der Muskat *dehr moos•kaht*	nutmeg
die Nelke *dee nehl•kuh*	clove
die Niere *dee nee•ruh*	kidney
die Nudel *dee noo•dehl*	noodle
der Nugat *dehr noo•gaht*	nougat
die Nüsse *dee new•suh*	nuts
das Obst *dahs ohbst*	fruit
der Ochse *dehr ohkh•suh*	ox
der Ochsenschwanz *dehr ohk•sehn•shvahnts*	oxtail
der Oktopus *dehr ohk•toh•poos*	octopus
die Olive *dee oh•lee•veh*	olive
das Olivenöl *dahs oh•lee•vehn•erl*	olive oil
das Omelett *dahs ohm•leht*	omelet
der Orangenlikör *dehr oh•rahn•jehn•lee•ker*	orange liqueur
das Oregano *dahs oh•reh•gah•noh*	oregano
die Pampelmuse *dee pahm•puhl•moo•zuh*	grapefruit
der Pansen *dehr pahn•sehn*	tripe
die Papaya *dee pah•pah•yah*	papaya
der Paprika *dehr pah•pree•kuh*	paprika
die Paprikaschote *dee pah•pree•kah•shoh•tuh*	pepper (vegetable)
die Pastinake *dee pah•stee•nahk•uh*	parsnip

die Pekannuss *dee peh·kahn·noos*	pecan
das Perlhuhn *dahs pehrl·hoon*	guinea fowl
die Petersilie *dee peh·tehr·see·lee·uh*	parsley
der Pfannkuchen *dehr pfahn·koo·khuhn*	pancake
der Pfeffer *dehr pfeh·fehr*	pepper (seasoning)
der Pfirsich *dehr pfeer·zeekh*	peach
die Pflaume *dee pflow·muh*	plum
der Pilz *dehr pihlts*	mushroom
die Pizza *dee pee·tsah*	pizza
die Pommes frites *dee pohm freets*	French fries
der Porree *dehr poh·reh*	leek
der Portwein *dehr pohrt·vien*	port
die Preiselbeere *dee prie·zuhl·beh·ruh*	cranberry
der Rahmkäse *dehr rahm·kay·zuh*	cream cheese
der Reis *dehr ries*	rice
der Rettich *dehr reh·teekh*	radish
der Rhabarber *dehr rah·bahr·behr*	rhubarb
der Rinderbraten *dehr reen·dehr·brah·tuhn*	roast beef
das Rindfleisch *dahs rihnt·fliesh*	beef
der Rosenkohl *dehr roh·zuhn·kohl*	Brussels sprouts
die Rosine *dee roh·zee·nuh*	raisin
der Rosmarin *dehr rohs·mah·reen*	rosemary
die rote Johannisbeere *dee roh·tuh yoh·hah·nihs·beh·ruh*	red currant
der Rotkohl *dehr roht·kohl*	red cabbage
die Rübe *dee rew·beh*	beet/turnip
der Rum *dehr room*	rum
der Safran *dehr zahf·rahn*	saffron
der Saft *dehr zahft*	juice
die Sahne *dee zah·nuh*	cream
die Salami *dee zah·lah·mee*	salami

der Salat *dehr sah-laht*	lettuce/salad
der Salbei *dehr zahl-bie*	sage
das Salz *dahs zahlts*	salt
das Sandwich *dahs sahnd-weetsh*	sandwich
die Sardelle *dee sahr-dehl-uh*	anchovy
die Sardine *dee zahr-dee-nuh*	sardine
die Sauce *dee zows-uh*	sauce
die Sauerkirsche *dee zow-ehr-keer-shuh*	sour cherry
die saure Sahne *dee zow-ruh zah-nuh*	sour cream
die Schalotte *dee shah-loh-tuh*	shallot
die scharfe Pfeffersauce *dee shahr-fuh pfeh-fehr-zow-suh*	hot pepper sauce
das Schaumgebäck *dahs showm-guh-behk*	meringue
der Schellfisch *dehr shehl-fihsh*	haddock
der Schinken *dehr sheen-kuhn*	ham
die Schlagsahne *dee shlahg-zah-nuh*	whipped cream
die Schnecke *dee shnehk-uh*	snail
der Schnittlauch *dehr shniht-lowkh*	chives
das Schnitzel *dahs shniht-tzuhl*	chop
die Schokolade *dee shoh-koh-lah-duh*	chocolate
die Schulter *dee shool-tehr*	shoulder
die schwarze Johannisbeere *dee shvahr-tsuh yoh-hah-nees-beh-ruh*	black currant
das Schweinefleisch *dahs shvien-uh-fliesh*	pork
der Schwertfisch *dehr shvehrt-fihsh*	swordfish
der Scotch *dehr skohtsh*	scotch
der Seebarsch *dehr zeh-bahrsh*	sea bass
der Seehecht *dehr zeh-hehkht*	hake
der Seeteufel *dehr zeh-toy-fuhl*	monkfish
die Seezunge *dee zeh-tsoong-uh*	sole
der Sellerie *dehr zeh-luh-ree*	celery

der Senf *dehr zehnf*	mustard
der Sherry *dehr <u>shehr</u>·ee*	sherry
der Sirup *dehr <u>zew</u>·roop*	syrup
das Soda-Wasser *dahs <u>soh</u>·dah·vah·sehr*	soda water
die Sojabohne *dee <u>zoh</u>·yah·boh·nuh*	soybean [soya bean]
die Sojamilch *dee <u>zoh</u>·yah·mihlkh*	soymilk [soya milk]
die Sojasauce *dee <u>zoh</u>·yah·zow·suh*	soy sauce
die Sojasprossen *dee <u>soh</u>·jah·shproh·suhn*	bean sprouts
die Spaghetti *dee shpah·<u>geh</u>·tee*	spaghetti
das Spanferkel *dahs <u>shpahn</u>·fehr·kehl*	crunchy roasted suckling pig
der Spargel *dehr <u>shpahr</u>·gehl*	asparagus
der Spinat *dehr shpee·<u>naht</u>*	spinach
die Spirituosen *dee shpee·ree·<u>twoh</u>·zuhn*	spirits
die Stachelbeere *dee <u>shtah</u>·khehl·beh·ruh*	gooseberry
das Steak *dahs stehk*	steak
die Suppe *dee <u>zoo</u>·puh*	soup
die Süßigkeiten *dee <u>zew</u>·seekh·kie·tuhn*	candy [sweets]
die Süßkartoffel *dee <u>zews</u>·kahr·toh·fuhl*	sweet potato
die süßsaure Sauce *dee <u>zews</u>·zow·ruh <u>zow</u>·suh*	sweet and sour sauce
der Süßstoff *dehr <u>zews</u>·shtohf*	sweetener
der Tee *dehr teh*	tea
der Thunfisch *dehr <u>toon</u>·fihsh*	tuna
der Thymian *dehr <u>tew</u>·mee·ahn*	thyme
der Tintenfisch *dehr <u>teen</u>·tuhn·fihsh*	squid
der Toast *dehr tohst*	toast
das Tofu *dahs <u>toh</u>·foo*	tofu
die Tomate *dee <u>toh</u>·mah·tuh*	tomato
das Tonic *dahs <u>toh</u>·neek*	tonic water
die Trüffel *dee <u>trew</u>·fuhl*	truffles
der Truthahn *dehr <u>troot</u>·hahn*	turkey

die Vanille *dee vah-nee-luh*	vanilla
die Wachtel *dee vahkh-tehl*	quail
die Waffel *dee vah-fuhl*	waffle
die Walnuss *dee vahl-noos*	walnut
das Wasser *dahs vah-sehr*	water
die Wassermelone *dee vah-sehr-meh-loh-nuh*	watermelon
der Wein *dehr vien*	wine
die Weintrauben *dee vien-trow-buhn*	grapes
der Weizen *dehr vie-tsuhn*	wheat
der Wermut *dehr vehr-moot*	vermouth
der Whisky *dehr vees-kee*	whisky
das Wild *dahs vihlt*	game/venison
der Wodka *dehr vohd-kah*	vodka
die Wurst *dee voorst*	sausage
der Zackenbarsch *dehr tsah-kehn-bahrsh*	sea perch
das Zicklein *dahs tsihk-lien*	kid (young goat)
die Ziege *dee tsee-guh*	goat
der Ziegenkäse *dehr tsee-guhn-kay-zuh*	goat cheese
der Zimt *dehr tsihmt*	cinnamon
die Zitrone *dee tsee-troh-nuh*	lemon
die Zucchini *dee tsoo-kee-nee*	zucchini [courgette]
der Zucker *dehr tsoo-kehr*	sugar
die Zunge *dee tsoong-uh*	tongue
die Zwiebel *dee tsvee-buhl*	onion

People

ESSENTIAL

Hello!	**Hallo!** hah·<u>loh</u>
How are you?	**Wie geht es Ihnen?** vee geht ehs <u>eehn</u>·uhn
Fine, thanks.	**Gut, danke.** goot <u>dahn</u>·kuh
Excuse me!	**Entschuldigung!** ehnt·<u>shool</u>·dee·goong
Do you speak English?	**Sprechen Sie Englisch?** <u>shpreh</u>·khuhn zee <u>ehn</u>·gleesh
What's your name?	**Wie heißen Sie?** vee <u>hie</u>·suhn zee
My name is...	**Mein Name ist ...** mien <u>nahm</u>·uh ihst ...
Nice to meet you.	**Schön, Sie kennenzulernen.** shern zee <u>keh</u>·nehn·tsoo·lehr·nehn
Where are you from?	**Woher kommen Sie?** <u>voh</u>·hehr <u>koh</u>·muhn zee
I'm from the U.S./U.K.	**Ich komme aus den USA/Großbritannien.** eekh <u>koh</u>·muh ows dehn oo·ehs·<u>ah</u>/ grohs·bree·<u>tah</u>·nee·ehn
What do you do for a living?	**Was machen Sie beruflich?** vahs <u>mah</u>·khuhn zee beh·<u>roof</u>·likh
I work for...	**Ich arbeite für ...** eekh <u>ahr</u>·bie·tuh fewr ...
I'm a student.	**Ich bin Student.** eekh bihn shtoo·<u>dehnt</u>
I'm retired.	**Ich bin Rentner.** eekh been <u>rehnt</u>·nehr
Do you like...?	**Mögen Sie ...?** <u>mer</u>·guhn zee ...
Goodbye.	**Auf Wiedersehen.** owf <u>vee</u>·dehr·zehn
See you later.	**Bis bald.** bihs bahld

When addressing anyone but a very close friend, it is polite to use a title: **Herr** (Mr.), **Frau** (Miss/Ms./Mrs.) or **Herr Dr.** (Dr.), and to speak to him or her using **Sie**, the formal form of 'you', until you are asked to use the familiar **Du**.

Language Difficulties

Do you speak English?	**Sprechen Sie Englisch?** _shpreh•khehn zee ehn•gleesh_
Does anyone here speak English?	**Spricht hier jemand Englisch?** _shpreekht heer yeh•mahnt ehn•gleesh_
I don't speak (much) German.	**Ich spreche kein (nicht viel) Deutsch.** _eekh shpreh•khuh kien (neekht feel) doych_
Can you speak more slowly, please?	**Können Sie bitte langsamer sprechen?** _ker•nuhn zee biht•tuh lahng•sahm•ehr shpreh•khuhn_
Can you repeat that, please?	**Können Sie das bitte wiederholen?** _ker•nuhn zee dahs biht•tuh vee•dehr•hoh•luhn_
Excuse me?	**Wie bitte?** _vee biht•tuh_
What was that?	**Was haben Sie gesagt?** _vahs hah•buhn zee guh•zahgt_
Can you spell it?	**Können Sie das buchstabieren?** _ker•nuhn zee dahs book•shtah•bee•ruhn_

YOU MAY HEAR...

Ich spreche nur wenig Englisch.
eekh shpreh•khuh noor veh•neek ehn•gleesh
Ich spreche kein Englisch.
eekh shpreh•khuh kien ehn•gleesh

I only speak a little English.
I don't speak English.

Write it down, please.	**Bitte schreiben Sie es auf.**
	biht•tuh shrie•buhn zee ehs owf
Can you translate this into English for me?	**Können Sie das für mich ins Englische übersetzen?** *ker•nuhn zee dahs fewr meekh ihns ehn•glee•shuh ew•behr•zeh•tsuhn*
What does... mean?	**Was bedeutet ...?** *vahs beh•doyt•eht ...*
I understand.	**Ich verstehe.** *eekh fehr•shteh•uh*
I don't understand.	**Ich verstehe nicht.** *eekh fehr•shteh•uh neekht*
Do you understand?	**Verstehen Sie?** *fehr•shteh•uhn zee*

Making Friends

Hello!	**Hallo!** *hah•loh*
Good morning.	**Guten Morgen.** *goo•tuhn mohr•guhn*
Good afternoon.	**Guten Tag.** *goo•tuhn tahk*
Good evening.	**Guten Abend.** *goo•tuhn ah•behnt*
My name is...	**Mein Name ist ...** *mien nahm•uh ihst ...*
What's your name?	**Wie heißen Sie?** *vee hie•sehn zee*
I'd like to introduce you to...	**Ich möchte Sie gern ... vorstellen.** *eekh merkh•tuh zee gehrn ... fohr•shteh•luhn*
Pleased to meet you.	**Angenehm.** *ahn•guh•nehm*

| How are you? | **Wie geht es Ihnen?** *vee geht ehs eehn·uhn* |
| Fine, thanks. And you? | **Gut, danke. Und Ihnen?** *goot dahn·kuh oont eehn·uhn* |

In Germany, it's polite to shake hands, both when you meet and say goodbye. Relatives and close friends may hug or kiss cheeks.

Travel talk

I'm here on business.	**Ich bin geschäftlich hier.** *eekh bihn guh·shehft·leekh heer*
I'm here on vacation.	**Ich mache hier Urlaub.** *eekh mahkh·uh heer oor·lowb*
I'm studying here.	**Ich bin zum Studieren hier.** *eekh bihn tsoom shtoo·dee·ruhn heer*
I'm staying for...	**Ich bleibe ...** *eekh blie·buh ...*
I've been here...	**Ich bin seit ... hier.** *eekh been ziet ... heer*
a day	**einem Tag** *ien·uhm tahk*
a week	**einer Woche** *ien·uhr voh·khuh*
a month	**einem Monat** *ien·uhm moh·naht*
Where are you from?	**Woher kommen Sie?** *voh·hehr koh·muhn zee*
I'm from...	**Ich komme aus ...** *eekh koh·muh ows ...*

For Numbers, see page 165.

Personal

Who are you with?	**Mit wem sind Sie hier?** *miht vehm zihnt zee heer*
I'm here alone.	**Ich bin allein hier.** *eekh bihn ah·lien heer*
How old are you?	**Wie alt sind Sie?** *vee ahlt zihnt zee*
I'm...	**Ich bin ...** *eekh bihn ...*

I'm with...	**Ich bin mit ... hier.** *eekh been miht ... heer*
my husband/wife	**meinem Mann/meiner Frau** *mie-nuhm mahn/*
	mie-nuhr frow
my boyfriend/	**meinem Freund/meiner Freundin**
my girlfriend	*mie-nuhm froynt/mie-nuhr froyn-dihn*
my friend	**meinem Freund** *mie-nuhm froynt*
my friends	**meinen Freunden** *mie-nuhn froyn-duhn*
my colleague	**meinem Kollegen** *mie-nuhm koh-leh-guhn*
my colleagues	**meinen Kollegen** *mie-nuhn koh-leh-guhn*
When's your birthday?	**Wann haben Sie Geburtstag?**
	vahn hah-buhn zee guh-boorts-tahk
Are you married?	**Sind Sie verheiratet?** *zihnt zee fehr-hie-rah-tuht*
I'm...	**Ich bin ...** *eekh bihn ...*
single/in a	**ledig/in einer Beziehung** *leh-deek/ihn*
relationship	*ien-uhr beh-tsee-oong*
engaged	**verlobt** *fehr-lohbt*
married	**verheiratet** *fehr-hie-rah-tuht*
divorced	**geschieden** *geh-shee-dehn*
separated	**getrennt lebend** *geh-trehnt leh-buhnd*
widowed	**verwitwet** *fehr-viht-veht*
Do you have children/	**Haben Sie Kinder/Enkelkinder?** *hah-buhn*
grandchildren?	*zee kihn-dehr/ehn-kehl-kihn-dehr*

For Numbers, see page 165.

Work & School

What are you	**Was studieren Sie?** *vahs shtoo-dee-ruhn zee*
studying?	
I'm studying	**Ich studiere Deutsch.** *eekh shtoo-dee-ruh doych*
German.	
What do you do	**Was machen Sie beruflich?**
for a living?	*vahs mah-khuhn zee beh-roof-leekh*

I...	**Ich ...** *eekh ...*
work full-time/ part-time	**arbeite Vollzeit/Teilzeit** _ahr_•bie•tuh _fohl_•tsiet/_tiel_•tsiet
do freelance work	**bin Freiberufler** bihn _frie_•beh•roo•flehr
am a consultant	**bin Berater** bihn beh•_rah_•tehr
am unemployed	**bin arbeitslos** bihn _ahr_•biets•lohs
work at home	**arbeite zu Hause** _ahr_•bie•tuh tsoo _how_•zuh
Who do you work for?	**Für wen arbeiten Sie?** fewr vehn _ahr_•bie•tuhn zee
I work for...	**Ich arbeite für ...** eekh _ahr_•bie•tuh fewr ...
Here's my business card.	**Hier ist meine Visitenkarte.** heer ihst _mie_•nuh vih•_zee_•tuhn•kahr•tuh

For Business Travel, see page 137.

Weather

What's the forecast?	**Wie ist die Wettervorhersage?** *vee ihst dee _veh_•tehr•fohr•hehr•zahg•uh*
What beautiful/ terrible weather!	**Was für ein schönes/schlechtes Wetter!** *vahs fewr ien _sher_•nuhs/_shlehkht_•uhs veh•tehr*
It's...	**Es ist ...** *ehs ihst ...*
cool/warm	**kühl/warm** *kewl/vahrm*
cold/hot	**kalt/heiß** *kahlt/hies*
rainy/sunny	**regnerisch/sonnig** _rehg_•nuh•reesh/_zoh_•neek
There is snow/ice.	**Es gibt Schnee/Eis.** *ehs gihbt shneh/ies*
Do I need a jacket/ an umbrella?	**Brauche ich eine Jacke/einen Regenschirm?** _brow_•khuh eekh _ien_•uh _yah_•kuh/ _ien_•uhn _reh_•guhn•sheerm

For Temperature, see page 171.

Romance

ESSENTIAL

Would you like to go out for a drink/dinner?	**Möchten Sie mit mir auf einen Drink/zum Essen gehen?** _merkh_•tuhn zee miht meer owf _ien_•uhn treenk/tsoom _eh_•suhn _geh_•uhn
What are your plans for tonight/tomorrow?	**Was haben Sie heute Abend/morgen vor?** vahs _hah_•buhn zee _hoy_•tuh _ah_•buhnt/_mohr_•guhn fohr
Can I have your number?	**Kann ich Ihre Telefonnummer haben?** kahn eekh _ee_•ruh teh•leh•_fohn_•noo•mehr _hah_•buhn
Can I join you?	**Kann ich mitkommen?** kahn eekh _miht_•koh•muhn
Can I get you a drink?	**Darf ich Ihnen einen Drink ausgeben?** dahrf eekh _eehn_•uhn _ien_•uhn treenk _ows_•geh•buhn
I like/love you.	**Ich mag/liebe dich.** eekh mahk/_lee_•buh deekh

The Dating Game

Would you like to go out... for coffee?	**Möchten Sie mit mir Kaffee trinken gehen?** _mehrkh_•tuhn zee miht meer _ien_•uhn kah•_feh_ trihnk•uhn _geh_•uhn
Would you like to go out for a drink?	**Möchten Sie mit mir etwas trinken gehen?** merkht•uhn zee eht•vahs thrihn•khun geh•huhn
Would you like to go out for dinner?	**Möchten Sie mit mir etwas essen gehen?** merkht•uhn zee eht•vahs ehs•suhn geh•huhn
What are your plans for... ?	**Was haben Sie ... vor?** vahs _hah_•buhn zee ... fohr
today	**heute** _hoy_•tuh
tonight	**heute Abend** _hoy_•tuh _ah_•buhnt
tomorrow	**morgen** _mohr_•guhn
this weekend	**dieses Wochenende** _dee_•zuhs voh•khuhn•_ehn_•duh

Where would you like to go?	**Wohin möchten Sie gern gehen?** _voh_·hihn _merkh_·tuhn zee gehrn _geh_·uhn
I'd like to go…?	**Ich möchte gern … gehen.** eekh _merkh_·tuh gehrn … _geh_·uhn
Do you like…?	**Mögen Sie …?** _mer_·guhn zee …
Can I have your number/e-mail?	**Kann ich Ihre Telefonnummer/E-Mail haben?** kahn eekh _ee_·ruh teh·leh·_fohn_·noo·mehr/ _ee_·mehl _hah_·buhn
Are you on Facebook/Twitter?	**Sind Sie bei Facebook/Twitter? (polite form)** zihnt zee by face·book/twit·ter
Can I join you?	**Kann ich mitkommen?** kahn eekh _miht_·koh·muhn
You're very attractive.	**Sie sind sehr attraktiv.** zee zihnt zehr aht·rahk·_teef_
Let's go somewhere quieter.	**Lassen Sie uns an einen ruhigeren Ort gehen.** _lah_·suhn zee oons ahn _ien_·uhn _roo_·ee·geh·ruhn ohrt _geh_·uhn

For Communications, see page 49.

Accepting & Rejecting

| I'd love to. | **Gerne.** _gehr_·nuh |
| Where should we meet? | **Wo wollen wir uns treffen?** voh _voh_·luhn veer oons _treh_·fuhn |

I'll meet you at the bar/your hotel.	**Ich treffe Sie an der Bar/Ihrem Hotel.**
	eekh treh•fuh zee ahn dehr bahr/ee•ruhm hoh•tehl
I'll come by at...	**Ich komme um ... vorbei.**
	eekh koh•muh oom ... fohr•bie
What is your address?	**Wie ist Ihre Adresse?** *vee ihsht ee•ruh*
	ah•drehs•uh
I'm busy.	**Ich bin beschäftigt.** *eekh been beh•shehf•teekt*
I'm not interested.	**Ich habe kein Interesse.** *eekh hah•buh kien*
	ihn•teh•reh•suh
Leave me alone.	**Lassen Sie mich in Ruhe.**
	lah•sehn zee meekh ihn roo•uh
Stop bothering me!	**Hören Sie auf, mich zu belästigen!**
	her•ruhn zee owf meekh tsoo buh•lay•steeg•uhn

For Time, see page 166.

Getting Intimate

Can I hug/kiss you?	**Kann ich dich umarmen/küssen?**
	kahn eekh deekh oom•ahr•muhn/kew•zuhn
Yes.	**Ja.** *yah*
No.	**Nein.** *nien*
Stop!	**Stopp!** *shtohp*
I like/love you.	**Ich mag/liebe dich.** *eekh mahk/lee•buh deekh*

Sexual Preferences

Are you gay?	**Bist du schwul?** *beesht doo shvool*
I'm...	**Ich bin ...** *eekh been ...*
heterosexual	**heterosexuell** *heh•tuh•roh•sehks•oo•ehl*
homosexual	**homosexuell** *hoh•moh•sehks•oo•ehl*
bisexual	**bisexuell** *bee•sehks•oo•ehl*
Do you like men/women?	**Magst du Männer/Frauen?** *mahgst doo*
	meh•nehr/frow•uhn

Leisure Time

Sightseeing

ESSENTIAL

Where's the tourist information office?	**Wo ist das Touristeninformationsbüro?** *voh ihst dahs too•ree•stuhn•een•fohr•mah•syohns•bew•roh*
What are the main sights?	**Was sind die wichtigsten Sehenswürdigkeiten?** *vahs zihnt dee veekh•teeg•stuhn zeh•uhns•vewr•deekh•kie•tuhn*
Do you offer tours in English?	**Haben Sie Führungen in Englisch?** *hah•buhn zee few•roong•uhn een ehn•gleesh*
Can I have a map/ guide?	**Kann ich einen Stadtplan/Reiseführer haben?** *kahn eekh ien•uhn shtaht•plahn/ rie•seh•fewhr•ehr hah•buhn*

Tourist Information

Do you have information on...?	**Haben Sie Informationen über ...?** *hah•buhn zee ihn•fohr•mah•syoh•nuhn ew•buhr ...*
Can you recommend...?	**Können Sie ... empfehlen?** *ker•nuhn zee ... ehm•pfeh•luhn*
a bus tour	**eine Busreise** *ien•uh boos•rie•zuh*
an excursion to...	**einen Ausflug nach ...** *ien•uhn ows•flook nahkh ...*
a sightseeing tour	**eine Stadtrundfahrt** *ien•uh shtaht•roond•fahrt*

On Tour

I'd like to go on the tour to...	**Ich möchte gern an der ... Führung teilnehmen.** *eekh merkht•uh gehrn ahn dehr ... fewhr•oong tiel•nehm•uhn*
When's the next tour?	**Wann ist die nächste Führung?** *vahn ihst dee nehkhst•uh fewhr•oong*

Tourist information offices are located throughout Germany. Look for the 'i' symbol or ask your hotel concierge where the nearest office is located. Tourist information offices can recommend destinations, attractions, local events and festivals, and help you find hotels, tours, transportation and other services. Visit the **Deutsche Zentrale für Tourismus**, **DZT** (German center for tourism), website for more information.

Are there tours in English?	**Gibt es Führungen in Englisch?** *gihpt ehs fewhr•oong•uhn ihn ehng•lihsh*
Is there an English guide book/audio guide?	**Gibt es einen englischsprachigen Reiseführer/Audio-Guide?** *gihpt ehs ien•uhn ehng•lihsh•shprahkh•ee•guhn riez•uh•fewhr•ehr/ ow•dee•oh•gied*
What time do we leave/return?	**Wann fahren wir ab/kommen wir wieder?** *vahn fahhr•uhn veer ap/kohm•uhn veer veed•ehr*
We'd like to see...	**Wir möchten gern ... sehen.** *veer merkht•uhn gehrn ... zeh•uhn*
Can we stop here...?	**Können wir hier anhalten ...?** *ker•nuhn veer heer ahn•hahlt•uhn ...*
to take photos	**um Fotos zu machen** *oom foht•ohs tsoo mahkh•uhn*
for souvenirs	**um Andenken zu kaufen** *oom ahn•dehnk•uhn tsoo kowf•uhn*
for the toilets	**um auf die Toilette zu gehen** *oom owf dee toy•leht•uh tsoo geh•uhn*
Is it disabled-accessible?	**Ist es behindertengerecht?** *ihst ehs beh•hihn•dehrt•uhn•geh•rehkht*

For Tickets, see page 19.

Seeing the Sights

Where's . . .?	**Wo ist . . .?**	*voh ihst . . .*
the battleground	**das Schlachtfeld**	*dahs shlahkht•fehlt*
the botanical garden	**der botanische Garten**	*dehr boh•tahn•eesh•uh gahr•tuhn*
the castle	**das Schloss**	*dahs shlohs*
the downtown area	**das Stadtzentrum**	*dahs shtadt•tsehnt•room*
the fountain	**der Brunnen**	*dehr broon•uhn*
the library	**die Bücherei**	*dee bewkh•eh•rie*
the market	**der Markt**	*dehr mahrkt*
the museum	**das Museum**	*dahs moo•zeh•oom*
the old town	**die Altstadt**	*dee ahlt•shtahdt*
the opera house	**das Opernhaus**	*dahs oh•pehrn•hows*
the palace	**der Palast**	*dehr pah•lahst*
the park	**der Park**	*dehr pahrk*
the ruins	**die Ruine**	*dee ro•ee•nuh*
the shopping area	**das Einkaufszentrum**	*dahs ien•kowfs•tsehn•troom*
the theater	**das Theater**	*dahs teh•ah•tehr*
the tower	**der Turm**	*dehr toorm*
the town hall	**das Rathaus**	*dahs raht•hows*
the town square	**der Rathausplatz**	*dehr raht•hows•plats*
Can you show me on the map?	**Können Sie mir das im Stadtplan zeigen?**	*ker•nuhn zee meer dahs ihm shtadt•plahn tsie•guhn*
It's . . .	**Es ist . . .**	*ehs ihst . . .*
amazing	**erstaunlich**	*ehr•shtown•leekh*
beautiful	**wunderschön**	*voond•ehr•shern*
boring	**langweilig**	*lahng•viel•eek*
interesting	**interessant**	*ihn•teh•reh•sahnt*
magnificent	**großartig**	*groh•sahr•teek*
romantic	**romantisch**	*roh•mahnt•eesh*
strange	**seltsam**	*zehlt•zahm*

107

stunning	**umwerfend** <u>oom</u>•vehrf•uhnt
terrible	**schrecklich** <u>shrehk</u>•leekh
ugly	**hässlich** <u>hehs</u>•leekh
I (don't) like it.	**Es gefällt mir (nicht).** ehs guh•<u>fehlt</u> meer (neekht)

For Asking Directions, see page 34.

Religious Sites

Where's…?	**Wo ist …?** voh ihst …
the cathedral	**die Kathedrale** dee kah•teh•<u>drahl</u>•uh
the Catholic/ Protestant church	**die katholische/evangelische Kirche** dee kah•<u>toh</u>•leesh•uh/eh•vahn•<u>gehl</u>•eesh•uh <u>keer</u>•khuh
the mosque	**die Moschee** dee moh•<u>sheh</u>
the shrine	**der Schrein** dehr shrien
the synagogue	**die Synagoge** dee zewn•uh•<u>goh</u>•guh
the temple	**der Tempel** dehr <u>tehm</u>•pehl
What time is mass/ the service?	**Wann ist die Messe/der Gottesdienst?** vahn ihst dee <u>mehs</u>•suh/dehr <u>goht</u>•ehs•deenst

Shopping

ESSENTIAL

Where's the market/mall [shopping centre]?	**Wo ist der Markt/das Einkaufszentrum?** *voh ihst dehr mahrkt/dahs ien•kowfs•tsehn•troom*	
I'm just looking.	**Ich schaue mich nur um.** *eekh show•uh meekh noor oom*	
Can you help me?	**Können Sie mir helfen?** *kern•uhn zee meer hehlf•uhn*	
I'm being helped.	**Ich werde schon bedient.** *eekh vehrd•uh shohn beh•deent*	
How much?	**Wie viel kostet das?** *vee feel kohs•tuht dahs*	
That one, please.	**Dieses bitte.** *dee•zuhs biht•tuh*	
That's all.	**Das ist alles.** *dahs ihst ahl•uhs*	
Where can I pay?	**Wo kann ich bezahlen?** *voh kahn eekh beh•tsahl•uhn*	
I'll pay in cash/by credit card.	**Ich zahle bar/mit Kreditkarte.** *eekh tsahl•uh bahr/miht kreh•deet•kahr•tuh*	
A receipt, please.	**Eine Quittung, bitte.** *ien•uh kvih•toong biht•tuh*	

At the Shops

Where's...?	**Wo ist ...?** *voh ihst ...*	
the antiques store	**das Antiquitätengeschäft** *dahs ahn•tee•kwee•tay•tuhn•guh•shehft*	
the bakery	**die Bäckerei** *dee beh•keh•rie*	
the bank	**die Bank** *dee bahnk*	
the bookstore	**der Buchladen** *dehr bookh•lahd•uhn*	

the clothing store	**das Bekleidungsgeschäft**
	dahs buh-klied-oongs-guh-shehft
the delicatessen	**das Feinkostgeschäft** *dahs fien-kohst-guh-shehft*
the department store	**das Kaufhaus** *dahs kowf-hows*
the gift shop	**der Geschenkwarenladen**
	dehr guh-shehnk-vah-ruhn-lah-duhn
the health food store	**das Reformhaus** *dahs reh-fohrm-hows*
the jeweler	**das Schmuckgeschäft** *dahs shmook-guh-shehft*
the liquor store [off-licence]	**das Spirituosengeschäft**
	dahs shpee-ree-twoh-zuhn-guh-shehft
the market	**der Markt** *dehr mahrkt*
the music store	**das Musikgeschäft** *dahs moo-zeek-guh-shehft*
the pastry shop	**die Konditorei** *dee kohn-dee-toh-rie*
the pharmacy [chemist]	**die Apotheke** *dee ah-poh-tehk-uh*
the produce [grocery] store	**das Lebensmittelgeschäft**
	dahs lehb-uhns-miht-uhl-guh-shehft
the shoe store	**das Schuhgeschäft** *dahs shooh-guh-shehft*
the shopping mall [shopping centre]	**das Einkaufszentrum**
	dahs ien-kowfs-tsehn-troom
the souvenir store	**der Andenkenladen** *dehr ahn-dehnk-uhn-lah-duhn*
the supermarket	**der Supermarkt** *dehr zoo-pehr-mahrkt*
the tobacconist	**der Tabakladen** *dehr tah-bahk-lahd-uhn*
the toy store	**das Spielzeuggeschäft** *dahs shpeel-tsoyg-geh-shehft*

Ask an Assistant

| When do you open/close? | **Wann öffnen/schließen Sie?** *vahn erf-nuhn/ shlees-uhn zee* |
| Where's…? | **Wo ist …?** *voh ihst …* |

the cashier	**die Kasse** *dee <u>kah</u>•suh*
the escalator	**die Rolltreppe** *dee <u>rohl</u>•trehp•uh*
the elevator [lift]	**der Fahrstuhl** *dehr <u>fahr</u>•shtool*
the fitting room	**die Umkleidekabine** *dee <u>oom</u>•klied•uh•kah•bee•nuh*
the store directory	**die Liste mit den Geschäften?**
	dee lihs•tuh miht dehn guh•sheft•tuhn
Can you help me?	**Können Sie mir helfen?** <u>kern</u>•uhn zee meer <u>hehl</u>•fuhn
I'm just looking.	**Ich schaue mich nur um.** *eekh <u>show</u>•uh*
	meekh noor oom
I'm already being	**Ich werde schon bedient.** *eekh <u>vehrd</u>•uh*
helped.	*shohn buh•<u>deent</u>*
Do you have…?	**Haben Sie …?** <u>hah</u>•buhn zee …

YOU MAY HEAR…

Kann ich Ihnen helfen? *kahn eekh <u>eehn</u>•uhn <u>hehlf</u>•uhn*

Can I help you?

Einen Moment. <u>ien</u>•uhn moh•<u>mehnt</u>

One moment.

Was möchten Sie? *vahs <u>merkht</u>•uhn zee*

What would you like?

Noch etwas? *nohkh <u>eht</u>•vahs*

Anything else?

YOU MAY SEE...

GEÖFFNET/GESCHLOSSEN	open/closed
ÜBER MITTAG GESCHLOSSEN	closed for lunch
EINGANG	entrance
UMKLEIDEKABINE	fitting room
KASSE	cashier
NUR BARZAHLUNG MÖGLICH	cash only
KREDITKARTENZAHLUNG MÖGLICH	credit cards accepted
ÖFFNUNGSZEITEN	business hours
AUSGANG	exit

Can you show me…?	**Können Sie mir … zeigen?** _kern_•nuhn zee meer … _tsieg_•uhn
Can you ship/wrap it?	**Können Sie das versenden/einpacken?** _kern_•uhn zee dahs fehr•_zehn_•duhn/ien•pahk•uhn
How much?	**Wie viel kostet es?** vee feel _kohs_•tuht ehs
That's all.	**Das ist alles.** dahs ihst _ahl_•uhs

For Clothing, see page 117.

For Meals & Cooking, see page 67.

For Souvenirs, see page 123.

Personal Preferences

I'd like something…	**Ich möchte etwas …** eekh _merkht_•uh _eht_•vahs …
cheap/expensive	**Billiges/Teueres** _bihl_•ee•guhs/_toy_•ehr•uhs
larger/smaller	**Größeres/Kleineres** _grers_•eh•ruhs/_klien_•eh•ruhs
nicer	**Schöneres** _shern_•uh•ruhs
from this region	**aus dieser Region** ows _deez_•ehr rehg•_yohn_
Around…euros.	**Ungefähr … Euro.** _oon_•guh•fehr … _oy_•roh
Can you show me…?	**Können Sie mir … zeigen?** _kern_•uhn zee meer … _tsieg_•uhn

Wie möchten Sie zahlen? *vee merkht·uhn zee tsahl·uhn*	How are you paying?
Ihre Kreditkarte wurde abgelehnt. *eehr·uh kreh·deet·kahr·tuh voor·duh ahp·guh·lehnt*	Your credit card has been declined.
Ihren Ausweis, bitte. *eehr·uhn ows·vies biht·tuh*	ID, please.
Wir nehmen keine Kreditkarten. *veer neh·muhn kie·nuh kreh·deet·kahr·tuhn*	We don't accept credit cards.
Bitte nur Bargeld. *biht·tuh noor bahr·gehlt*	Cash only, please.
Haben Sie Wechselgeld/kleine Scheine? *hah·buhn zee vehkh·zuhl·gehlt/klien·uh shien·uh*	Do you have change/ small bills [notes]?

Is that your best price?	**Ist das Ihr bester Preis?** *ihst dahs eehr behst·ehr pries*
Can you give me a discount?	**Können Sie mir einen Rabatt geben?** *kern·uhn zee meer ien·uhn rah·baht geh·buhn*

For Numbers, see page 165.

Making a Complaint

I'd like...	**Ich möchte ...** *eekh merkht·uh ...*
to exchange this	**das umtauschen** *dahs oom·tow·shuhn*
a refund	**gern mein Geld zurück** *gehrn mien gehld tsoo·rewk*
to see the manager	**mit dem Manager sprechen** *miht dehm mahn·ah·jehr shprehkh·uhn*

Is it real?	**Ist das echt?** *ihst dahs ehkht*
That's not quite what I want.	**Das ist nicht ganz das, was ich möchte.** *dahs ihst neekht gahnts dahs vahs eekh <u>merkht</u>·u*
No, I don't like it.	**Das gefällt mir nicht.** *dahs guh·<u>fehlt</u> meer neek*
It's too expensive.	**Es ist zu teuer.** *ehs ihst tsoo <u>toy</u>·ehr*
I have to think about it.	**Das muss ich mir überlegen.** *dahs moos eekh meer <u>ewb</u>·ehr·leh·guhn*
I'll take it.	**Ich nehme es.** *eekh <u>nehm</u>·uh ehs*

Paying & Bargaining

How much?	**Wie viel kostet es?** *vee feel <u>kohs</u>·tuht ehs*
I'll pay…	**Ich zahle …** *eekh <u>tsah</u>·luh …*
in cash	**bar** *bahr*
by credit card	**mit Kreditkarte** *miht kreh·<u>deet</u>·kahr·tuh*
by traveler's cheque	**mit Reiseschecks** *miht <u>riez</u>·uh·shehks*
A receipt, please.	**Die Quittung, bitte.** *dee <u>kviht</u>·oong <u>biht</u>·tuh*
That's too much.	**Das ist zu viel.** *dahs ihst tsoo veel*
I'll give you…	**Ich gebe Ihnen …** *eekh <u>gehb</u>·uh <u>eehn</u>·uhn …*
I have only… euros.	**Ich habe nur … Euro.** *eekh <u>hah</u>·buh noor … <u>oy</u>·roh*

In Germany, cash is the preferred form of payment. Credit cards are accepted in most larger stores, gas stations, hotels and restaurants. Credit cards may not be accepted by smaller businesses, so be sure to ask before making a purchase. Traveler's checks are not very popular in Germany. If taken, they should be exchanged for cash at a currency exchange office or bank, though a fee will be charged for the exchange. Some banks do not accept traveler's checks.

Services

Can you recommend...?	**Können Sie ... empfehlen?** _kern_·uhn zee ... _ehm_·_pfeh_·luhn
a barber	**einen Herrenfriseur** _ien_·uhn _hehr_·uhn·frih·zer
a dry cleaner	**eine Reinigung** _ien_·uh _rien_·ee·goong
a hairstylist	**einen Friseur** _ien_·uhn frih·_zer_
a laundromat [launderette]	**einen Waschsalon** _ien_·uhn _vahsh_·zah·lohn
a nail salon	**ein Nagelstudio** ien _nah_·gehl·shtood·yoh
a spa	**ein Wellness-Center** ien _vehl_·nuhs·_sehn_·tehr
a travel agency	**ein Reisebüro** ien _rie_·zuh·bew·roh
Can you...this?	**Können Sie das ...?** _kern_·uhn zee dahs ...
alter	**ändern** _ehn_·dehrn
clean	**reinigen** _rien_·ee·guhn
fix	**reparieren** reh·pah·_reer_·uhn
press	**bügeln** _bewg_·uhln
When will it be ready?	**Wann wird es fertig sein?** vahn veerd ehs _fehr_·teekh zien

Hair & Beauty

I'd like...	**Ich möchte ...** eekh _merkht_·uh ...
an appointment for today/tomorrow	**einen Termin für heute/morgen** _ien_·uhn tehr·_meen_ fewr _hoy_·tuh/_mohr_·guhn
some color/ highlights	**die Haare/Strähnchen gefärbt bekommen** dee _hah_·ruh/_shtrehnkh_·uhn guh·_ferbt_ buh·_kohm_·uhn
my hair styled/ blow-dried	**mein Haar stylen/fönen lassen** mien hahr _shtew_·luhn/_fern_·uhn _lahs_·uhn
a haircut	**einen Haarschnitt** _ien_·uhn _hahr_·shniht
an eyebrow/bikini wax	**eine Haarentfernung an den Augenbrauen/der Bikinizone** _ien_·uh _hahr_·ehnt·fehr·noong ahn dehn _ow_·guhn·brow·uhn/dehr bee·_kee_·nee·tsoh·nuh

a facial	**eine Gesichtsbehandlung**
	ien•uh guh•zeekhts•beh•hahnd•loong
a manicure/	**eine Maniküre/Pediküre** _ien•uh_
pedicure	_mahn•eh•kewruh/pede•eh•kewruh_
a (sports) massage	**eine (Sport-)Massage** _ien•uh (shport-) mah•sahdj•uh_
a trim	**die Haare nachschneiden lassen**
	dee hahr•uh nahkh•shnayd•uhn lahs•uhn

Not too short.	**Nicht zu kurz.** _neekht tsoo koorts_
Shorter here.	**Hier kürzer.** _heer kewrts•ehr_
Do you offer…?	**Machen Sie …?** _mahk•uhn zee …_
acupuncture	**Akupunktur** _ah•koo•poonk•toor_
aromatherapy	**Aromatherapie** _ah•roh•mah•teh•rah•pee_
oxygen treatment	**Sauerstoffbehandlung**
	zow•ehr•shtohf•beh•hahnd•loong
Do you have	**Haben Sie eine Sauna?** _hah•buhn zee ien•uh_
a sauna?	_zown•ah_

Health resorts, day spas and hotel spas are popular destinations, and there are hundreds throughout Germany. Most spa towns have the word **Bad** in their names, for example: Bad Reichenhall, Europe's largest saline source, in Bavaria; Baden-Baden, considered the best and most fashionable; Wiesbaden, one of Germany's oldest cities and considered second best only to Baden-Baden; Bad Homburg, at the foot of Taunus Hills, once the summer retreat of Prussian kings; and Bad Nauheim, famous because both William Randolph Hearst and Elvis Presley were once guests experiencing the healing powers of the carbonic acid springs.

Tipping varies by spa; ask about the tipping policy when booking or upon arrival.

Antiques

How old is it?	**Wie alt ist es?** *vee ahlt ihst ehs*
Do you have anything from the... period?	**Haben Sie etwas aus der ... Zeit?** *hah•buhn zee eht•vahs ows dehr ... tsiet*
Do I have to fill out any forms?	**Muss ich irgendwelche Formulare ausfüllen?** *moos eekh eer•guhnd•vehlkh•uh fohr•moo•lahr•uh ows•fewl•uhn*
Is there a certificate of authenticity?	**Gibt es ein Echtheitszeugnis?** *gihpt ehs ien ehkht•hiets•tsoyg•nuhs*
Can you ship/wrap it?	**Können Sie es liefern/einpacken?** *ker•nuhn zee ehs lee•fuhrn/ien•pahk•kuhn*

Clothing

I'd like...	**Ich möchte ...** *eekh merkht•uh ...*
Can I try this on?	**Kann ich das anprobieren?** *kahn eekh dahs ahn•proh•bee•ruhn*
It doesn't fit.	**Es passt nicht.** *ehs pahst neekht*
It's too...	**Es ist zu ...** *ehs ihst tsoo ...*
big/small	**groß/klein** *grohs/klien*
short/long	**kurz/lang** *koorts/lahng*
tight/loose	**eng/weit** *ehng/viet*

| Do you have this in size…? | **Haben Sie das in der Größe … ?**
 hah·buhn zee dahs ihn dehr _grers_·uh … |
| Do you have this in a bigger/ smaller size? | **Haben Sie das in einer größeren/kleineren Größe?** _hah_·buhn zee dahs ihn _ien_·ehr grers·ehr·uhn/klien·uh·ruhn _grers_·uh |

For Numbers, see page 165.

Colors

I'd like something…	**Ich möchte etwas …** eekh _merkht_·uh _eht_·vahs …
beige	**Beiges** _behdj_·uhs
black	**Schwarzes** _shvahrtz_·uhs
blue	**Blaues** _blow_·uhs
brown	**Braunes** _brown_·uhs
green	**Grünes** _grewn_·uhs
gray	**Graues** _grow_·uhs
orange	**Oranges** _oh_·rahnj·uhs
pink	**Pinkes** _peenk_·uhs
purple	**Violettes** vee·oh·_leht_·uhs
red	**Rotes** _roht_·uhs
white	**Weißes** _vies_·uhs
yellow	**Gelbes** _gehlb_·uhs

YOU MAY SEE...

HERRENABTEILUNG	men's (department)
DAMENABTEILUNG	women's (department)
KINDERABTEILUNG	children's (department)

Clothes & Accessories

a backpack	**der Rucksack**	*dehr rook•zahk*
a belt	**der Gürtel**	*dehr gewrt•uhl*
a bikini	**der Bikini**	*dehr bih•kee•nee*
a blouse	**die Bluse**	*dee bloo•zuh*
a bra	**der BH**	*dehr beh•hah*
briefs [underpants]	**der Schlüpfer**	*dehr shlewp•fehr*
panties	**die Unterhosen**	*dee oont•ehr•hoh•suhn*
a coat	**der Mantel**	*dehr mahnt•ehl*
a dress	**das Kleid**	*dahs klied*
a hat	**der Hut**	*dehr hoot*
a jacket	**die Jacke**	*dee yah•kuh*

YOU MAY HEAR...

Das steht Ihnen gut.
dahs shteht eehn•uhn goot

That looks great on you.

Passt es? *pahst ehs*

How does it fit?

Wir führen Ihre Größe nicht.
veer fewhr•uhn eehr•uh grers•uh neekht

We don't have your size.

jeans	**die Jeans** *dee djeens*
pajamas	**der Schlafanzug** *dehr shlahf·ahn·tsoog*
pants [trousers]	**die Hose** *dee hohz·uh*
pantyhose [tights]	**die Strumpfhose** *dee shtroompf·hoh·zuh*
a purse [handbag]	**die Handtasche** *dee hahnd·tahsh·uh*
a raincoat	**der Regenmantel** *dehr rehg·uhn·mahn·tuhl*
a scarf	**der Schal** *dehr shahl*
a shirt	**das Hemd** *dahs hehmt*
shorts	**die kurze Hose** *dee koortz·uh hohz·uh*
a skirt	**der Rock** *dehr rohk*
socks	**die Socken** *dee zohk·uhn*
a suit	**der Anzug** *dehr ahn·tsoog*
sunglasses	**die Sonnenbrille** *dee zohn·uhn·brihl·uh*
a sweater	**der Pullover** *dehr pool·oh·fehr*
a sweatshirt	**das Sweatshirt** *dahs sveht·shehrt*
a swimsuit	**der Badeanzug** *dehr bah·deh·ahn·tsoog*
a T-shirt	**das T-Shirt** *dahs tee·shert*
a tie	**die Krawatte** *dee krah·vah·tuh*
underwear	**die Unterwäsche** *dee oon·tehr·vehsh·uh*

Fabric

I'd like...	**Ich möchte ...** *eekh merkht·uh ...*
cotton	**Baumwolle** *bowm·vohl·uh*
denim	**Denim** *dehn·ihm*
lace	**Spitze** *shpihts·uh*
leather	**Leder** *lehd·ehr*
linen	**Leinen** *lien·uhn*
silk	**Seide** *zied·uh*
wool	**Wolle** *vohl·uh*
Is it machine washable?	**Ist es waschmaschinenfest?** *ihst ehs vahsh·mah·sheen·uhn·fehst*

Shoes

I'd like…	**Ich möchte …** _eekh merkht•uh …_
high-heels/flats	**Schuhe mit Absatz/ohne Absatz**
	shoo•uh miht ahp•zahts/ohn•uh ahb•zahts
boots	**Stiefel** _shtee•fuhl_
loafers	**Slipper** _slihp•ehr_
sandals	**Sandalen** _zahn•dahl•uhn_
shoes	**Schuhe** _shoo•uh_
slippers	**Badelatschen** _bah•duh•lahtsh•uhn_
sneakers	**Turnschuhe** _toorn•shoo•huh_
In size…	**In der Größe …** _ihn dehr grers•uh …_

For Numbers, see page 165.

For Numbers, see page 165.

Sizes

small (S)	**klein** _klein_
medium (M)	**mittel** _miht•tuhl_
large (L)	**gross** _grohs_
extra large (XL)	**extra gross** _ehks•trah grohs_
petite	**die Kurzgröße** _dee koorts•grer•suh_
plus size	**die Übergröße** _dee ew•buhr•grer•suh_

Newsagent & Tobacconist

Do you sell English-language newspapers?	**Haben Sie englischsprachige Zeitungen?** _hah•buhn zee ehng•leesh•shprah•khee•guh tsie•toong•uhn_
I'd like…	**Ich möchte …** _eekh merkht•uh …_
candy [sweets]	**Süßigkeiten** _zews•eekh•kiet•uhn_
chewing gum	**Kaugummi** _kow•goo•mee_
a chocolate bar	**einen Schokoladenriegel** _ien•uhn shoh•koh•lahd•uhn•ree•guhl_
a cigar	**eine Zigarre** _ien•uh tsee•gahr•uh_

a pack/carton of cigarettes	**eine Schachtel/Stange Zigaretten** _ien_•uh _shahkht_•uhl/_shtahng_•uh tsee•gahr•_eht_•uhn
a lighter	**ein Feuerzeug** ien _foy_•ehr•tsoyg
a magazine	**eine Zeitschrift** _ien_•uh _tsiet_•shrihft
matches	**Streichhölzer** _shtriekh_•herlts•uhr
a newspaper	**eine Zeitung** _ien_•uh _tsie_•toong
a pen	**einen Stift** _ien_•uhn shtihft
a postcard	**eine Postkarte** _ien_•uh _pohst_•kahr•tuh
a road/town map of…	**eine Straßenkarte/einen Stadtplan vonen …** _ien_•uh _shtrahsuhn_•kahrt•uh/_ien_•uhn _shtaht_•plahn fohn
stamps	**Briefmarken** _breef_•mahrk•uhn

Photography

I'd like a/an… camera.	**Ich möchte eine … Kamera.** eekh _merkht_•uh _ien_•uh … _kah_•meh•ruh
automatic	**automatische** ow•toh•_maht_•ihsh•uh
digital	**digitale** _dihd_•juh•tuhl
disposable	**Wegwerf-** _vehk_•vehrf-
I'd like…	**Ich möchte …** eekh _merkht_•uh …
a battery	**eine Batterie** _ien_•uh bah•tuh•_ree_
digital prints	**digitale Ausdrucke** _dihd_•juh•tuhl _ows_•drook•uh
a memory card	**eine Speicherkarte** _ien_•uh _shpie_•khuhr•kahrt•uh
Can I print digital photos here?	**Kann ich hier Digitalfotos ausdrucken lassen?** kahn eekh heer dihd•jih•_tahl_•foh•tohs _ows_•droo•kuhn _lahs_•uhn

In addition to small, medium and large, many clothing articles are labeled by continental size. As that size varies by manufacturer, be sure to try on any article before buying.

Souvenirs

Can I see this/that?	**Kann ich das sehen?**	*kahn eekh dahs <u>zeh</u>•uhn*
It's in the window/ display case.	**Es ist im Schaufenster/in der Vitrine.**	*ehs ihst ihm <u>show</u>•fehn•stehr/ihn dehr vih•<u>tree</u>•nuh*
I'd like...	**Ich möchte ...**	*eekh <u>merkht</u>•uh ...*
a battery	**eine Batterie**	*<u>ien</u>•uh bah•tuh•<u>ree</u>*
a bracelet	**ein Armband**	*ien <u>ahrm</u>•bahnt*
a brooch	**eine Brosche**	*<u>ien</u>•uh brohsh•uh*
a clock	**eine Uhr**	*<u>ien</u>•uh oohr*
earrings	**Ohrringe**	*<u>oh</u>•reeng•uh*
a necklace	**eine Kette**	*<u>ien</u>•uh <u>keht</u>•uh*
a ring	**einen Ring**	*<u>ien</u>•uhn reeng*
a watch	**eine Uhr**	*<u>ien</u>•uh oohr*
I'd like...	**Ich möchte ...**	*eekh <u>merkht</u>•uh ...*
a beer stein	**einen Bierkrug**	*ien•uh beer•kroog*
a bottle of wine	**eine Flasche Wein**	*ien•uh flahsh•uh vien*
a box of chocolates	**eine Schachtel Pralinen**	*ien•uh shahkht•uhl prah•lee•nuhn*
a doll	**eine Puppe**	*ien•uh poo•puh*
a key ring	**ein Schlüsselring**	*ien shlews•uhl•reeng*
a postcard	**eine Postkarte**	*ien•uh post•kahr•tuh*

pottery	**Töpferwaren** _terp·fuhr·vah·ruhn_
a T-shirt	**ein T-Shirt** _ien tee·shehrt_
a toy	**ein Spielzeug** _ien shpeel·tsoyg_
copper	**Kupfer** _koop·fehr_
crystal	**Kristall** _krihs·tahl_
diamonds	**Diamanten** _dee·ah·mahn·tuhn_
white/yellow gold	**Weißgold/Gelbgold** _vies·gohlt/gehlb·gohlt_
pearls	**Perlen** _pehr·luhn_
pewter	**Zinn** _tsihn_
platinum	**Platin** _plah·teen_
sterling silver	**Sterlingsilber** _shtehr·leeng·zihl·behr_
Is this real?	**Ist das echt?** _ihst dahs ehkht_
Can you engrave it?	**Können Sie etwas eingravieren?**
	ker·nuhn zee eht·vahs ien·grah·vee·ruhn

One of Germany's most famous products is the Black Forest cuckoo clock. Though very expensive, these clocks will last for generations if properly cared for. Another popular and less expensive souvenir is a traditional German beer stein. Collector beer steins are made from clay, glass or pewter and can be brightly painted, with or without a lid and engraved. Germany is also known for its toys: wooden figurines, porcelain dolls and model trains. Other souvenirs include: **lederhosen** (traditional German pants), lace and porcelain.

Sport & Leisure

ESSENTIAL

When's the game?	**Wann findet das Spiel statt?** *vahn fihnd•uht dahs shpeel shtaht*
Where's . . . ?	**Wo ist . . . ?** *voh ihst . . .*
the beach	**der Strand** *dehr shtrahnd*
the park	**der Park** *dehr pahrk*
the pool	**der Pool** *dehr pool*
Is it safe to swim here?	**Kann man hier schwimmen?** *kahn mahn heer shvihm•uhn*
Can I hire golf clubs?	**Kann ich Golfschläger ausleihen?** *kahn eekh gohlf•shlelig•ehr ows•lie•uhn*
How much per hour?	**Wie viel kostet es pro Stunde?** *vee feel kohs•tuht ehs proh shtoond•uh*
How far is it to . . . ?	**Wie weit ist es bis zum** *m* **/zur** *f* **. . . ?** *vee viet ihst ehs bihs tsoom /tsoor . . .*
Show me on the map, please.	**Zeigen Sie es mir bitte auf dem Stadtplan.** *tsieg•uhn zee ehs meer biht•tuh owf dehm shtaht•plahn*

Watching Sport

When's . . . ?	**Wann findet . . . statt?** *vahn fihnd•uht . . . shtaht*
the baseball game	**das Baseballspiel** *dahs behs•bahl•shpeel*
the basketball game	**das Basketballspiel** *dahs bahs•kuht•bahl•shpeel*
the boxing match	**der Boxkampf** *dehr bohx•kahmpf*
the cricket match	**das Cricket-Turnier** *dahs krih•kuht•toor•neer*
the cycling race	**das Radrennen** *dahs rahd•rehn•uhn*

the golf tournament	**das Golfturnier** dahs <u>gohlf</u>•toor•neer
the soccer [football] game	**das Fußballspiel** dahs <u>foos</u>•bahl•shpeel
the tennis match	**das Tennismatch** dahs <u>tehn</u>•ihs•mahch
the volleyball game	**das Volleyballspiel** dahs <u>voh</u>•lee•bahl•shpeel
Who's playing?	**Wer spielt?** vehr shpeelt
Where's the racetrack/stadium?	**Wo ist die Rennbahn/das Stadion?** voh ihst dee <u>rehn</u>•bahn/dahs <u>shtah</u>•dyohn
Where can I place a bet?	**Wo kann ich eine Wette abschließen?** voh kahn eekh <u>ien</u>•uh <u>veh</u>•tuh <u>ahp</u>•shlees•uhn

For Tickets, see page 19.

Playing Sport

Where is/are...?	**Wo ist/sind ...?** voh ihst/zihnt ...
the golf course	**der Golfplatz** dehr <u>gohlf</u>•plahts
the gym	**die Sporthalle** dee <u>shpohrt</u>•hah•luh
the park	**der Park** dehr pahrk
the tennis courts	**die Tennisplätze** dee <u>tehn</u>•ihs•pleht•suh
How much per...	**Wie viel kostet es pro ...** vee feel <u>kohs</u>•tuht ehs proh ...
day	**Tag** tak
hour	**Stunde** <u>shtoond</u>•uh
game	**Spiel** shpeel
round	**Runde** <u>roond</u>•uh
Can I rent [hire]...?	**Kann ich ... ausleihen?** kahn eekh ... <u>ows</u>•lie•huhn
golf clubs	**Golfschläger** <u>gohlf</u>•shlehg•ehr
equipment	**eine Ausrüstung** <u>ien</u>•uh <u>ows</u>•rews•toong
a racket	**einen Schläger** <u>ien</u>•uhn <u>shlehg</u>•ehr

Are there lessons?	**Kann man Stunden nehmen?**
	kahn mahn shtoond•uhn neh•muhn
I'm a beginner.	**Ich bin Anfänger.** *eekh bihn ahn•fehng•ehr*
I'm experienced.	**Ich bin erfahren.** *eekh been ehr•fahr•uhn*
A trail [piste] map, please.	**Bitte einen Pistenplan.** *biht•tuh ien•uhn pees•tuhn•plahn*

YOU MAY SEE...

SCHLEPPLIFT	drag lift
SEILBAHN	cable car
SESSELLIFT	chair lift
ANFÄNGER	novice
FORTGESCHRITTENE	intermediate
KÖNNER	expert
PISTE GESCHLOSSEN	trail [piste] closed

Germany's most popular sport is **Fußball** (soccer); in fact, Germany has won the World Cup three times. Tennis is another popular sport; the German Tennis Federation boasts membership of more than one million. Other popular sports include biking, hiking, handball, basketball, volleyball, ice hockey, golf and horseback riding. Casinos are found throughout Germany. The spa towns, in particular, are home to well-known casinos.

At the Beach/Pool

Where's the beach/pool?	**Wo ist der Strand/Pool?** *voh ihst dehr shtrahnt/pool*
Is there a...?	**Gibt es einen ...?** *gihpt ehs ien•uhn ...*
kiddie pool	**Pool für Kinder** *pool fewr kihnd•ehr*
indoor/outdoor pool	**Hallenbad/Freibad** *hahl•ehn•baht/frie•baht*
lifeguard	**Rettungsschwimmer** *reht•oongs•shvihm•ehr*

Germany's main beach areas are located along the North Sea and Baltic Sea coasts. There are numerous types of beaches in Germany, including family, adults-only and nude beaches. A few of the more popular areas include Sylt, known for its nude beaches; Büsum, an intimate small town with calm North Sea waters; Helgoland, a Frisian island in the North Sea; Heiligendamm, Germany's oldest seaside resort; Heringsdorf, on the island of Usedom; and Kühlungsborn and Warnemünde, located on the Baltic Sea.

Is it safe to swim/dive?	**Ist es sicher zu schwimmen/tauchen?** *ihst ehs <u>sihk</u>•hehr tsoo <u>shvihm</u>•uhn/<u>towkh</u>•uhn*
Is it safe for children?	**Ist es kindgerecht?** *ihst ehs <u>kihnt</u>•guh•rehkht*
I'd like to rent hire…	**Ich möchte gern … ausleihen.** *eekh <u>merkht</u>•uh gehrn … <u>ows</u>•lie•uhn*
a deck chair	**einen Liegestuhl** *ien•uhn <u>leeg</u>•uh•shtoohl*
diving equipment	**eine Tauchausrüstung** *ien•uh <u>towkh</u>•ows•rew•stoong*
a jet ski	**einen Jet Ski** *ien•uhn djeht skee*
a motorboat	**ein Motorboot** *ien <u>moht</u>•ohr•boht*
a rowboat	**ein Ruderboot** *ien <u>rood</u>•ehr•boht*
snorkeling equipment	**eine Schnorchelausrüstung** *ien•uh <u>shnohr</u>•khehl•ows•rew•stoong*
a surfboard	**ein Surfboard** *ien <u>soorf</u>•bohrd*
a towel	**ein Handtuch** *ien <u>hahnd</u>•tookh*
an umbrella	**einen Schirm** *ien•uhn sheerm*
water skis	**Wasserski** *<u>vahs</u>•ehr•shee*
a windsurfer	**ein Surfbrett** *ien serf•breht*
For…hours.	**Für … Stunden.** *fewr … <u>shtoond</u>•uhn*

Winter Sports

A lift pass for a day/ five days, please.	**Einen Liftpass für einen Tag/fünf Tage, bitte.** *ien•uhn <u>lihft</u>•pahs fewr ien•uhn tahk/fewnf <u>tahg</u>•uh <u>biht</u>•tuh*
I'd like to hire…	**Ich möchte gerne … ausleihen.** *eekh <u>merkht</u>•uh <u>gehr</u>•nuh … <u>ows</u>•lie•uhn*
boots	**Stiefel** *<u>shteef</u>•uhl*
a helmet	**einen Helm** *ien•uhn hehlm*
poles	**Stöcke** *<u>shterk</u>•uh*
skis	**Skier** *skee•ehr*
a snowboard	**ein Snowboard** *ien <u>snohw</u>•bohrd*
snowshoes	**Schneeschuhe** *<u>shneh</u>•shoo•uh*
These are too big/small.	**Diese sind zu groß/klein.** *<u>dee</u>•zuh zihnt tsoo grohs/klien*

Winter offers plenty of opportunities for outdoor activity in Germany. Alpine skiing, snowboarding, cross-country skiing, ice skating, tobogganing and hiking are just some of the options available to winter travelers.

Out in the Country

A map of..., please.	**Eine Karte ..., bitte.** _ien_·uh _kahrt_·uh ... _biht_·tuh
this region	**dieser Region** _deez_·uhr rehg·_yohn_
the walking routes	**mit Wanderrouten** miht _vahnd_·ehr·root·uhn
the bike routes	**mit Radrouten** miht _rahd_·root·uhn
the trails	**mit Wanderwegen** miht _vahnd_·ehr·veh·guhn
Is it...?	**Ist es ...?** ihst ehs ...
easy	**leicht** liekht
difficult	**schwierig** _shveer_·eeg
far	**weit** viet
steep	**steil** shtiel
How far is it to...?	**Wie weit ist es bis ...?** vee viet ihst ehs bihs ...
Show me on the map, please.	**Zeigen Sie es mir bitte auf der Karte.** _tsieg_·uhn zee ehs meer _biht_·tuh owf dehr _kahrt_·uh
I'm lost.	**Ich habe mich verlaufen.** eekh _hahb_·uh meekh fehr·_lowf_·uhn
Where's...?	**Wo ist ...?** voh ihst ...
the bridge	**die Brücke** dee _brew_·kuh
the cave	**die Höhle** dee _her_·luh
the canyon	**der Canyon** dehr _kahn_·yohn
the cliff	**die Klippe** dee _klih_·puh
the desert	**die Wüste?** dee vews·tuh
the farm	**der Bauernhof** dehr _bow_·ehrn·hohf
the field	**das Feld** dahs fehld
the forest	**der Wald** dehr vahld
the hill	**der Hügel** dehr _hew_·gehl
the lake	**der See** dehr zeh
the mountain	**der Berg** dehr behrg
the nature preserve	**das Naturschutzgebiet** dahs _nah_·toor·shoots·guh·beet
the viewpoint	**der Aussichtspunkt** dehr _ows_·seekhts·poonkt

the park	**der Park** *dehr pahrk*
the path	**der Pfad** *dehr pfahd*
the peak	**der Gipfel** *dehr <u>gihp</u>•fuhl*
the picnic area	**der Picknickplatz** *dehr <u>pihk</u>•nihk•plahts*
the pond	**der Teich** *dehr tiekh*
the ravine	**die Schlucht** *dee shlookht*
the river	**der Fluss** *dehr floos*
the sea	**das Meer** *dahs mehr*
the (hot) spring	**die (heiße) Quelle** *dee (<u>hie</u>•suh) <u>kveh</u>•luh*
the stream	**der Strom** *dehr shtrom*
the valley	**das Tal** *dahs tahl*
the village	**das Dorf** *dahs dohrf*
the vineyard	**das Weingut** *dahs <u>vien</u>•goot*
the waterfall	**der Wasserfall** *dehr <u>vahs</u>•ehr•fahl*

Going Out

ESSENTIAL

What's there to do at night?	**Was kann man dort abends unternehmen?** *vahs kahn mahn dohrt <u>ahb</u>•uhnds oon•tehr•<u>nehm</u>•uhn*
Do you have a program of events?	**Haben Sie ein Veranstaltungsprogramm?** *hah•buhn zee ien fehr•<u>ahn</u>•shtahlt•oongs•prohg•rahm*
What's playing tonight?	**Was wird heute Abend aufgeführt?** *vahs vihrd <u>hoyt</u>•uh <u>ahb</u>•uhnd <u>owf</u>•guh•fewrt*
Where's …?	**Wo ist …?** *voh ihst …*
the downtown area	**das Stadtzentrum** *dahs <u>shtadt</u>•tsehn•troom*
the bar	**die Bar** *dee bahr*
the dance club	**der Tanzclub** *dee <u>tahnts</u>•kloop*
Is there a cover charge?	**Kostet es Eintritt?** *<u>kohs</u>•tuht ehs <u>ien</u>•triht*

Entertainment

Can you recommend...?	**Können Sie ... empfehlen?** _kern_·uhn zee ... ehm·_pfeh_·luhn
a concert	**ein Konzert** ien kohn·_tsehrt_
a movie	**einen Film** _ien_·uhn feelm
an opera	**eine Oper** _ien_·uhn _oh_·pehr
a play	**ein Theaterstück** ien teh·_ah_·tehr·shtewk
When does it start/end?	**Wann beginnt/endet es?** vahn beh·_gihnt_/_ehnd_·eht ehs
Where's ...?	**Wo ist ...?** voh ihst ...
the concert hall	**die Konzerthalle** dee kohn·_tsehrt_·hah·luh
the opera house	**das Opernhaus** dahs _oh_·pehrn·hows

YOU MAY HEAR...

Bitte schalten Sie Ihre Handys aus.
biht·tuh _shahlt_·uhn zee _eehr_·uh _hehnd_·ees ows

Turn off your mobile [cell] phones, please.

the theater	**das Theater** *dahs teh·ah·tehr*
the arcade	**die Spielhalle?** *dee shpeel·hah·luh*
What's the dress code?	**Wie ist die Kleiderordnung?** *vee ihst dee klied·ehr·ohrd·noong*
I like...	**Mir gefällt ...** *meer guh·fehlt ...*
classical music	**klassische Musik** *klahs·ihsh·uh moo·zeek*
folk music	**Volksmusik** *fohlks·moo·zeek*
jazz	**Jazz** *djehz*
pop music	**Popmusik** *pohp·moo·zeek*
rap	**Rap** *rehp*

For Tickets, see page 19.

Nightlife

What's there to do at night?	**Was kann man dort abends unternehmen?** *vahs kahn mahn dohrt ah·uhnds oont·ehr·nehm·uhn*
Can you recommend...?	**Können Sie ... empfehlen?** *kern·uhn zee ... ehm·pfeh·luhn*
a bar	**eine Bar** *ien·uh bahr*
a cabaret	**eine Kabarettvorstellung** *ie·nuh kah·bah·reht·fohr·shteh·loong*
a casino	**ein Casino** *ien kah·see·noh*

Listings of regional events can be found in local newspapers.
The local tourist information office and your hotel concierge can
be useful sources of information about local events, and may also be
able to help you obtain tickets and plan transportation.

a dance club	**einen Tanzclub** _ien_·uhn _tahnts_·kloop
a gay club	**einen Schwulenclub** _ien_·uhn _shvoo_·luhn·kloop
a jazz club	**einen Jazzclub** _ien_·uhn _yahts_·kloop
a club with German music	**ein Club mit deutscher Musik** _ien cloob meet doyt·shuhr muh·seek_
Is there live music?	**Gibt es dort Livemusik?** _gihpt ehs dohrt liev·moo·zeek_
How do I get there?	**Wie komme ich dorthin?** _vee kohm·uh eekh dohrt·hihn_
Is there a cover charge?	**Kostet es Eintritt?** _kohs·tuht ehs ien·triht_
Let's go dancing.	**Lass uns tanzen gehen.** _ahs oons tahnt·suhn geh·uhn_
Is this area safe at night?	**Ist dieses Gebiet bei Nacht sicher?** _ihst dee·zuhs geh·beet bie nahkht zeek·hehr_

Special Requirements

Business Travel

ESSENTIAL

I'm here on business.	**Ich bin geschäftlich hier.**
	eekh been guh·shehft·leekh heer
Here's my business card.	**Hier ist meine Visitenkarte.** *heer ihst*
	mien·uh vih·zee·tuhn·kahr·tuh
Can I have your card?	**Kann ich Ihre Karte haben?**
	kahn eekh ihhr·uh kahrt·uh hah·buhn
I have a meeting with…	**Ich habe ein Meeting mit …**
	eekh hahb·uh ien mee·teeng miht …
Where's…?	**Wo ist…?** *voh ihst*
the convention hall	**der Kongressaal** *dehr kohn·grehs·sahl*
the meeting room	**das Konferenzzimmer**
	dahs kohn·fehr·ehnts·tsihm·her

Germans are generally formal and so are their greetings.
Business introductions are always accompanied by a handshake.
Address business colleagues by title: **Herr** (Mr.), **Frau** (Miss/Ms./
Mrs.) or **Herr Dr.** (Dr.) and the person's last name. **Herr Professor** and
Frau Professor are also used, but usually without a last name.

On Business

I'm here for…	**Ich bin für … hier.** *eekh been fuer … heer*
a seminar	**ein Seminar** *ien zehm·ee·nahr*
a conference	**eine Konferenz** *ien·uh kohn·feh·rehnts*
a meeting	**ein Meeting** *ien mee·teeng*

138

My name is...	**Mein Name ist ...** *mien nahm·uh ihst ...*
May I introduce my colleague...?	**Darf ich Ihnen meinen Kollegen ... vorstellen?** *dahrf eekh eehn·uhn mien·uhn koh·leh·guhn ... fohr·shtehl·uhn*
Pleasure to meet you.	**Freut mich.** *froyt meekh*
I have a meeting/an appointment with...	**Ich habe ein Meeting/einen Termin mit ...** *eekh hahb·uh ien mee·teeng/ien·uhn tehr·meen miht ...*
I'm sorry I'm late.	**Es tut mir leid, dass ich spät bin.** *ehs toot meer lied dahs eekh shpayt bih*
I need an interpreter.	**Ich brauche einen Dolmetscher.** *eek browkh·uh ien·uhn dohl·meh·chehr*
You can contact me at the...Hotel.	**Sie können mich im ... Hotel erreichen.** *zee kern·uhn meekh ihm ... hoh·tehl ehr·riekh·uhn*

YOU MAY HEAR...

Haben Sie einen Termin? *hah·buhn zee ien·uhn tehr·meen*	Do you have an appointment?
Mit wem? *meet vehm*	With whom?
Er *m*/Sie *f* ist in einem Meeting. *ehr/zee ihst ihn ien·uhm mee·teeng*	He/She is in a meeting.
Einen Moment, bitte. *ien·uhn moh·mehnt biht·tuh*	One moment, please.
Nehmen Sie Platz. *nehm·uhn zee plats*	Have a seat.
Möchten Sie etwas zu trinken? *merkht·uhn zee eht·vahs tsoo trihnk·uhn*	Would you like something to drink?
Vielen Dank für Ihr Kommen. *feel·uhn dahnk fewr eehr kohm·uhn*	Thank you for coming.

I'm here until…	**Ich bin bis … hier.** *eekh bihn bihs … heer*
I need to…	**Ich muss …** *eekh moos …*
make a call	**telefonieren** *tehl•eh•fohn•eer•uhn*
make a photocopy	**eine Kopie machen** *ien•uh koh•pee•uh mahkh•uhn*
send an e-mail	**eine E-Mail senden** *ien•uh ee•mehl zehnd•uhn*
send a fax	**ein Fax senden** *ien fahx zehnd•uhn*
send a package (for next-day delivery)	**ein Paket schicken (per Express)** *ien pah•keht shihk•uhn (pehr ehks•prehs)*
It was a pleasure to meet you.	**Es war schön, Sie kennenzulernen.** *ehs vahr shern zee keh•nehn•tsoo•lehr•nehn*

For Communications, see page 49.

Traveling with Children

ESSENTIAL

Is there a discount for kids?	**Gibt es Ermäßigung für Kinder?** *gihpt ehs ehr·meh·see·goong fewr kihn·dehr*
Can you recommend a babysitter?	**Können Sie einen Babysitter empfehlen?** *kern·uhn zee ien·uhn beh·bee·siht·ehr ehm·pfeh·luhn*
Do you have a child's seat/highchair?	**Haben Sie einen Kindersitz/Kinderstuhl?** *hah·buhn zee ien·uhn kihnd·ehr·zihts/ kihnd·ehr·shtoohl*
Where can I change the baby?	**Wo kann ich das Baby wickeln?** *voh kahn eekh dahs beh·bee vihk·uhln*

Out & About

Can you recommend something for kids?	**Können Sie etwas für Kinder empfehlen?** _kern•uhn zee eht•vahs fewr kihnd•ehr ehm•pfeh•luhn_
Where's…?	**Wo ist …?** _voh ihst …_
the amusement park	**der Vergnügungspark** _dehr fehrg•new•goongs•pahrk_
the arcade	**die Spielhalle?** _dee shpeel•hah•luh_
the kiddie [paddling] pool	**das Kinderbecken** _dahs kihnd•ehr•beh•kuhn_
the park	**der Park** _dehr pahrk_
the playground	**der Spielplatz** _dehr shpeel•plats_
the zoo	**der Zoo** _dehr tsoh_
Are kids allowed?	**Sind Kinder erlaubt?** _zihnt kihnd•ehr ehr•lowbt_
Is it safe for kids?	**Ist es für Kinder geeignet?** _ihst ehs fewr kihnd•ehr guh•ieg•nuht_
Is it suitable for… year olds?	**Ist es für … Jahre alte Kinder geeignet?** _ihst ehs fewr … yah•ruh ahlt•uh kihnd•ehr guh•ieg•nuht_

For Numbers, see page 165.

YOU MAY HEAR…

Wie süß! _vee zews_	How cute!
Wie heißt er _m_ /sie _f_? _vee hiest ehr/zee_	What's his/her name?
Wie alt ist er _m_ /sie _f_? _vee ahlt ihst ehr/zee_	How old is he/she?

Baby Essentials

Do you have…?	**Haben Sie …?** _hah·buhn zee_ …
a baby bottle	**eine Babyflasche** _ien·uh beh·bee·flahsh·uh_
baby food	**Babynahrung** _beh·bee·nahr·oong_
baby wipes	**feuchte Babytücher** _foykh·tuh beh·bee·tewkh·ehr_
a car seat	**einen Kindersitz** _ien·uhn kihnd·ehr·zihts_
a children's menu/ portion	**ein Kindermenü/eine Kinderportion** _ien·uhn kihnd·ehr·meh·new/ien·uh kihnd·ehr·pohrtz·yohn·uhn_
a child's seat/ highchair	**einen Kindersitz/Kinderstuhl** _ien·uhn kihnd·ehr·zihts/kihnd·ehr·shtoohl_
a crib/cot	**ein Gitterbett/Kinderbett** _ien giht·tehr·beht/kihnd·ehr·beht_
diapers [nappies]	**Windeln** _vihnd·uhln_
formula [baby food]	**Babynahrung** _beh·bee·nah·roong_
a pacifier [dummy]	**einen Schnuller** _ien·uhn shnool·ehr_
a playpen	**einen Laufstall** _ien·uhn lowf·shtahl_
a stroller [pushchair]	**einen Kinderwagen** _ien·uhn kihnd·ehr·vahg·uhn_
Can I breastfeed the baby here?	**Kann ich das Baby hier stillen?** _kahn eekh dahs beh·bee heer shtihl·uhn_
Where can I breastfeed/change the baby?	**Wo kann ich das Baby stillen/wickeln?** _voh kahn eekh dahs beh·bee shtihl·uhn/vihk·uhln_

For Dining with Children, see page 65.

Babysitting

Can you recommend a babysitter?	**Können Sie einen Babysitter empfehlen?** _kern·uhn zee ien·uhn beh·bee·siht·ehr ehm·pfeh·luhn_
What is the cost?	**Was sind die Kosten?** _vahs zihnt dee kohs·tuhn_

I'll be back by…	**Ich bin um … zurück.** *eekh been oom … tsoo·rewk*
If you need to	**Ich bin unter … zu erreichen.**
contact me, call…	*eekh been oont·ehr … tsoo ehr·riekh·uhn*

For Time, see page 166

Health & Emergency

Can you recommend	**Können Sie einen Kinderarzt empfehlen?**
a pediatrician?	*kern·uhn zee ien·uhn kihnd·ehr·ahrtst ehm·pfeh·luhn*
My child is	**Mein Kind ist allergisch auf …**
allergic to…	*mien kihnt ihst ah·lehrg·eesh owf …*
My child is missing.	**Mein Kind ist weg.** *mien kihnt ihst vehk*
Have you seen	**Haben Sie einen Jungen/ein Mädchen gesehen?**
a boy/girl?	*hah·buhn zee ien·uhn yoong·uhn/ien meht·khuhn*
	guh·zeh·uhn

For Meals & Cooking, see page 67.

For Health, see page 150.

For Police, see page 148.

Disabled Travelers

ESSENTIAL

Is there…?	**Gibt es …?** *gihpt ehs …*
access for the disabled	**einen Zugang für Behinderte** *ien•uhn tsoo•gahng fewr beh•hihnd•ehrt•uh*
a wheelchair ramp	**eine Rollstuhlrampe** *ien•uh rohl•shtool•rahm•puh*
a disabled-accessible toilet	**eine Behindertentoilette** *ien•uh beh•hihn•dehrt•uhn•toy•leh•tuh*
I need…	**Ich brauche …** *eekh browkh•uh …*
assistance	**Hilfe** *hihlf•uh*
an elevator [a lift]	**einen Fahrstuhl** *ien•uhn fahr•shtool*
a ground-floor room	**ein Zimmer im Erdgeschoss** *ien tsihm•ehr ihm ehrd•guh•shohs*

Asking for Assistance

I'm...	**Ich bin ...** *eekh bihn ...*
disabled	**behindert** *beh•hihn•dehrt*
visually impaired	**sehbehindert** *zeh•buh•hihn•dehrt*
hearing impaired/ deaf	**hörgeschädigt/taub** *her•guh•sheh•deegt/towb*
I'm unable to walk far/use the stairs.	**Ich kann nicht weit laufen/die Treppe benutzen.** *eekh kahn neekht viet low•fuhn/dee trehp•uh beh•noot•suhn*
Please speak louder.	**Bitte sprechen Sie lauter.** *biht•tuh shprehkh•uhn zee lowt•ehr*
Can I bring my wheelchair?	**Kann ich meinen Rollstuhl mitbringen?** *kahn eekh mien•uhn rohl•shtoohl miht•brihng•uhn*
Are guide dogs permitted?	**Sind Blindenhunde erlaubt?** *zihnt blihnd•uhn•hoond•uh ehr•lowbt*
Can you help me?	**Können Sie mir helfen?** *kern•uhn zee meer hehlf•uhn*
Please open/hold the door.	**Bitte öffnen/halten Sie die Tür.** *biht•tuh erf•nuhn/hahlt•uhn zee dee tewr*

In an Emergency

Emergencies

ESSENTIAL

Help!	**Hilfe!** _hihlf_·uh
Go away!	**Gehen Sie weg!** _geh_·uhn zee vehk
Stop, thief!	**Haltet den Dieb!** _hahlt_·uht dehn deeb
Get a doctor!	**Holen Sie einen Arzt!** _hohl_·uhn zee _ien_·uhn ahrtst
Fire!	**Feuer!** _foy_·ehr
I'm lost.	**Ich habe mich verlaufen.** eekh _hahb_·uh meekh fehr·_lowf_·uhn
Can you help me?	**Können Sie mir helfen?** _kern_·uhn zee meer _hehlf_·uhn

YOU MAY HEAR...

Füllen Sie dieses Formular aus.
fewl·uhn zee _deez_·uhs fohr·moo·_lahr_ ows

Fill out this form.

Ihren Ausweis, bitte.
eehr·uhn ows·vies _biht_·tuh

Your ID, please.

Wann/Wo ist es passiert?
vahn/voh ihst ehs _pah_·seert

When/Where did it happen?

Wie sah er _m_ /sie _f_ aus?
vee zah ehr/zee ows

What does he/she look like?

Police

ESSENTIAL

Call the police!	**Rufen Sie die Polizei!** _roof_•uhn zee dee poh•leet•_sie_
Where's the police station?	**Wo ist das Polizeirevier?** voh ihst dahs poh•leet•_sie_•ruh•veer
There was an accident/attack.	**Es gab einen Unfall/Überfall.** ehs gahb _ien_•uhn _oon_•fahl/_ewb_•ehr•fahl
My child is missing.	**Mein Kind ist weg.** mien kihnt ihst vehk
I need an interpreter.	**Ich brauche einen Dolmetscher.** eekh _browkh_•uh _ien_•uhn _dohl_•mech•ehr
I need to contact my lawyer/make a phone call.	**Ich muss mit meinem Anwalt sprechen/ telefonieren.** eekh moos miht _mien_•uhm _ahn_•vahlt _shpreh_•khehn/tehl•eh•fohn•_eer_•uhn
I'm innocent.	**Ich bin unschuldig.** eekh bihn _oon_•shoold•eekh

In an emergency, dial: **110** for the police
112 for the fire brigade
115 for the ambulance

Crime & Lost Property

I want to report…	**Ich möchte … melden.** eekh _merkht_•uh … _mehld_•uhn
a mugging	**einen Überfall** _ien_•uhn _ewb_•ehr•fahl
a rape	**eine Vergewaltigung** _ien_•uh fehr•guh•_vahlt_•ee•goong
a theft	**einen Diebstahl** _ien_•uhn _deeb_•shtahl

I've been mugged	**Ich wurde überfallen**
	eekh voor•duh ewb•ehr•fahl•uhn
I've been robbed	**Ich wurde beraubt** _eekh voor•duh beh•rowbt_
I've lost…	**Ich habe … verloren.**
	eekh hahb•uh … fehr•lohr•uhn
…was stolen.	**… wurde gestohlen.** … _voor•duh_
	geh•shtohl•uhn
My backpack	**Mein Rucksack** _mien rook•zahk_
My bicycle	**Mein Fahrrad** _mien fahr•ahd_
My camera	**Meine Kamera** _mien•uh kah•meh•rah_
My (hire) car	**Mein Mietauto** _mien meet•ow•toh_
My computer	**Mein Computer** _mien kohm•pjoo•tehr_
My credit card	**Meine Kreditkarte** _mien•uh kreh•deet•kahrt•uh_
My jewelry	**Mein Schmuck** _mien shmook_
My money	**Mein Geld** _mien gehlt_
My passport	**Mein Reisepass** _mien riez•uh•pahs_
My purse [handbag]	**Meine Handtasche** _mien•uh hahnd•tahsh•uh_
My traveler's checks [cheques]	**Meine Reiseschecks** _mien•uh riez•uh•shehks_
My wallet	**Meine Brieftasche** _mien•uh breef•tahsh•uh_

I need a police report.	**Ich brauche einen Polizeibericht.**
	eekh browkh·uh ien·uhn poh·leet·sie·beh·reekht
Where is the British/American/Irish embassy?	**Wo ist die britische/amerikanische/irische Botschaft?** *voh ihst dee brih·tih·shuh/ah·meh·rih·kah·nih·shuh/eer·ih·shuh boht·shaft*

Health

ESSENTIAL

I'm sick.	**Ich bin krank.** *eekh bihn krahnk*
I need an English-speaking doctor.	**Ich brauche einen englischsprechenden Arzt.** *eekh browkh·uh ien·uhn ehng·glihsh·shprehkh·ehnd·uhn ahrtst*
It hurts here.	**Es tut hier weh.** *ehs toot heer veh*
I have a stomachache.	**Ich habe Magenschmerzen.** *eekh hahb·uh mahg·uhn·shmehrt·suhn*

Finding a Doctor

Can you recommend a doctor/dentist?	**Können Sie einen Arzt/Zahnarzt empfehlen?** *kern·uhn zee ien·uhn ahrtst/tsahn·ahrtst ehm·pfeh·luhn*
Can the doctor come here?	**Kann der Arzt herkommen?** *kahn dehr ahrtst hehr·kohm·uhn*
I need an English-speaking doctor.	**Ich brauche einen englischsprechenden Arzt.** *eekh browkh·uh ien·uhn ehng·gleesh·shprehkh·ehnd·uhn ahrtst*
What are the office hours?	**Wann sind die Sprechstunden?** *vahn zihnt dee shprekh·shtoond·uhn*
It's urgent.	**Es ist dringend.** *ehs ihst dreeng·uhnt*

I'd like an appointment for...	**Ich möchte einen Termin für ...** *eekh merkht·uh ien·uhn tehr·meen fewr ...*
today	**heute** *hoy·tuh*
tomorrow	**morgen** *mohr·guhn*
as soon as possible	**so bald wie möglich** *zoh bahld vee merg·leekh*

Symptoms

I'm bleeding.	**Ich blute.** *eekh bloot·uh*
I'm constipated.	**Ich habe Verstopfung.** *eekh hahb·uh fehr·shtohpf·oong*
I'm dizzy.	**Mir ist schwindlig.** *meer ihst shvihnd·leekh*
I'm nauseous.	**Mir ist schlecht.** *meer ihst shlehkht*
I'm vomiting.	**Ich übergebe mich.** *eekh ewb·ehr·gehb·uh meekh*
It hurts here.	**Es tut hier weh.** *ehs toot heer veh*
I have...	**Ich habe ...** *eekh hahb·uh ...*
an allergic reaction	**eine allergische Reaktion** *ien·uh ah·lehr·geesh·uh reh·ahk·syon*
chest pain	**Brustschmerzen** *broost·shmehrt·suhn*
cramps	**Krämpfe** *krehmp·fuh*
diarrhea	**Durchfall** *doorkh·fahl*
an earache	**Ohrenschmerzen** *oht·uhn·shmehrt·suhn*
a fever	**Fieber** *feeb·ehr*
pain	**Schmerzen** *shmehrt·suhn*
a rash	**einen Ausschlag** *ien·uhn ows·shlahg*
a sprain	**eine Verstauchung** *ien·uh fehr·shtowkh·oong*
some swelling	**eine Schwellung** *ien·uh shvehl·oong*
a sore throat	**Halsschmerzen** *hahls·shmehrt·suhn*
a stomachache	**Magenschmerzen** *mahg·uhn·shmehrt·suhn*
sunstroke	**einen Sonnenstich** *ien·uhn zohn·uhn·shteekh*
I've been sick [ill] for...days.	**Ich bin seit ... Tagen krank.** *eekh bihn ziet ... tahg·uhn krahnk*

YOU MAY HEAR...

Was stimmt nicht mit Ihnen?
vahs shtihmt neekht miht eehn•uhn

What's wrong?

Wo tut es weh? *voh toot ehs veh*

Where does it hurt?

Tut es hier weh? *toot ehs heer veh*

Does it hurt here?

Nehmen Sie Medikamente?
nehm•uhn zee mehd•ee•kah•mehnt•uh

Are you on
medication?

Sind Sie auf irgendetwas allergisch?
zihnt zee owf eer•guhnd•eht•vahs ah•lehr•geesh

Are you allergic to
anything?

Öffnen Sie Ihren Mund.
erf•nuhn zee eehr•uhn moont

Open your mouth.

Tief einatmen. *teef ien•aht•muhn*

Breathe deeply.

Bitte husten. *biht•tuh hoos•tuhn*

Cough, please.

Gehen Sie ins Krankenhaus.
geh•uhn zee ihns krahnk•uhn•hows

Go to the hospital.

Es ist ... *ehs ihst ...*

It's...

   gebrochen *geh•brohkh•uhn*

broken

   ansteckend *ahn•shtehk•uhnt*

contagious

   infiziert *een•fee•tseert*

infected

   verstaucht *fehr•shtowkht*

sprained

   nichts Ernstes *neekhts ehrnst•uhs*

nothing serious

Conditions

I'm...	**Ich bin ...** *eekh bih ...*
anemic	**anämisch** *ah•nay•meesh*
asthmatic	**Asthmatiker** *ahst•maht•eek•ehr*
diabetic	**Diabetiker** *dee•ah•beht•eek•her*
epileptic	**Epileptiker/Epileptikerin** *eh•pih•lehp•tih•kuhr/ eh•pih•lehp•tih•kuh•rihn*

I'm allergic to antibiotics/penicillin.	**Ich bin allergisch auf Antibiotika/Penicillin.** *eekh bihn <u>ah</u>·lehrg·eesh owf ahn·tee·bee·<u>oh</u>·tee·kah/ peh·nih·<u>sihl</u>·ihn*
I have…	**Ich habe …** *eekh <u>hahb</u>·uh …*
arthritis	**Arthritis** <u>ahr</u>·tree·tihs
a heart condition	**eine Herzkrankheit** <u>ien</u>·uh hehrts·krahnk·hiet
high/low blood pressure	**hohen/niedrigen Blutdruck** <u>hoh</u>·uhn/ <u>need</u>·ree·gehn <u>bloot</u>·drook
I'm on…	**Ich nehme …** *eekh <u>nehm</u>·uh …*

For Meals & Cooking, see page 67.

Treatment

Do I need a prescription/ medicine?	**Brauche ich ein Rezept/Medikament?** <u>browkh</u>·uh eekh ien reh·<u>tsehpt</u>/mehd·ee·kah·<u>mehnt</u>
Can you prescribe a generic drug? [unbranded medication]	**Können Sie ein ähnliches, günstiges Medikament verschreiben?** <u>kern</u>·uhn zee ien ehn·<u>lee</u>·khehs <u>gewn</u>·stee·guhs meh·dee·kah·<u>mehnt</u> fehr·<u>shrieb</u>·uhn
Where can I get it?	**Wo kann ich es bekommen?** *voh kahn eekh ehs buh·<u>kohm</u>·uhn*
Is this over the counter?	**Ist es rezeptfrei?** *ihst ehs reh·<u>tsehpt</u>·frie*

For What to Take, see page 156.

Hospital

Notify my family, please.	**Bitte benachrichtigen Sie meine Familie.** *<u>biht</u>·tuh buh·<u>nahkh</u>·reekh·tih·guhn zee <u>mien</u>·uh fah·<u>mee</u>·lee·uh*
I'm in pain.	**Ich habe Schmerzen.** *eekh <u>hahb</u>·uh <u>shmehrt</u>·suhn*
I need a doctor/nurse.	**Ich brauche einen Arzt/eine Schwester.** *eekh <u>browkh</u>·uh <u>ien</u>·uhn ahrtst/<u>ien</u>·uh <u>shvehs</u>·tehr*

| When are visiting hours? | **Wann ist die Besuchszeit?** *vahn ihst dee beh•zookhs•tsiet* |
| I'm visiting... | **Ich besuche ...** *eekh beh•zookh•uh ...* |

Dentist

I have...	**Ich habe ...** *eekh hahb•uh ...*
a broken tooth	**einen kaputten Zahn** *ien•uhn kah•poot•uhn tsahn*
a lost filling	**eine Füllung verloren** *ien•uh fewl•oong fehr•lohr•uhn*
a toothache	**Zahnschmerzen** *tsahn•shmehrts•uhn*
Can you fix this denture?	**Können Sie diese Prothese reparieren?** *kern•uhn zee deez•uh proh•teh•zuh reh•pah•reer•uhn*

Gynecologist

I have cramps/ a vaginal infection.	**Ich habe Krämpfe/eine Scheideninfektion.** *eekh hahb•uh krehmp•fuh/ ie•nuh shnied•uhn•ihn•fehk•tyohn*
I missed my period.	**Meine Periode ist ausgeblieben.** *mien•uh pehr•yoh•duh ihst ows•geh•bleeb•uhn*
I'm on the Pill.	**Ich nehme die Pille.** *eekh nehm•uh dee pihl•uh*
I'm (one/two/three/ four/five/six/seven/ eight/nine months) pregnant.	**Ich bin (im ersten/zweiten/dritten/vierten/ fünften/sechsten/siebten/achten/neunten Monat) schwanger.** *eekh bihn (ihm ehrs•thun/ tsvai•thun/dree•thun/feer•thun/ewnf•thun/sehks•thun/ seeb•thun/ahkh•thun/noyn•thun moh•naht) shvahn•guhr*
I'm not pregnant.	**Ich bin nicht schwanger.** *eekh bihn (neekht) shvahng•ehr*
My last period was...	**Meine letzte Periode war ...** *mien•uh lehts•uh pehr•yohd•uh vahr ...*

Optician

I've lost…	**Ich habe … verloren.** eekh _hahb_•uh … fehr•_lohr_•uhn
a contact lens	**eine Kontaktlinse** _ien_•uh _kohn_•tahkt•lihnz•uh
my glasses	**meine Brille** _mien_•uh _brihl_•uh
a lens	**ein Brillenglas** ien _brihl_•uhn•glahs

Payment & Insurance

How much?	**Wie viel kostet es?** vee feel _kohs_•tuht ehs
Can I pay by credit card?	**Kann ich mit Kreditkarte bezahlen?** kahn eekh miht kreh•_deet_•kahr•tuh beht•_sahl_•uhn
I have insurance.	**Ich bin versichert.** eekh bihn fehr•_zeekh_•ehrt
I need a receipt for my insurance.	**Ich brauche eine Quittung für meine Versicherung.** eekh _browkh_•uh _ien_•uh _kviht_•oong fewr _mien_•uh fehr•_zeekh_•ehr•oong

Pharmacy

ESSENTIAL

Where's the pharmacy?	**Wo ist die Apotheke?** voh ihst dee ah•poh•_tehk_•uh
What time does it open/close?	**Wann öffnet/schließt sie?** vahn _erf_•nuht/ shleest zee
What would you recommend for…?	**Was empfehlen Sie bei …?** vahs ehm•_pfeh_•luhn zee bie …
How much do I take?	**Wie viel muss ich einnehmen?** vee feel moos eekh ei•_nehm_•uhn

What to Take

How much do I take?	**Wie viel muss ich einnehmen?**
	vee feel moos eekh <u>ien</u>•nehm•uhn
How often?	**Wie oft?** *vee ohft*
Is it safe for children?	**Ist es für Kinder geeignet?**
	ihst ehs fewr <u>kihnd</u>•ehr geh•<u>ieg</u>•nuht
I'm taking...	**Ich nehme ...** *eekh <u>neh</u>•muh ...*

In Germany, there is a distinction between **Apotheke** (pharmacy) and **Drogerie** (drugstore).
Die Apotheke, usually featuring a large red A sign, dispenses prescription and over-the-counter medication.
Die Drogerie sells toiletries and other personal items. Pharmacies are open 9:00 a.m. to 6:30 p.m. Monday to Friday, and from 9:00 a.m. to 1:00 p.m. (sometimes 4:00 p.m) on Saturday. Most large cities and towns have at least one 24-hour pharmacy. Closed pharmacies will have a sign on the door indicating the nearest 24-hour location.

YOU MAY SEE...

EINMAL/DREIMAL AM TAG	once/three times a day
TABLETTE	tablet
TROPFEN	drop
TEELÖFFEL	teaspoon
NACH/VOR/MIT DEN MAHLZEITEN	after/before/with meals
AUF LEEREN MAGEN	on an empty stomach
IM GANZEN SCHLUCKEN	swallow whole
KANN BENOMMENHEIT VERURSACHEN	may cause drowsiness
NUR ZÜR ÄUSSEREN ANWENDUNG	for external use only

Are there side effects?	**Gibt es Nebenwirkungen?** _gihpt ehs nehb_•uhn•veerk•oong•uhn
I need something for...	**Ich brauche etwas gegen ...** _ihkh browkh_•uh _eht_•vahs _geh_•guhn ...
a cold	**eine Erkältung** _ien_•uh ehr•_kehlt_•oong
a cough	**Husten** _hoos_•tuhn
diarrhea	**Durchfall** _doorkh_•fahl
a headache	**Kopfschmerzen** _kohpf_•shmehr•tsuhn
insect bites	**Insektenstiche** _een_•_zehkt_•uhn•shteekh•uh
motion [travel] sickness	**die Reisekrankheit** _dee riez_•uh•krahnk•hiet
a sore throat	**Halsschmerzen** _hahls_•shmehrt•suhn
sunburn	**Sonnenbrand** _zohn_•uhn•brahnt
a toothache	**Zahnschmerzen** _tsahn_•shmehr•tsuhn
an upset stomach	**eine Magenverstimmung** _ien_•uh _mahg_•uhn•fehr•shtihm•oong

Basic Supplies

I'd like...	**Ich hätte gern ...** *eekh heh·tuh gehrn ...*
acetaminophen [paracetamol]	**Paracetamol** *pah·rah·seht·ah·mohl*
antiseptic cream	**eine antiseptische Creme** *ahn·tee·zehp·tee·shuh krehm*
aspirin	**Aspirin** *ahs·pih·reen*
bandages	**Pflaster** *pflahs·tehr*
a comb	**einen Kamm** *ien·uhn kahm*
condoms	**Kondome** *kohn·dohm·uh*
contact lens solution	**Kontaktlinsenlösung** *kohn·tahkt·lehnz·uhn·lerz·oong*
deodorant	**Deodorant** *deh·oh·doh·rahnt*
a hairbrush	**eine Haarbürste** *ien·uh hahr·bewr·stuh*
hairspray	**Haarspray** *hahr·shpraye*
ibuprofen	**Ibuprofen** *ee·boo·proh·fuhn*
insect repellent	**Insektenspray** *ihn·zehkt·uhn·shpray*
lotion	**Lotion** *loht·syohn*
a nail file	**eine Nagelfeile** *ien·uh nahg·ehl·fie·luh*
a (disposable) razor	**(Wegwerf-) Rasierer** *vehk·vehrf rah·zeer·ehr*
razor blades	**Rasierklingen** *rah·zeer·kleeng·uhn*
rubbing alcohol [surgical spirit]	**Franzbranntwein** *frahnts·brahnt·vien*
sanitary napkins [towels]	**Monatsbinden** *moh·nahts·bihnd·uhn*
shampoo/ conditioner	**Shampoo/Spülung** *shahm·poo/shpewl·oong*
soap	**Seife** *zie·fuh*
sunscreen	**Sonnenmilch** *zohn·nuhn·mihlkh*
tampons	**Tampons** *tahm·pohns*

tissues	**Taschentücher** _tahsh_·uhn·tewkh·ehr
toilet paper	**Toilettenpapier** _toy·leht_·uhn·pah·peer
toothpaste	**Zahnpasta** _tsahn_·pahs·tah

For Baby Essentials, see page 142.

The Basics

Grammar

Regular Verbs

Regular verbs in German are conjugated as in the table below. Note that the past is expressed with **haben** (to have) or **sein** (to be) plus the past participle. The future is formed with **werden** (will) plus the infinitive.

BEZAHLEN (to pay)		Present	Past	Future
I	**ich**	bezahl**e**	habe bezahlt	werde bezahlen
you (inf.)	**du**	bezahl**st**	hast bezahlt	wirst bezahlen
he/she/it	**er/sie/es**	bezahl**t**	hat bezahlt	wird bezahlen
we	**wir**	bezahl**en**	haben bezahlt	werden bezahlen
you (pl.) (inf.)	**ihr**	bezahl**t**	habt bezahlt	werdet bezahlen
they/you	**sie/Sie**	bezahl**en**	haben bezahlt	werden bezahlen

Example: **Ich bezahle bar.** I'll pay in cash.
Er _m_ **/sie** _f_ **bezahlt mit Kreditkarte.** He/She will pay with credit card.

MACHEN (to do, make)		Present	Past	Future
I	**ich**	mache	habe gemacht	werde machen
you (inf.)	**du**	machst	hast gemacht	wirst machen
he/she/it	**er/sie/es**	macht	hat gemacht	wird machen
we	**wir**	machen	haben gemacht	werden machen
you (pl.) (inf.)	**ihr**	macht	habt gemacht	werdet machen
they/you	**sie/Sie**	machen	haben gemacht	werden machen

Examples: **Ich mache hier Urlaub.** I'm here on vacation.
Was machen Sie beruflich? What do you do (for work)?

Irregular Verbs

There are a number of irregular verbs in German. Two common irregular verbs in German are **haben** (to have) and **sein** (to be). Conjugations follow:

HABEN (to have)		Present	Past	Future
I	**ich**	habe	habe gehabt	werde haben
you (inf.)	**du**	hast	hast gehabt	wirst haben
he/she/it	**er/sie/es**	hat	hat gehabt	wird haben
we	**wir**	haben	haben gehabt	werden haben
you (pl.) (inf.)	**ihr**	habt	habt gehabt	werdet haben
they/you	**sie/Sie**	haben	haben gehabt	werden haben

Example: **Ich habe einen Koffer.** I have one suitcase.
Ihr habt viel zu tun. You guys have a lot to do.

SEIN (to be)		Present	Past	Future
I	**ich**	bin	bin gewesen	werde sein
you (inf.)	**du**	bist	bist gewesen	wirst sein
he/she/it	**er/sie/es**	ist	ist gewesen	wird sein
we	**wir**	sind	sind gewesen	werden sein
you (pl.) (inf.)	**ihr**	seid	seid gewesen	werdet sein
they/you	**sie/Sie**	sind	sind gewesen	werden sein

Example: **Ich bin geschäftlich hier.** I am here on business.
Wir sind glücklich. We are happy.

Word Order

German is similar to English in terms of word order for simple sentences; it
follows the subject-verb-object pattern.
Example: **Wir lassen unser Gepäck hier.** We leave our luggage here.
When the sentence doesn't begin with a subject, the word order changes: the
verb and the subject are inverted.
Examples:

	Er	**ist**	**in Berlin.**		He is in Berlin.
Heute	**ist**	**er**	**in Berlin.**		Today he is in Berlin.
	Wir	**sind**	**in Berlin**	**gewesen.**	We were in Berlin.

To ask a question, begin with the verb and follow with the subject, as in
English. Example: **Seid ihr in Köln gewesen?** Have you been to Cologne?
(Literally: Have you to Cologne been?)

Negation

The negative is formed by putting **nicht** after the verb.
Example: **Ich bin Thomas**. I am Thomas.
Ich bin nicht Thomas. I am not Thomas.
If a noun is used, the negation is made by adding **kein** (masculine and neuter),
or **keine** (feminine). For plural nouns, always add **keine**.
Example: **Wir haben keine Einzelzimmer.** We don't have any single rooms.

Imperatives

Whereas in English the imperative always looks like the infinitive ('Go!'), in
German it is derived from the **du-/Sie-** form of the present tense. In the **du-**
form, the **-st** is dropped. All other forms are identical to the present tense. The
verb always comes first in commands.

		Go!
du	you (inf.)	**Geh!**
ihr	you (pl.) (inf.)	**Geht!**
Sie	you	**Gehen Sie!**
wir	we	**Gehen wir!** (Let's go!)

Nouns & Articles

In German, all nouns are capitalized. German nouns are also gender-specific; they can be masculine, feminine or neuter. There is no easy way to determine whether a noun is masculine, feminine or neuter.

There are three definite articles (the) in German: **der**, **die** and **das**. Masculine words use **der**, feminine words use **die** and neuter words use **das**. The only way to tell whether a word is masculine, feminine or neuter is to look at the article. For this reason, it is best to memorize the article when learning the word. For plural nouns using a definite article, all genders use **die**.

Definite examples: **der Mann** (the man), **die Männer** (the men); **die Frau** (the woman), **die Frauen** (the women); **das Kind** (neuter) (the child), **die Kinder** (neuter) (the children)

There are four cases in German. The definite articles are as follows:

	masculine	feminine	neuter	plural (all genders)
nominative	**der**	**die**	**das**	**die**
accusative	**den**	**die**	**das**	**die**
dative	**dem**	**der**	**dem**	**den**
genitive	**des**	**der**	**des**	**der**

German uses two indefinite articles (a/an): **ein** and **eine**. Masculine and neuter nouns use **ein**, and feminine nouns use **eine**. For plural nouns, the indefinite article is dropped, as in English.

Indefinite examples: **ein Zug** (a train), **Züge** (trains); **eine Karte** (a map), **Karten** (maps)

Adjectives

Adjectives must agree with the nouns they modify. Adjective endings change based on the article used and the case. For masculine nouns, **−er** is added to the adjective after an indefinite article and **−e** is added after a definite article.

Example: **ein kleiner Herr** a short gentleman

der kleine Herr the short gentleman

For feminine nouns, **−e** is added to the adjective after both an indefinite and a definite article.

Example: **eine kluge Frau** an intelligent woman

die kluge Frau the intelligent woman

For neuter nouns, **−es** is added to the adjective after an indefinite article, while **−e** is added to the adjective after a definite article.

Example: **ein großes Land** a big country

das große Land the big country

Comparatives & Superlatives

In German, the comparative of an adjective is usually formed by adding **−er** to the end of the adjective.

Examples: **klein** (small), **kleiner** (smaller); **billig** (cheap), **billiger** (cheaper); **groß** (big), **größer** (bigger)

The superlative is formed by adding **−sten** or **−esten** to the end of the adjective. If the adjective has a vowel of **a**, **o** or **u**, it may change to **ä**, **ö** or **ü** in the comparative and superlative forms.

Examples: **klein** (small), **kleinsten** (smallest); **billig** (cheap), **billigsten** (cheapest); **groß** (big); **größten** (biggest)

Possessive Adjectives

Possessive adjectives must agree in gender and number with the noun they are associated with.

	singular		
	masculine/neuter	**feminine**	**plural**
my	**mein**	**meine**	**meine**
your (inf.)	**dein**	**deine**	**deine**
his/its	**sein**	**seine**	**seine**
her/their	**ihr**	**ihre**	**ihre**
your (pl.) (inf.)	**Ihr**	**Ihre**	**Ihre**
our	**unser**	**unsere**	**unsere**

Example: **Wir lassen unser Gepäck im Hotel.** We leave our luggage in the hotel.

Possessive Pronouns

Possessive pronouns agree in gender and number with the noun they replace.

	Masculine	**Feminine**	**Neuter**
mine	**meiner**	**meine**	**meines**
yours (inf.)	**deiner**	**deine**	**deines**
his/its	**seiner**	**seine**	**seines**
hers/theirs	**ihrer**	**ihre**	**ihres**
ours	**unserer**	**unsere**	**unseres**
yours (pl.) (inf.)	**eurer**	**eure**	**eures**

Example: **Wem gehört der Schlüssel?** Whose key is this?
Das ist meiner. It's mine.

Adverbs & Adverbial Expressions

In German, adverbs are usually identical to adjectives but, unlike adjectives, their endings don't change.
Examples:
Adjective: **das <u>gute</u> Essen** the good food
Adverb: **Sie sprechen <u>gut</u> Deutsch.** You speak German well.

Numbers

ESSENTIAL

0	**null**	*nool*
1	**eins**	*iens*
2	**zwei**	*tsvie*
3	**drei**	*drie*
4	**vier**	*feer*
5	**fünf**	*fewnf*
6	**sechs**	*zehks*
7	**sieben**	<u>*zeeb*</u>*•uhn*
8	**acht**	*ahkht*
9	**neun**	*noyn*
10	**zehn**	*tsehn*
11	**elf**	*ehlf*
12	**zwölf**	*tsverlf*
13	**dreizehn**	<u>*driet*</u>*•sehn*
14	**vierzehn**	<u>*feert*</u>*•sehn*
15	**fünfzehn**	<u>*fewnf*</u>*•tsehn*
16	**sechszehn**	<u>*zehk*</u>*•tsehn*
17	**siebzehn**	<u>*zeep*</u>*•tsehn*
18	**achtzehn**	<u>*ahkht*</u>*•tsehn*
19	**neunzehn**	<u>*noyn*</u>*•tsehn*
20	**zwanzig**	<u>*tsvahnt*</u>*•seek*
21	**einundzwanzig**	<u>*ien*</u>*•oond•tsvahn•tseek*
22	**zweiundzwanzig**	<u>*tsvie*</u>*•oond•tsvahn•tseek*
30	**dreißig**	<u>*drie*</u>*•seekh*
31	**einunddreißig**	<u>*ien*</u>*•oont•drie•seekh*
40	**vierzig**	<u>*feert*</u>*•seek*
50	**fünfzig**	<u>*fewnf*</u>*•tseeg*

60	**sechzig** _zehkht_·seeg	
70	**siebzig** _zeeb_·tseeg	
80	**achtzig** _ahkht_·tseeg	
90	**neunzig** _noynt_·seek	
100	**einhundert** _ien_·hoon·dehrt	
101	**einhunderteins** _ien_·hoon·dehr·tiens	
200	**zweihundert** _tsvie_·hoon·dehrt	
500	**fünfhundert** _fewnf_·hoon·dehrt	
1,000	**eintausend** _ien_·tow·zuhnt	
10,000	**zehntausend** _tsehn_·tow·zuhnt	
1,000,000	**eine Million** _ien_·uh mihl·_yohn_	

Ordinal Numbers

first	**erste** _ehrs_·tuh
second	**zweite** _tsviet_·uh
third	**dritte** _driht_·tuh
fourth	**vierte** _feer_·tuh
fifth	**fünfte** _fewnf_·tuh
once	**einmal** _ien_·mahl
twice	**zweimal** _tsvie_·mahl
three times	**dreimal** _drie_·mahl

Time

ESSENTIAL

What time is it?	**Wie spät ist es?** vee shpayt ihst ehs
It's midday.	**Es ist zwölf.** ehs ihst tsverlf
At midnight.	**Um Mitternacht.** oom _miht_·tehr·nahkht

From one o'clock to two o'clock.	**Von eins bis zwei.** *fohn iens bihs tsvie*
Five past three.	**Fünf nach drei.** *fewnf nahkh drie*
A quarter to four.	**Viertel vor vier.** <u>*feert*</u>*•uhl fohr feer*
5:30 a.m./5:30 p.m.	**Fünf Uhr dreißig/Siebzehn Uhr dreißig** *fewnf oohr <u>drie</u>•seeg/<u>zeeb</u>•tsuhn oohr <u>drie</u>•seeg*

Germans use the 24-hour clock in formal contexts (radio, TV, transportation schedules and digital clocks) or when confusion might otherwise arise. The morning hours from 1:00 a.m. to noon are the same as in English. After that, just add 12: so 1:00 p.m. would be 13:00, 5:00 p.m. would be 17:00 and so on. This system eliminates the necessity of 'a.m.' and 'p.m.' markers. When the 12-hour clock is used, **morgens** (in the morning) and **abends** (in the evening) are added after the number for clarity.

Days

ESSENTIAL

Monday	**Montag** <u>*mohn*</u>*•tahk*
Tuesday	**Dienstag** <u>*deens*</u>*•tahk*
Wednesday	**Mittwoch** <u>*miht*</u>*•vohkh*
Thursday	**Donnerstag** <u>*dohn*</u>*•ehrs•tahk*
Friday	**Freitag** <u>*frie*</u>*•tahk*
Saturday	**Samstag** <u>*zahms*</u>*•tahk*
Sunday	**Sonntag** *zohn•tahk*

Dates

yesterday	**gestern** _gehs_·tehrn
today	**heute** _hoy_·tuh
tomorrow	**morgen** _mohr_·guhn
day	**Tag** tahk
week	**Woche** _vohkh_·uh
month	**Monat** _moh_·naht
year	**Jahr** yahr

German calendars and weeks, like the U.K., are arranged
Monday through Sunday (in contrast to the U.S., where calendars
run Sunday through Saturday).

Months

January	**Januar** _yahn_·wahr
February	**Februar** _fehb_·rooahr
March	**März** mehrts
April	**April** ah·_prihl_
May	**Mai** mie

June	**Juni** _yoo•nee_
July	**Juli** _yoo•lee_
August	**August** _ow•goost_
September	**September** _zehp•tehm•behr_
October	**Oktober** _ohk•toh•behr_
November	**November** _noh•vehm•behr_
December	**Dezember** _deh•tsehm•behr_

Germany follows a day-month-year format instead of the month-day-year format used in the U.S.
For example: July 25, 2008; 25/07/08 = 7/25/2008 in the U.S.

Seasons

in...	**im ...** _ihm ..._
spring	**Frühling** _frewh•leeng_
summer	**Sommer** _zohm•ehr_
fall [autumn]	**Herbst** _hehrbst_
winter	**Winter** _vihnt•ehr_

Holidays

January 1: New Year's Day, **Neujahrstag**
January 6: Epiphany, **Heilige Drei Könige**
May 1: Labor Day, **Tag der Arbeit**
August 15: Assumption Day, **Mariä Himmelfahrt**
October 3: German Unity Day, **Tag der Deutschen Einheit**
November 1: All Saint's Day, **Allerheiligen**
December 25: Christmas, **Erster Weihnachtstag**
December 26: St. Stephen's Day [Boxing Day], **Zweiter Weihnachtstag**

The Easter (movable) holidays are:
Ascension Day, **Christ Himmelfahrt**
Easter Sunday, **Ostersonntag**
Easter Monday, **Ostermontag**
Feast of Corpus Christi, **Fronleichnam**
Good Friday, **Karfreitag**
Pentecost, **Pfinstsonntag**
Pentecost Monday, **Pfinstmontag**

One of Germany's most famous festivals is **Oktoberfest**, held each September in Munich. This food and beer festival extends for more than two weeks and is attended by about six million visitors from around the world. Another popular festival is **Karneval**, celebrated with parades and parties the week before Lent in areas that have substantial Catholic populations. Christmas festivities and markets are also very popular in Germany. Locals and tourists alike visit these markets to purchase local handmade crafts such as toys, wooden carvings, marionettes, candles, lambskin shoes and much more. There are plenty of food vendors available with numerous tasty treats to try.

Conversion Tables

When you know	Multiply by	To find
ounces	*28.3*	grams
pounds	*0.45*	kilograms
inches	*2.54*	centimeters
feet	*0.3*	meters
miles	*1.61*	kilometers
square inches	*6.45*	sq. centimeters
square feet	*0.09*	sq. meters

square miles	2.59	sq. kilometers
pints (U.S./Brit)	0.47/0.56	liters
gallons (U.S./Brit)	3.8/4.5	liters
Fahrenheit	5/9, after −32	Centigrade
Centigrade	9/5, then +32	Fahrenheit

Kilometers to Miles Conversions

1 km – 0.62 mi	**20 km** – 12.4 mi
5 km – 3.10 mi	**50 km** – 31.0 mi
10 km – 6.20 mi	**100 km** – 61.0 mi

Measurement

1 gram	**ein Gramm** *ien grahm*	= 0.035 oz.
1 kilogram (kg)	**ein Kilogramm** *ien kee·loh·grahm*	= 2.2 lb
1 liter (l)	**ein Liter** *ien lee·tehr*	= 1.06 U.S/0.88 Brit. quarts
1 centimeter (cm)	**ein Zentimeter** *ien tsehn·tee·muh·tehr*	= 0.4 inch
1 meter (m)	**ein Meter** *ien meh·tehr*	= 39.37 inches/ 3.28 ft.
1 kilometer (km)	**ein Kilometer** *ien kee·loh·meh·tehr*	= 0.62 mile

Temperature

−40° C – −40° F	**−1° C** – 30° F	**20° C** – 68° F
−30° C – −22° F	**0° C** – 32° F	**25° C** – 77° F
−20° C – −4° F	**5° C** – 41° F	**30° C** – 86° F
−10° C – 14° F	**10° C** – 50° F	**35° C** – 95° F
−5° C – 23° F	**15° C** – 59° F	

Oven Temperature

100° C – 212° F	**175° C** – 347° F	**204° C** – 400° F
121° C – 250° F	**177° C** – 350° F	**220° C** – 428° F
149° C – 300° F	**180° C** – 356° F	**250° C** – 482° F
150° C – 302° F	**200° C** – 392° F	**260° C** – 500° F

Dictionary

English–German

A

accept v akzeptieren
access n der Zutritt
accident der Unfall
accommodation die Unterkunft
account n (bank) das Konto
acupuncture die Akupunktur
adapter der Adapter
address n die Adresse
admission (price) der Eintritt
after nach;
  ~noon der Nachmittag;
  ~shave das Aftershave
age n das Alter
agency die Agentur
AIDS AIDS
air n die Luft; **~ conditioning** die
  Klimaanlage; **~-dry**
  lufttrocknen; **~ pump**
  die Luftpumpe; **~line**
  die Fluggesellschaft; **~mail**
  die Luftpost; **~plane** das Flugzeug;
  ~port der Flughafen
aisle der Gang; **~ seat** der Platz
  am Gang

allergic allergisch; **~ reaction**
  die allergische Reaktion
allow erlauben
alone allein
alter v umändern
alternate route die Alternativroute
aluminum foil die Aluminiumfolie
amazing erstaunlich
ambulance der Krankenwagen
American adj amerikanisch
amusement park
  der Vergnügungspark
anemic anämisch
anesthesia die Anästhesie
animal das Tier
ankle das Fußgelenk
antibiotic n das Antibiotikum
antiques store
  das Antiquitätengeschäft
antiseptic cream die antiseptische
  Creme
apartment das Apartment
appendix (body part)
  der Blinddarm
appetizer die Vorspeise

adj adjective	**BE** British English	**prep** preposition
adv adverb	**n** noun	**v** verb

appointment der Termin
arcade die Spielhalle
area code die Ortsvorwahl
arm n **(body part)** der Arm
aromatherapy die Aromatherapie
around (the corner) um;
~ **(price)** ungefähr
arrival Ankunft
arrive ankommen
artery die Arterie
arthritis die Arthritis
art die Kunst
Asian adj asiatisch
aspirin das Aspirin
asthmatic asthmatisch
ATM der Bankautomat;
~ **card** die Bankkarte
attack v angreifen
attraction (place)
die Sehenswürdigkeit
attractive attraktiv
Australia das Australien
Australian adj australisch
automatic automatisch;
~ **car** das Auto mit
Automatikschaltung
available verfügbar

B
baby das Baby;
~ **bottle** die Babyflasche;

~ **wipe** das Baby-Pflegetuch;
~**sitter** der Babysitter
back (body part) der Rücken;
~**ache** die Rückenschmerzen;
~**pack** der Rucksack
bag die Tasche
baggage [BE] das Gepäck;
~ **claim** die Gepäckausgabe;
~ **ticket** der Gepäckschein
bake v backen
bakery die Bäckerei
ballet das Ballett
bandage das Pflaster
bank n die Bank
bar (place) die Bar
barbecue (device) n der Grill
barber der Herrenfriseur
baseball der Baseball
basket (grocery store)
der Einkaufskorb
basketball der Basketball
bathroom das Bad
battery die Batterie
battleground das Schlachtfeld
be v sein
beach der Strand
beautiful wunderschön; ~ schön
bed n das Bett; ~ **and breakfast**
die Pension
before vor
begin beginnen

beginner der Anfänger

behind (direction) hinter

beige adj beige

belt der Gürtel

best adj beste; ~ **before** mindestens haltbar bis

better besser

bicycle das Fahrrad

big groß; ~**ger** größerger

bike route die Radroute

bikini der Bikini

bill n **(money)** der Geldschein; ~ n **(of sale)** die Rechnung

bird der Vogel

birthday der Geburtstag

black adj schwarz

bladder die Blase

bland fad

blanket die Decke

bleed bluten

blender der Mixer

blood das Blut; ~ **pressure** der Blutdruck

blouse die Bluse

blue adj blau

board v einsteigen; ~**ing pass** die Bordkarte

boat n das Boot

boil v kochen

bone n der Knochen

book n das Buch;

~**store** der Buchladen

boot n der Stiefel

boring langweilig

botanical garden der botanische Garten

bother v belästigen

bottle n die Flasche; ~ **opener** der Flaschenöffner

bowl n die Schüssel

boxing match der Boxkampf

boy der Junge; ~**friend** der Freund

bra der BH

bracelet das Armband

brake (car) die Bremse

breaded paniert

break v **(bone)** brechen

breakdown (car) die Panne

breakfast n das Frühstück

break-in (burglary) n der Einbruch

breast die Brust; ~**feed** v stillen

breathe atmen

bridge die Brücke

briefs (clothing) der Schlüpfer

bring bringen

British adj britisch

broken kaputt; ~ **(bone)** gebrochen

brooch die Brosche

broom der Besen

brother der Bruder

brown *adj* braun
bug (insect) *n* das Insekt
building das Gebäude
burn *v* brennen
bus *n* der Bus;
  ~ station der Busbahnhof;
  ~ stop die Bushaltestelle;
  ~ ticket die Busfahrkarte;
  ~ tour die Busreise
business *adj* Geschäfts-;
  ~ card die Visitenkarte;
  ~ center das Geschäftszentrum;
  ~ class die Business-Class;
  ~ hours die Öffnungszeiten
butcher *n* der Fleischer
buttocks der Po
buy *v* kaufen
bye auf Wiedersehen

C

cabaret das Kabarett
cable car die Seilbahn
cafe (place) das Café
call *v* **(phone)** anrufen;
  ~ *n* der Anruf **~ collect** ein
  R-Gespräch führen
calorie die Kalorie
camera die Kamera;
  ~ case die Kameratasche; **digital**
  ~ die Digitalkamera
camp *v* campen; **~ing stove**

der Campingkocher; **~site** der
Campingplatz
can opener der Dosenöffner
Canada das Kanada
Canadian *adj* kanadisch
cancel stornieren
candy die Süßigkeit
canned good die Konserve
canyon der Canyon
car das Auto;
  ~ hire [BE] die Autovermietung; **~**
  park [BE] der Parkplatz;
  ~ rental die Autovermietung; **~**
  seat der Autositz
carafe die Karaffe
card *n* die Karte;
  ATM ~ die Bankkarte;
  credit ~ die Kreditkarte;
  debit ~ die EC-Karte;
  phone ~ die Telefonkarte
carry-on *n* **(piece of hand**
luggage) das Handgepäckstück
cart (grocery store) der
Einkaufswagen; **~ (luggage)** der
Gepäckwagen
carton (of cigarettes) die Stange
(Zigaretten);
  ~ (of groceries) die Packung
cash *n* das Bargeld;
  ~ *v* einlösen
cashier der Kassierer

casino das Casino
castle das Schloss
cathedral die Kathedrale
cave n die Höhle
CD die CD
cell phone das Handy
Celsius Celsius
centimeter der Zentimeter
certificate das Zertifikat
chair n der Stuhl;
~ **lift** der Sessellift
change v **(baby)** wickeln;
~ **(buses)** umsteigen;
~ **(money)** wechseln;
~ n **(money)** das Wechselgeld
charge v **(credit card)**
belasten; ~ **(cost)** verlangen
cheap billig; ~**er** billiger
check v **(luggage)**
aufgeben; ~ **(on something)**
prüfen; n **(payment)** der
Scheck; ~**-in** das Check-in;
~**ing account** das Girokonto;
~**-out** das Check-out
Cheers! Prost!
chemical toilet die
Campingtoilette
chemist [BE] die Apotheke
chest (body part) die Brust;
~ **pain** die Brustschmerzen
chewing gum der Kaugummi

child das Kind;
~**'s seat** der Kinderstuhl
children's menu das Kindermenü
children's portion die Kinderportion
Chinese adj chinesisch
chopsticks die Stäbchen
church die Kirche
cigar die Zigarre
cigarette die Zigarette
class n die Klasse;
business ~ die Business-Class;
economy ~ die Economy-Class;
first ~ die erste Klasse
classical music die
klassische Musik
clean v reinigen; ~ adj
(clothes) sauber; ~**ing**
product das Reinigungsmittel
clear v **(on an ATM)** löschen
cliff die Klippe
cling film [BE] die Klarsichtfolie
close v **(a shop)** schließen
closed geschlossen
clothing die Bekleidung;
~ **store** das Bekleidungsgeschäft
club n der Club
coat der Mantel
coin die Münze
colander das Sieb
cold n **(sickness)** die Erkältung; ~
adj **(temperature)** kalt

colleague der Kollege
cologne das Kölnischwasser
color n die Farbe
comb n der Kamm
come v kommen
complaint die Beschwerde
computer der Computer
concert das Konzert;
  ~ **hall** die Konzerthalle
condition (medical) die
  Beschwerden
conditioner (hair) die Spülung
condom das Kondom
conference die Konferenz
confirm bestätigen
congestion (medical) der Blutstau
connect (internet) verbinden
connection (travel/internet)
  die Verbindung; ~ **flight** der
  Anschlussflug
constipated verstopft
consulate das Konsulat
consultant der Berater
contact v kontaktieren
contact lens die Kontaktlinse;
  ~ **solution** Kontaktlinsenlösung
contagious ansteckend
convention hall der Kongresssaal
conveyor belt das Förderband
cook v kochen
cool adj **(temperature)** kalt

copper n das Kupfer
corkscrew n der Korkenzieher
cost v kosten
cotton die Baumwolle
cough v husten;
  ~ n der Husten
country code die Landesvorwahl
cover charge der Preis pro Gedeck
cream (ointment) die Creme
credit card die Kreditkarte
crew neck der runde Halsausschnitt
crib das Kinderbett
crystal n **(glass)** das Kristall
cup n die Tasse
currency die Währung; ~ **exchange**
  der Währungsumtausch; ~
  exchange office die Wechselstube
current account [BE] das
  Girokonto
customs der Zoll
cut v schneiden;
  ~ n **(injury)** der Schnitt
cute süß
cycling das Radfahren

D

damage v beschädigen
dance v tanzen; ~ **club** der
  Tanzclub; ~**ing** das Tanzen
dangerous gefährlich
dark adj dunkel

date *n* **(calendar)** das Datum
day der Tag
deaf *adj* taub
debit card die EC-Karte
deck chair der Liegestuhl
declare *v* **(customs)** deklarieren
decline *v* **(credit card)** ablehnen
deep *adj* tief
degree (temperature) das Grad
delay *v* verzögern
delete *v* **(computer)** löschen
delicatessen das Feinkostgeschäft
delicious lecker
denim das Denim
dentist der Zahnarzt
denture die Zahnprothese
deodorant das Deodorant
department store das Kaufhaus
departure (plane) der Abflug
deposit *v* **(money)** einzahlen;
  ~ *n* **(bank)** die Einzahlung
desert *n* die Wüste
detergent das Waschmittel
develop *v* **(film)** entwickeln
diabetic *adj* diabetisch; *n* der
  Diabetiker
dial *v* wählen
diamond der Diamant
diaper die Windel
diarrhea der Durchfall
diesel der Diesel

difficult schwierig
digital digital; ~ **camera**
  die Digitalkamera;
  ~ **photo** das Digitalfoto;
  ~ **print** der digitale Ausdruck
dining room das Esszimmer
dinner das Abendessen
direction die Richtung
dirty schmutzig
disabled *adj* **(person)**
  behindert; ~ **accessible [BE]**
  behindertengerecht
disconnect (computer) trennen
discount *n* der Rabatt; die
  Ermäßigung
dishes (kitchen) das Geschirr
dishwasher der Geschirrspüler
dishwashing liquid
  das Geschirrspülmittel
display *n* **(device)** das Display; ~
  case die Vitrine
disposable *n* der Einwegartikel; ~
  razor der Einweg-Rasierer
dive *v* tauchen
diving equipment
  die Tauchausrüstung
divorce *v* sich scheiden lassen
dizzy *adj* schwindelig
doctor *n* der Arzt
doll *n* die Puppe
dollar (U.S.) der Dollar

domestic inländisch;
  ~ flight der Inlandsflug
door die Tür
dormitory der Schlafsaal
double bed das Doppelbett
downtown *n* das Stadtzentrum
dozen das Dutzend
drag lift der Schlepplift
dress (clothing) das Kleid;
  ~ code die Kleiderordnung
drink *v* trinken; **~** *n* das Getränk;
  ~ menu die Getränkekarte; **~ing
  water** das Trinkwasser
drive *v* fahren
driver's license number die
  Führerscheinnummer
drop *n* **(medicine)** der Tropfen
drowsiness die Schläfrigkeit
dry clean chemisch reinigen;
  ~er's die chemische Reinigung
dubbed synchronisiert
during während
duty (tax) der Zoll; **~-free** zollfrei
DVD die DVD

E

ear das Ohr; **~ache** die
  Ohrenschmerzen
earlier früher
early früh
earring der Ohrring

east *n* der Osten
easy leicht
eat *v* essen
economy class die Economy-Class
elbow *n* der Ellenbogen
electric outlet die Steckdose
elevator der Fahrstuhl
e-mail *v* eine E-Mail senden;
  ~ *n* die E-Mail; **~ address** die
  E-Mail-Adresse
emergency der Notfall;
  ~ exit der Notausgang
empty *v* entleeren
end *v* beenden; **~** *n* das Ende
engaged (person) verlobt
English *adj* englisch; **~** *n*
  (language) das Englisch
engrave eingravieren
enjoy genießen
enter *v* **(place)** eintreten
entertainment die Unterhaltung
entrance der Eingang
envelope der Umschlag
epileptic *adj* epileptisch;
  ~ *n* der Epileptiker
equipment die Ausrüstung
escalator die Rolltreppe
e-ticket das E-Ticket
EU resident der EU-Bürger
euro der Euro
evening *n* der Abend

excess baggage das Übergepäck

exchange v umtauschen;
~ n (**place**) die Wechselstube; ~
rate der Wechselkurs

excursion der Ausflug

excuse v entschuldigen

exhausted erschöpft

exit v verlassen; ~ n der Ausgang

expensive teuer

experienced erfahren

expert der Experte

exposure (film) die Belichtung

express adj Express-; ~ **bus**
der Expressbus; ~ **train** der
Expresszug

extension (phone) die Durchwahl

extra adj zusätzlich; ~ **large**
extragroß

extract v (**tooth**) ziehen

eye das Auge

eyebrow wax
die Augenbrauenkorrektur

F

face n das Gesicht

facial n die kosmetische
Gesichtsbehandlung

family n die Familie

fan n (**appliance**) der Ventilator

far (distance) weit

farm der Bauernhof

far-sighted weitsichtig

fast adj schnell

fat free fettfrei

father der Vater

fax v faxen; ~ n das Fax;
~ **number** die Faxnummer

fee n die Gebühr

feed v füttern

ferry n die Fähre

fever n das Fieber

field (sports) der Platz

fill v (**car**) tanken

fill out v (**form**) ausfüllen

filling n (**tooth**) die Füllung

film n (**camera**) der Film

fine n (**fee for breaking law**)
die Strafe

finger n der Finger; ~**nail** der
Fingernagel

fire n das Feuer;
~ **department** die Feuerwehr; ~
door die Feuertür

first adj erste; ~ **class** erste Klasse

fit n (**clothing**) die Passform

fitting room die Umkleidekabine

fix v (**repair**) reparieren

fixed-price menu das Festpreismenü

flash photography das
Fotografieren mit Blitzlicht

flashlight das Blitzlicht

flight n der Flug

flip-flops die Badelatschen
floor n (**level**) die Etage
florist der Florist
flower n die Blume
folk music die Volksmusik
food das Essen; ~ **processor** die Küchenmaschine
foot n der Fuß
football game [BE] das Fußballspiel
for für
forecast n die Vorhersage
forest n der Wald
fork n die Gabel
form n (**document**) das Formular
formula (baby) die Babynahrung
fort die Festung
fountain n der Springbrunnen
free adj frei
freelance work die freiberufliche Arbeit
freezer der Gefrierschrank
fresh frisch
friend der Freund
frozen food die Tiefkühlkost
frying pan die Bratpfanne
full-time adj Vollzeit-

G

game n das Spiel
garage n (**parking**) die Garage; ~ n (**for repairs**) die Autowerkstatt

garbage bag der Abfallbeutel
gas (car) das Benzin; ~ **station** die Tankstelle
gate (airport) das Gate
gay adj (**homosexual**) schwul; ~ **bar** die Schwulenbar; ~ **club** der Schwulenclub
gel n (**hair**) das Gel
generic drug das Generikum
German adj deutsch; ~ n (**language**) das Deutsch
Germany Deutschland
get off (a train/bus/ subway) aussteigen
gift n das Geschenk; ~ **shop** der Geschenkwarenladen
girl das Mädchen; ~**friend** die Freundin
give v geben
glass (drinking) das Glas; ~ (**material**) das Glas
glasses die Brille
go v (**somewhere**) gehen
gold n das Gold
golf n das Golf; ~ **course** der Golfplatz; ~ **tournament** das Golfturnier
good adj gut; ~ n die Ware; ~ **afternoon** guten Tag ~ **day** guten Tag; ~ **evening** guten Abend; ~ **morning** guten

Morgen; **~bye** auf Wiedersehen
gram das Gramm
grandchild das Enkelkind
grandparents die Großeltern
gray *adj* grau
green *adj* grün
grocery store das
Lebensmittelgeschäft
ground floor das Erdgeschoss
groundcloth die Unterlegplane
group *n* die Gruppe
guide *n* **(book)** der Reiseführer; ~ *n*
(person) der Fremdenführer ~ **dog**
der Blindenhund
gym *n* **(place)** der Fitnessraum
gynecologist der Gynäkologe

H

hair das Haar; **~brush** die
Haarbürste; **~cut** der Haarschnitt;
~ **dryer** der Fön; ~ **salon**
der Friseursalon; **~spray** das
Haarspray; **~style**
die Frisur; ~ **stylist** der Friseur
halal halal
half *adj* halb; ~ *n* die Hälfte;
~ **hour** die halbe Stunde;
~-kilo das halbe Kilo
hammer *n* der Hammer
hand *n* die Hand; ~ **luggage**
das Handgepäck; ~ **wash** die

Handwäsche; **~bag [BE]** die
Handtasche
handicapped behindert;
~-accessible
behindertengerecht
hangover der Kater
happy glücklich
hat der Hut
have *v* haben; ~ **sex** Sex haben
hay fever der Heuschnupfen
head (body part) *n* der Kopf;
~ache die Kopfschmerzen;
~phones die Kopfhörer
health die Gesundheit; ~ **food**
store das Reformhaus
hearing impaired hörgeschädigt
heart das Herz; ~ **condition**
die Herzkrankheit
heat *v* heizen; **~er** das Heizgerät;
~ing [BE] die Heizung
hectare der Hektar
hello Hallo
helmet der Helm
help *v* helfen; ~ *n* die Hilfe
here hier
hi Hallo
high hoch; **~chair** der Kindersitz;
~lights (hair)
die Strähnchen; **~way**
die Autobahn
hiking boots die Wanderschuhe

hill n der Berg
hire v [BE] **(a car)** mieten;
~ **car** [BE] das Mietauto
hockey das Hockey
holiday [BE] der Urlaub
horsetrack die Pferderennbahn
hospital das Krankenhaus
hostel die Jugendherberge
hot (spicy) scharf;
~ **(temperature)** heiß;
~ **spring** heiße Quelle;
~ **water** heißes Wasser
hotel das Hotel
hour die Stunde
house n das Haus; ~**hold
goods** die Haushaltswaren;
~**keeping services** der
Hotelservice
how wie; ~ **much** wie viel
hug v umarmen
hungry hungrig
hurt v wehtun
husband der Ehemann

I

ibuprofen das Ibuprofen
ice n das Eis; ~ **hockey** das
Eishockey
icy eisig
identification die Identifikation
ill krank

in in
include v beinhalten
indoor pool (public) das Hallenbad
inexpensive preisgünstig
infected infiziert
information (phone) die Auskunft;
~ **desk** die Information
insect das Insekt: ~ **bite** der
Insektenstich; ~ **repellent** der
Insektenschutz
insert v **(card)** einführen
insomnia die Schlaflosigkeit
instant message die instant
Message
insulin das Insulin
insurance die Versicherung;
~ **card** die Versicherungskarte;
~ **company** die
Versicherungsgesellschaft
interesting interessant
intermediate fortgeschritten
international international;
~ **flight** der internationale Flug; ~
student card der internationale
Studentenausweis
internet das Internet;
~ **cafe** das Internetcafé;
~ **service** der Internetservice
interpreter der Dolmetscher
intersection die Kreuzung
intestine der Darm

introduce v **(person)** vorstellen
invoice n **[BE]** die Rechnung
Ireland das Irland
Irish adj irisch
iron v bügeln; ~ n **(clothes)** das Bügeleisen
Italian adj italienisch

J

jacket n die Jacke
Japanese adj japanisch
jar n **(for jam etc.)** das Glas
jaw n der Kiefer
jazz n der Jazz; ~ **club** der Jazzclub
jeans die Jeans
jet ski n die Jet-Ski
jeweler der Juwelier
jewelry der Schmuck
join v **(go with somebody)** mitkommen
joint n **(body part)** das Gelenk

K

key n der Schlüssel; ~ **card** die Schlüsselkarte; ~**ring** der Schlüsselring
kiddie pool das Kinderbecken
kidney (body part) die Niere
kilo das Kilo; ~**gram** das Kilogramm; ~**meter** der Kilometer
kiss v küssen

kitchen die Küche; ~ **foil [BE]** die Aluminiumfolie
knee n das Knie
knife das Messer
kosher adj koscher

L

lace n **(fabric)** die Spitze
lactose intolerant laktoseintolerant
lake der See
large groß
last adj letzte
late (time) spät
launderette [BE] der Waschsalon
laundromat der Waschsalon
laundry (place) die Wäscherei ~ **service** der Wäscheservice
lawyer n der Anwalt
leather n das Leder
leave v **(hotel)** abreisen; ~ **(plane)** abfliegen
left adj, adv **(direction)** links
leg n das Bein
lens die Linse
less weniger
lesson n die Lektion; **take** ~**s** Unterricht nehmen
letter n der Brief
library die Bücherei
life jacket die Schwimmweste

lifeguard der Rettungsschwimmer
lift n [BE] der Fahrstuhl; ~ n
  (**ride**) die Mitfahrgelegenheit; ~
  pass der Liftpass
light n (**cigarette**) das Feuer;
  ~ n (**overhead**) die Lampe;
  ~**bulb** die Glühbirne
lighter n das Feuerzeug
like v mögen
line n (**train/bus**) die Linie
linen das Leinen
lip n die Lippe
liquor store das Spirituosengeschäft
liter der Liter
little wenig
live v leben; ~ **music** Livemusik
liver (**body part**) die Leber
loafers die Halbschuhe
local n (**person**) der Einheimische
lock v abschließen; ~ n das Schloss
locker das Schließfach
log off v (**computer**) abmelden
log on v (**computer**) anmelden
long adj lang; ~-**sighted** [BE]
  weitsichtig; ~-**sleeved** langärmlig
look v schauen; ~ **for something**
  etwas suchen
loose (**fit**) locker
lose v (**something**) verlieren
lost verloren; ~-**and-found** das
  Fundbüro

lotion die Lotion
louder lauter
love v (**someone**) lieben;
  ~ n die Liebe
low adj niedrig
luggage das Gepäck; ~ **cart**
  der Gepäckwagen; ~ **locker** das
  Gepäckschließfach;
  ~ **ticket** der Gepäckschein
lunch n das Mittagessen
lung die Lunge
luxury car das Luxusauto

M

machine washable
  maschinenwaschbar
magazine das Magazin
magnificent großartig
mail v mit der Post schicken; ~
  n die Post; ~**box** der Briefkasten
main attraction die Hauptattraktion
main course das Hauptgericht
mall das Einkaufszentrum
man (**adult male**) der Mann
manager der Manager
manicure n die Maniküre
manual car das Auto mit
  Gangschaltung
map n die Karte;
  ~ n (**town**) der Stadtplan
market n der Markt

married verheiratet
marry heiraten
mass n (**church service**) die Messe
massage n die Massage
match n das Spiel
meal die Mahlzeit
measure v (**someone**) Maß nehmen
measuring cup der Messbecher
measuring spoon der Messlöffel
mechanic n der Mechaniker
medication (drugs) die
  Medikamente
medicine das Medikament
medium (steak) medium
meet v treffen
meeting n (**business**) das Meeting;
  ~ **room** das Konferenzzimmer
membership card der
  Mitgliedsausweis
memorial (place) das Denkmal
memory card die Speicherkarte
mend v (**clothes**) ausbessern
menstrual cramps die
  Menstruationskrämpfe
menu (restaurant) die Speisekarte
message die Nachricht
meter n (**parking**) die Parkuhr; ~ n
  (**measure**) der Meter
microwave n die Mikrowelle
midday [BE] der Mittag
midnight die Mitternacht

mileage die Meilenzahl
mini-bar die Mini-Bar
minute die Minute
missing (not there) weg
mistake n der Fehler
mobile home der Wohnwagen
mobile phone [BE] das Handy
mobility die Mobilität
monastery das Kloster
money das Geld
month der Monat
mop n der Wischmopp
moped das Moped
more mehr
morning n der Morgen
mosque die Moschee
mother n die Mutter
motion sickness die Reisekrankheit
motor n der Motor;
  ~ **boat** das Motorboot;
  ~**cycle** das Motorrad;
  ~**way [BE]** die Autobahn
mountain der Berg;
  ~ **bike** das Mountainbike
mousse (hair) der Schaumfestiger
mouth n der Mund
movie der Film; ~ **theater**
  das Kino
mug v überfallen
multiple-trip ticket
  der Mehrfachfahrschein

muscle n der Muskel
museum das Museum
music die Musik; **~ store** das Musikgeschäft

N

nail file die Nagelfeile
nail salon das Nagelstudio
name n der Name
napkin die Serviette
nappy [BE] die Windel
nationality die Nationalität
nature preserve das Naturreservat
nausea die Übelkeit
nauseous übel
near nahe; **~-sighted** kurzsichtig
nearby in der Nähe von
neck n der Nacken
necklace die Kette
need v brauchen
newspaper die Zeitung
newsstand der Zeitungskiosk
next adj nächste
nice schön
night die Nacht; **~club** der Nachtclub
no nein; **~ (not any)** kein
non-alcoholic nichtalkoholisch
non-smoking adj Nichtraucher
noon n der Mittag
north n der Norden

nose die Nase
note n **[BE] (money)** der Geldschein
nothing nichts
notify v benachrichtigen
novice der Anfänger
now jetzt
number n die Nummer
nurse n die Krankenschwester

O

office das Büro; **~ hours** die Bürozeiten
off-licence [BE] das Spirituosengenschäft
oil n das Öl
OK okay
old adj alt
on the corner an der Ecke
once (one time) einmal
one ein; **(counting)** eins; **~-day (ticket)** Tages-; **~-way ticket (airline)** das einfache Ticket, **(bus/train/ subway)** die Einzelfahrkarte; **~-way street** die Einbahnstraße
only nur
open v öffnen; **~** adj offen
opera die Oper; **~ house** das Opernhaus
opposite n das Gegenteil
optician der Optiker

orange *adj* (color) orange
orchestra das Orchester
order *v* (restaurant) bestellen
outdoor pool das Freibad
outside *prep* draußen
over *prep* (direction) über; **~done**
(meat) zu lang
gebraten; **~heat** *v* (car)
überhitzen; **~look** *n* (scenic
place) der Aussichtsplatz; **~night**
über Nacht; **~-the-counter**
(medication) rezeptfrei
oxygen treatment
die Sauerstoffbehandlung

P

p.m. nachmittags
pacifier der Schnuller
pack *v* packen
package *n* das Paket
pad *n* [BE] die Monatsbinde
paddling pool [BE]
das Kinderbecken
pain der Schmerz
pajamas der Pyjama
palace der Palast
pants die Hose
pantyhose die Strumpfhose
paper *n* (material) das Papier; **~**
towel das Papierhandtuch
paracetamol [BE] das Paracetamol

park *v* parken; **~** *n* der Park; **~ing**
garage das Parkhaus;
~ing lot der Parkplatz;
~ing meter die Parkuhr
parliament building
das Parlamentsgebäude
part (for car) das Teil;
~-time *adj* Teilzeit-
pass through *v* (travel)
durchreisen
passenger der Passagier
passport der Reisepass;
~ control die Passkontrolle
password das Passwort
pastry shop die Konditorei
patch *v* (clothing) ausbessern
path der Pfad
pay *v* bezahlen; **~phone**
das öffentliche Telefon
peak *n* (of a mountain) der Gipfel
pearl *n* die Perle
pedestrian *n* der Fußgänger
pediatrician der Kinderarzt
pedicure *n* die Pediküre
pen *n* der Stift
penicillin das Penicillin
penis der Penis
per pro; **~ day** pro Tag;
~ hour pro Stunde;
~ night pro Nacht;
~ week pro Woche

perfume *n* das Parfüm
period (menstrual) die Periode; ~ **(of time)** der Zeitraum
permit *v* erlauben
petrol [BE] das Benzin; ~ **station** [BE] die Tankstelle
pewter das Zinn
pharmacy die Apotheke
phone *v* anrufen; ~ *n* das Telefon; ~ **call** das Telefonat; ~ **card** die Telefonkarte; ~ **number** die Telefonnummer
photo das Foto; ~**copy** die Fotokopie; ~**graphy** die Fotografie
pick up *v* **(person)** abholen
picnic area der Rastplatz
piece *n* das Stück
Pill (birth control) die Pille
pillow *n* das Kissen
pink *adj* rosa
piste [BE] die Piste; ~ **map** [BE] der Pistenplan
pizzeria die Pizzeria
place *v* **(a bet)** abgeben
plane *n* das Flugzeug
plastic wrap die Klarsichtfolie
plate *n* der Teller
platform [BE] **(train)** der Bahnsteig
platinum *n* das Platin
play *v* spielen; ~ *n* **(theatre)** das Stück; ~**ground** der Spielplatz;

~**pen** der Laufstall
please *adv* bitte
pleasure *n* die Freude
plunger die Saugglocke
plus size die Übergröße
pocket *n* die Tasche
poison *n* das Gift
poles (skiing) die Stöcke
police die Polizei; ~ **report** der Polizeibericht; ~ **station** das Polizeirevier
pond *n* der Teich
pool *n* der Pool
pop music die Popmusik
portion *n* die Portion
post *n* [BE] die Post; ~ **office** die Post; ~**box** [BE] der Briefkasten; ~**card** die Postkarte
pot *n* der Topf
pottery die Töpferwaren
pound *n* **(weight)** das Pfund; ~ **(British sterling)** das Pfund
pregnant schwanger
prescribe (medication) verschreiben
prescription das Rezept
press *v* **(clothing)** bügeln
price *n* der Preis
print *v* drucken; ~ *n* der Ausdruck
problem das Problem

produce *n* das Erzeugnis;
  ~ store das Lebensmittelgeschäft
prohibit verbieten
pronounce aussprechen
Protestant der Protestant
public *adj* öffentlich
pull *v* ziehen
purple *adj* violett
purse *n* die Handtasche
push *v* drücken; **~chair [BE]**
  der Kinderwagen

Q

quality *n* die Qualität
question *n* die Frage
quiet *adj* leise

R

racetrack die Rennbahn
racket *n* **(sports)** der Schläger
railway station [BE] der Bahnhof
rain *n* der Regen; **~coat** die
  Regenjacke; **~forest** der
  Regenwald; **~y** regnerisch
rap *n* **(music)** der Rap
rape *v* vergewaltigen;
  ~ n die Vergewaltigung
rare selten
rash *n* der Ausschlag
ravine die Schlucht
razor blade die Rasierklinge

reach *v* erreichen
ready bereit
real *adj* echt
receipt *n* die Quittung
receive *v* erhalten
reception (hotel) die Rezeption
recharge *v* aufladen
recommend empfehlen
recommendation die Empfehlung
recycling das Recycling
red *adj* rot
refrigerator der Kühlschrank
region die Region
registered mail das Einschreiben
regular *n* **(fuel)** das Normalbenzin
relationship die Beziehung
rent *v* mieten; **~ n** die Miete
rental car das Mietauto
repair *v* reparieren
repeat *v* wiederholen
reservation die Reservierung;
  ~ desk der Reservierungsschalter
reserve *v* **(hotel)** reservieren
restaurant das Restaurant
restroom die Toilette
retired *adj* **(from work)** in Rente
return *v* **(something)**
  zurückgeben; **~ [BE] (trip)**
  die Hin- und Rückfahrt
reverse *v* **(the charges) [BE]**
  ein R-Gespräch führen

rib *n* **(body part)** die Rippe
right *adj, adv* **(direction)** rechts; ~
  of way die Vorfahrt
ring *n* der Ring
river der Fluss
road map die Straßenkarte
rob *v* berauben
robbed beraubt
romantic *adj* romantisch
room *n* das Zimmer; ~ **key**
  der Zimmerschlüssel;
  ~ **service** der Zimmerservice
round trip die Hin- und Rückfahrt
route *n* die Route
rowboat das Ruderboot
rubbing alcohol der
  Franzbranntwein
rubbish *n* **[BE]** der Abfall;
  ~ **bag [BE]** der Abfallbeutel
rugby das Rugby
ruin *n* die Ruine
rush *n* die Eile

S

sad traurig
safe *adj* **(protected)** sicher;
  ~ *n* **(thing)** der Safe
sales tax die Mehrwertsteuer
same *adj* gleiche
sandals die Sandalen
sanitary napkin die Monatsbinde

sauna die Sauna
sauté *v* sautieren
save *v* **(computer)** speichern
savings (account) das Sparkonto
scanner der Scanner
scarf der Schal
schedule *v* planen; ~ *n* der Plan
school *n* die Schule
science die Wissenschaft
scissors die Schere
sea das Meer
seat *n* der Sitzplatz
security die Sicherheit
see *v* sehen
self-service *n* die Selbstbedienung
sell *v* verkaufen
seminar das Seminar
send *v* senden
senior citizen der Rentner
separated (person) getrennt lebend
serious ernst
service (in a restaurant)
  die Bedienung
sexually transmitted disease
  (STD) die sexuell übertragbare
  Krankheit
shampoo *n* das Shampoo
sharp *adj* scharf
shaving cream die Rasiercreme
sheet *n* **(bed)** die Bettwäsche
ship *v* versenden

shirt das Hemd
shoe store das Schuhgeschäft
shoe der Schuh
shop v einkaufen;
~ n das Geschäft
shopping n das Einkaufen;
~ area das Einkaufszentrum;
~ centre [BE] das
Einkaufszentrum;
~ mall das Einkaufszentrum
short kurz; ~-sleeved kurzärmelig
shorts die kurze Hose
short-sighted [BE] kurzsichtig
shoulder n die Schulter
show v zeigen
shower n (bath) die Dusche
shrine der Schrein
sick adj krank
side n die Seite; ~ dish die Beilage;
~ effect die Nebenwirkung; ~
order die Beilage
sightseeing das Besichtigen von
Sehenswürdigkeiten;
~ tour die Besichtigungstour
sign v (document) unterschreiben
silk die Seide
silver n das Silber
single adj (person) alleinstehend;
~ bed das Einzelbett;
~ print der Einzelabzug;
~ room das Einzelzimmer

sink n das Waschbecken
sister die Schwester
sit v sitzen
size n die Größe
ski v Ski fahren; ~ n der Ski;
~ lift der Skilift
skin n die Haut
skirt n der Rock
sleep v schlafen; ~er car
der Schlafwagen; ~ing bag
der Schlafsack; ~ing car [BE] der
Schlafwagen
slice n die Scheibe
slippers die Pantoffeln
slower langsamer
slowly langsam
small klein
smoke v rauchen
smoking (area) Raucher-
snack bar der Imbiss
sneakers die Turnschuhe
snowboard n das Snowboard
snowshoe n der Schneeschuh
snowy verschneit
soap n die Seife
soccer der Fußball
sock die Socke
some (with singular nouns) etwas;
~ (with plural nouns) einige
soother [BE] der Schnuller
sore throat die Halsschmerzen

south *n* der Süden
souvenir *n* das Souvenir;
  ~ store das Souvenirgeschäft
spa das Wellness-Center
spatula der Spatel
speak *v* sprechen
specialist (doctor) der Spezialist
specimen die Probe
speeding die
  Geschwindigkeitsüberschreitung
spell *v* buchstabieren
spicy scharf; **~ (not bland)** würzig
spine (body part) die Wirbelsäule
spoon *n* der Löffel
sports der Sport; **~ massage**
  die Sportmassage
sprain *n* die Verstauchung
stadium das Stadion
stairs die Treppe
stamp *v* **(ticket)** entwerten;
  ~ n (postage) die Briefmarke
start *v* beginnen
starter [BE] die Vorspeise
station *n* **(stop)** die Haltestelle;
  bus ~ der Busbahnhof;
  gas ~ die Tankstelle;
  petrol ~ [BE] die Tankstelle;
  subway ~ die U-Bahn-Haltestelle;
  train ~ der Bahnhof
statue die Statue
steakhouse das Steakhouse

steal *v* stehlen
steep *adj* steil
sterling silver das Sterlingsilber
sting *n* der Stich
stolen gestohlen
stomach der Magen; **~ache** die
  Bauchschmerzen
stool (bowel movement) der
  Stuhlgang
stop *v* **(bus)** anhalten;
  ~ n (transportation) die
  Haltestelle
store directory (mall)
  der Übersichtsplan
storey [BE] die Etage
stove *n* der Herd
straight *adv* **(direction)** geradeaus
strange seltsam
stream *n* der Strom
stroller (baby) der Kinderwagen
student (university) der Student;
  ~ (school) der Schüler
study *v* studieren;
  ~ing *n* das Studieren
stuffed gefüllt
stunning umwerfend
subtitle *n* der Untertitel
subway die U-Bahn; **~ station** die
  U-Bahn Haltestelle
suit *n* der Anzug; **~case** der Koffer
sun *n* die Sonne; **~block** das

Sonnenschutzmittel; **~burn**
der Sonnenbrand; **~glasses**
die Sonnenbrille; **~ny** sonnig;
~screen die Sonnencreme;
~stroke der Sonnenstich
super *n* **(fuel)** das Superbenzin;
~market der Supermarkt
surfboard das Surfboard
surgical spirit [BE] der
Franzbranntwein
swallow *v* schlucken
sweater der Pullover
sweatshirt das Sweatshirt
sweet *n* **[BE]** die Süßigkeit;
~ *adj* **(taste)** süß
swelling die Schwellung
swim *v* schwimmen;
~suit der Badeanzug
symbol (keyboard) das Zeichen
synagogue die Synagoge

T

table *n* der Tisch
tablet (medicine) die Tablette
take *v* nehmen
tampon *n* der Tampon
taste *v* **(test)** kosten
taxi *n* das Taxi
team *n* das Team
teaspoon der Teelöffel
telephone *n* das Telefon

temple (religious) der Tempel
temporary vorübergehend
tennis das Tennis
tent *n* das Zelt;
~ peg der Zelthering;
~ pole die Zeltstange
terminal *n* **(airport)** der Terminal
terrible schrecklich
text *v* **(send a message)**
eine SMS schicken;
~ *n* der Text
thank *v* danken; **~ you** vielen Dank
the der?, das (neuter), die/
theater das Theater
theft der Diebstahl
there dort
thief der Dieb
thigh der Oberschenkel
thirsty durstig
this dieser?, dieses (neuter), diese/
throat der Hals
thunderstorm das Gewitter
ticket *n* die Fahrkarte;
~ office der Fahrkartenschalter
tie *n* **(clothing)** die Krawatte
tight (fit) eng
tights [BE] die Strumpfhose
time die Zeit; **~table [BE]**
(transportation) der Fahrplan
tire *n* der Reifen
tired müde

tissue das Gewebe
tobacconist der Tabakhändler
today *adv* heute
toe *n* der Zeh
toenail der Zehnagel
toilet [BE] die Toilette;
  ~ paper das Toilettenpapier
tomorrow *adv* morgen
tongue *n* die Zunge
tonight heute Abend
to (direction) zu
tooth der Zahn
toothpaste die Zahnpasta
total *n* **(amount)** der Gesamtbetrag
tough *adj* **(food)** zäh
tour *n* die Tour
tourist der Tourist;
  ~ information office das
  Touristeninformationsbüro
tow truck der Abschleppwagen
towel *n* das Handtuch
tower *n* der Turm
town die Stadt; **~ hall** das Rathaus;
  ~ map der Stadtplan; **~ square**
  der Rathausplatz
toy das Spielzeug;
  ~ store der Spielzeugladen
track *n* **(train)** der Bahnsteig
traditional traditionell
traffic light die Ampel
trail *n* **(ski)** die Piste;

  ~ map der Pistenplan
trailer (car) der Anhänger
train *n* der Zug;
  ~ station der Bahnhof
transfer *v* **(change trains/**
  flights) umsteigen;
  ~ (money) überweisen
translate übersetzen
trash *n* der Abfall
travel *n* das Reisen;
  ~ agency das Reisebüro;
  ~ sickness die Reisekrankheit;
  ~ers check [cheque BE] der
  Reisescheck
tree der Baum
trim (hair) *v* nachschneiden
trip *n* die Reise
trolley [BE] **(grocery store)**
  der Einkaufswagen; **~** [BE]
  (luggage) der Gepäckwagen
trousers [BE] die Hose
T-shirt das T-Shirt
tumble dry maschinentrocknen
turn off *v* **(device)** ausschalten
turn on *v* **(device)** anschalten
TV der Fernseher
tyre [BE] der Reifen

U

ugly hässlich
umbrella der Regenschirm

unbranded medication [BE]
das Generikum
unconscious (faint) bewusstlos
underdone halb gar
underground *n* [BE] die U-Bahn; ~
station [BE] die U-Bahn-Haltestelle
underpants [BE] der Slip
understand *v* verstehen
underwear die Unterwäsche
United Kingdom (U.K.)
das Großbritannien
United States (U.S.)
die Vereinigten Staaten
university die Universität
unleaded (gas) bleifrei
upset stomach
die Magenverstimmung
urgent dringend
urine der Urin
use *v* benutzen
username der Benutzername
utensil das Haushaltsgerät

V

vacancy (room) das freie Zimmer
vacation der Urlaub
vaccination die Impfung
vacuum cleaner der Staubsauger
vaginal infection die vaginale
Entzündung
valid gültig

valley das Tal
valuable *adj* wertvoll
value *n* der Wert
van der Kleintransporter
VAT [BE] die Mehrwertsteuer
vegan *n* der Veganer;
~ *adj* vegan
vegetarian *n* der Vegetarier;
~ *adj* vegetarisch
vehicle registration
die Fahrzeugregistrierung
viewpoint (scenic) [BE]
der Aussichtsplatz
village das Dorf
vineyard das Weingut
visa das Visum
visit *v* besuchen; **~ing hours** die
Besuchszeiten
visually impaired sehbehindert
vitamin das Vitamin
V-neck der V-Ausschnitt
volleyball game das
Volleyballspiel
vomit *v* erbrechen;
~ing das Erbrechen

W

wait *v* warten;
~ *n* die Wartezeit
waiter der Kellner
waiting room der Warteraum

waitress die Kellnerin
wake *v* wecken;
  ~-up call der Weckruf
walk *v* spazieren gehen;
  ~ *n* der Spaziergang;
  ~ing route die Wanderroute
wallet die Geldbörse
war memorial
  das Kriegsdenkmal
warm *v* **(something)** erwärmen;
  ~ *adj* **(temperature)** warm
washing machine die
  Waschmaschine
watch *v* beobachten
waterfall der Wasserfall
wax *v* **(hair)** mit Wachs entfernen
  (Haare)
weather *n* das Wetter
week die Woche; **~end** das
  Wochenende
weekly wöchentlich
welcome *adj* willkommen; **you're**
  ~ gern geschehen
west *n* der Westen
what was
wheelchair der Rollstuhl;
  ~ ramp die Rollstuhlrampe
when *adv* **(at what time)** wann
where wo
white *adj* weiß; **~ gold** das
  Weißgold

who (question) wer
widowed verwitwet
wife die Ehefrau
window das Fenster;
  ~ case das Schaufenster
wine list die Weinkarte
wireless wireless; **~ phone** das
  schnurlose Telefon
with mit
withdraw *v* **(money)** abheben;
  ~al (bank) die Abhebung
without ohne
woman die Frau
wool die Wolle
work *v* arbeiten
wrap *v* einpacken
wrist das Handgelenk
write *v* schreiben

Y

year das Jahr
yellow *adj* gelb
yes ja
yesterday *adv* gestern
young *adj* jung
youth hostel
  die Jugendherberge

Z

zoo der Zoo

German–English

A

der Abend evening
das Abendessen dinner
der Abfall *n* trash [rubbish BE]
der Abfallbeutel garbage [rubbish BE] bag
abfliegen *v* leave (plane)
der Abflug departure (plane)
abgeben *v* place (a bet)
abheben *v* withdraw (money)
die Abhebung withdrawal (bank)
abholen *v* pick up (something)
ablehnen *v* decline (credit card)
abmelden *v* log off (computer)
der Abschleppwagen tow truck
abschließen *v* lock (door)
der Adapter adapter
die Adresse *n* address
das Aftershave aftershave
die Agentur agency
AIDS AIDS
die Akupunktur *n* acupuncture
akzeptieren *v* accept
allein alone; **~stehend** single (person)
allergisch allergic;
die allergische Reaktion allergic reaction
alt *adj* old

das Alter *n* age
die Alternativroute alternate route
die Aluminiumfolie aluminum [kitchen BE] foil
amerikanisch American
die Ampel traffic light
anämisch anemic
die Anästhesie anesthesia
der Anfänger beginner/novice
angreifen *v* attack
anhalten *v* stop
der Anhänger trailer
ankommen arrive
die Ankunft arrival
anmelden *v* log on (computer)
der Anruf *n* call
anrufen *v* call
anschalten *v* turn on (device)
ansteckend contagious
das Antibiotikum *n* antibiotic
das Antiquitätengeschäft antiques store
antiseptisch antiseptic
der Anwalt lawyer
die Anzahlung *n* deposit (car rental)
der Anzug *n* suit
das Apartment apartment
die Apotheke pharmacy [chemist BE]

arbeiten v work
arbeitslos adj unemployed
der Arm n arm (body part)
die Aromatherapie aromatherapy
die Arterie artery
die Arthritis arthritis
der Arzt doctor
asiatisch Asian
das Aspirin aspirin
asthmatisch asthmatic
atmen breathe (place)
attraktiv attractive
auf Wiedersehen goodbye
aufladen v recharge
das Auge eye
ausbessern v mend (clothing)
der Ausfluss discharge (bodily fluid)
ausfüllen v fill out (form)
der Ausgang n exit
ausgeschlafen well-rested
die Auskunft information (phone)
die Ausrüstung equipment
ausschalten turn off (device)
der Ausschlag rash
der Aussichtsplatz viewpoint [BE]
aussprechen pronounce
aussteigen get off (a train/bus/
  subway)
Australien Australia
der Australier Australian
das Auto car; ~ mit

Automatikschaltung
  automatic car; ~ mit
  Gangschaltung manual car
die Autobahn highway [motorway
  BE]
automatisch automatic
der Autositz car seat
die Autovermietung car rental
  [hire BE]

B

das Baby baby
die Babyflasche baby bottle
die Babynahrung formula (baby)
das Baby-Pflegetuch baby wipe
der Babysitter babysitter
backen bake
die Bäckerei bakery
das Bad bathroom
der Badeanzug swimsuit
die Badelatschen flip-flops
der Bahnhof train [railway BE]
  station
der Bahnsteig track [platform BE]
das Ballett ballet
die Bank bank (money)
der Bankautomat ATM
die Bankkarte ATM card
die Bar bar (place)
das Bargeld n cash
der Baseball baseball (game)

der Basketball basketball (game)
die Batterie battery
die Bauchschmerzen stomachache
der Bauernhof n farm
der Baum tree
die Baumwolle cotton
die Beaufsichtigung supervision
die Bedienung service (in a restaurant)
beenden v exit (computer)
beginnen begin
behindert handicapped;
~engerecht handicapped [disabled BE]-accessible
beige adj beige
die Beilage side order
das Bein leg
beinhalten include (tax)
die Bekleidung clothing
das Bekleidungsgeschäft clothing store
belasten v charge (credit card)
belästigen bother
die Belichtung exposure (film)
benachrichtigen notify
benutzen v use
der Benutzername username
das Benzin gas [petrol BE]
beobachten v watch
der Berater consultant
berauben rob

beraubt robbed
bereit ready
der Berg hill; ~ mountain
beschädigen v damage
beschädigt damaged
die Beschwerde complaint
die Beschwerden condition (medical)
der Besen broom
die Besichtigungstour sightseeing tour
besser better
bestätigen confirm
beste adj best
bestellen v order (restaurant)
besuchen v visit
die Besuchszeiten visiting hours
das Bett n bed
die Bettwäsche sheets
bewusstlos unconscious (condition)
bezahlen pay
die Beziehung relationship
der BH bra
der Bikini bikini
billig cheap
billiger cheaper
bitte please
die Blase bladder
blau adj blue
bleifrei unleaded (gas)
der Blinddarm appendix (body part)

der **Blindenhund** guide dog
das **Blitzlicht** flashlight
die **Blume** *n* flower
die **Bluse** blouse
das **Blut** blood
der **Blutdruck** blood pressure
bluten bleed
der **Blutstau** congestion
das **Boot** boat
die **Bordkarte** boarding pass
der **botanische Garten** botanical garden
der **Boxkampf** boxing match
die **Bratpfanne** frying pan
brauchen *v* need
braun *adj* brown
brechen *v* break
die **Bremse** brakes (car)
brennen *v* burn
der **Brief** letter
der **Briefkasten** mailbox [postbox BE]
die **Briefmarke** *n* stamp (postage)
die **Brille** glasses (optical)
bringen bring
britisch British
die **Brosche** brooch
die **Brücke** bridge
der **Bruder** brother
die **Brust** breast; ~ chest ~**schmerzen** chest pain

das **Buch** *n* book
die **Bücherei** library
der **Buchladen** bookstore
buchstabieren *v* spell
das **Bügeleisen** *n* iron (clothes)
bügeln *v* iron
das **Büro** office
die **Bürozeiten** office hours
der **Bus** bus; ~**bahnhof** bus station; ~**fahrschein** bus ticket
die **Bushaltestelle** bus stop;
die **Business-Class** business class
die **Bustour** bus tour

C

das **Café** cafe (place)
campen *v* camp
der **Campingkocher** camping stove
der **Campingplatz** campsite
die **Campingtoilette** chemical toilet
der **Canyon** canyon
das **Casino** casino
die **CD** CD
Celsius Celsius
das **Check-in** check-in
das **Check-out** check-out
chinesisch Chinese
der **Club** *n* club
der **Computer** computer
die **Creme** *n* cream (ointment)

D

danken thank
der Darm intestine
das (neuter) the
das Datum *n* date (calendar)
die Decke blanket
das Denkmal memorial (place)
das Deodorant deodorant
der the
das Deutsch German;
~**land** Germany
der Diabetiker *n* diabetic
der Diamant diamond
die the
der Dieb thief; ~**stahl** theft
diese this
der Diesel diesel
dieser this
dieses (neuter) this
digital digital
der Digitaldruck digital print
das Digitalfoto digital photo
die Digitalkamera digital camera
das Display *n* display
Dollar dollar (U.S.)
der Dolmetscher interpreter
das Doppelbett double bed
das Dorf village
dort there
der Dosenöffner can opener
draußen outside

dringend urgent
drucken *v* print
drücken *v* push
dunkel *adj* dark
der Durchfall diarrhea
durchreisen pass through
durstig thirsty
die Dusche *n* shower
das Dutzend dozen
die DVD DVD

E

echt real
die EC-Karte debit card
die Ecke *n* corner; **an der Ecke**
on the corner
die Economy-Class economy class
die Ehefrau wife
der Ehemann husband
die Eile *n* rush
die Einbahnstraße one-way street
einbrechen *v* break in (burglary)
einchecken *v* check in
einführen *v* insert
der Eingang entrance
eingravieren engrave
der Einheimische *n* local (person)
einkaufen *v* shop
das Einkaufen shopping
der Einkaufskorb basket
(grocery store)

der Einkaufswagen cart [trolley BE] (grocery store)

das Einkaufszentrum shopping mall [centre BE]; ~ shopping area (town)

einlösen v cash (check)

einmal once

einpacken v wrap (parcel)

eins one

das Einschreiben registered mail

einsteigen v board (bus)

eintreten v enter

der Eintritt admission (fee)

der Einwegartikel n disposable

der Einweg-Rasierer disposable razor

einzahlen v deposit (money)

die Einzahlung n deposit (bank)

der Einzelabzug single print

das Einzelbett single bed

das Einzelzimmer single room

das Eis n ice; ~**hockey** ice hockey

der Ellenbogen elbow

die E-Mail n e-mail; ~-**Adresse** e-mail address; ~ **senden** v e-mail

empfehlen recommend

die Empfehlung recommendation

eng tight (fit)

englisch English

der Enkel grandchild

entleeren v empty

entschuldigen v excuse

entwerten v stamp (ticket)

entwickeln v develop (film)

epileptisch adj epileptic

erbrechen v vomit

erfahren adj experienced

erhalten receive

die Erkältung n cold (sickness)

erklären explain

erlauben allow

ernst serious

erreichen v reach

erschöpft exhausted

erstaunlich amazing

erste Klasse first class

erste adj first

erwärmen v warm (something)

essen eat

das Essen food

das Esszimmer dining room

die Etage floor [storey BE]

das E-Ticket e-ticket

etwas something; ~ **mehr...** some more...

der EU-Bürger EU resident

der Euro euro

die Exkursion excursion

der Experte n expert

der Express n express; ~**bus** express bus

extra extra; **~ groß** extra large

F

die Fähre ferry
fahren v drive
die Fahrkarte ticket
der Fahrkartenschalter ticket office
das Fahrrad n bicycle
der Fahrradweg bike route
der Fahrstuhl elevator [lift BE]
die Fahrzeugregistrierung vehicle registration
die Familie family
die Farbe n color
das Fax n fax
faxen v fax
die Faxnummer fax number
der Fehler n mistake
fehlen be missing
der Urlaub vacation [holiday BE]
das Feinkostgeschäft delicatessen
das Fenster window
der Fernseher television
das Festpreismenü fixed-price menu
die Festung fort
fettfrei fat free
das Feuer n fire
die Feuertür fire door
die Feuerwehr fire department
das Feuerzeug lighter

das Fieber fever
filetiert fileted (food)
der Film film (camera); **~** movie (cinema)
der Finger n finger
der Fingernagel fingernail
der Fitnessraum gym (workout)
die Flasche n bottle
der Flaschenöffner bottle opener
der Fleischer butcher
der Florist florist
der Flug flight
die Fluggesellschaft airline
der Flughafen airport
das Flugzeug airplane
der Fluss river
der Fön hair dryer
das Förderband conveyor belt
das Formular n form
fortgeschritten intermediate
das Foto photo
die Fotografie photography
fotografieren take a photo
die Fotokopie photocopy
die Frage n question
der Franzbranntwein rubbing alcohol [surgical spirit BE]
die Frau woman
freiberufliche Arbeit freelance work
frei adj free

das Fremdenverkehrsbüro tourist information office
die Freude pleasure
der Freund boyfriend; friend
die Freundin girlfriend; friend
frisch fresh
die Frischhaltefolie plastic wrap
der Friseur barber, hairstylist
der Friseursalon hair salon
die Frisur hairstyle
früh early
das Frühstück breakfast
der Führer guide
die Führerscheinnummer driver's license number
das Fundbüro lost-and-found
für for
der Fuß foot; ~**ball** soccer
das Fußballspiel soccer match [football game BE]
der Fußgänger n pedestrian
das Fußgelenk n ankle
füttern v feed

G

die Gabel fork
der Gang aisle
die Garage garage
das Gate gate (airport)
das Gebäude building
geben v give

die Gebühr fee
der Geburtstag birthday
gefährlich dangerous
der Gefrierschrank freezer
das Gegenteil n opposite
gehen v go (somewhere)
gekocht stewed
das Gel gel (hair)
gelb adj yellow
das Gelbgold yellow gold
das Geld money
die Geldbörse wallet
der Geldschein n bill [note BE] (money)
das Gelenk joint (body part)
das Generikum generic drug [unbranded medication BE]
genießen v enjoy
das Gepäck baggage [luggage BE]
die Gepäckausgabe baggage claim
der Gepäckschein baggage [luggage BE] ticket
das Gepäckschließfach baggage [luggage BE] locker
der Gepäckwagen baggage [luggage BE] cart
geradeaus straight
gern geschehen you're welcome
das Geschäft business; ~ store
~**sverzeichnis** store directory;
~**szentrum** business center

das Geschenk gift
der Geschenkwarenladen
  gift shop
das Geschirr dishes (kitchen)
der Geschirrspüler dishwasher
das Geschirrspülmittel
  dishwashing liquid
geschlossen closed
die Geschwindigkeitsüber-
  schreitung speeding
das Gesicht *n* face
gestern yesterday
gestohlen stolen
die Gesundheit health
das Getränk *n* drink
die Getränkekarte drink menu
getrennt lebend separated
  (person)
das Gewitter thunderstorm
gewürfelt diced (food)
das Gift *n* poison
der Gipfel peak (of a mountain)
das Girokonto checking [current
  BE] account
das Glas glass
gleich same
glücklich happy
die Glühbirne lightbulb
golden golden
der Golfplatz golf course
das Golfturnier golf

tournament
das Grad degree (temperature)
das Gramm gram
grau *adj* gray
der Grill *n* barbecue
groß big; ~ large
großartig magnificent
das Großbritannien United
  Kingdom (U.K.)
die Größe *n* size
die Großeltern grandparents
größer bigger; ~ larger
grün *adj* green
die Gruppe *n* group
gültig valid
der Gürtel belt
gut *adj* good; *adv* well;
  ~en Abend good evening;
  ~en Morgen good morning;
  ~en Tag good day
der Gynäkologe gynecologist

H

das Haar hair
die Haarbürste hairbrush
der Harfestiger mousse (hair)
der Haarschnitt haircut
das Haarspray hairspray
haben *v* have
halal halal
halb half; **~gar** underdone;

die ~e Stunde half hour;
das ~e Kilo half-kilo
die Halbschuhe loafers
halbtags part-time
das Hallenbad indoor pool
Hallo hello
der Hals throat
die Halsschmerzen sore throat
die Haltestelle *n* stop
der Hammer *n* hammer
die Hand *n* hand
das Handgelenk wrist
das Handgepäck hand luggage
die Handtasche purse [handbag BE]
das Handtuch towel
Handwäsche hand wash
das Handy cell [mobile BE] phone
hässlich ugly
die Hauptattraktion main attraction
das Hauptgericht main course
das Haus *n* house
das Haushaltsgerät utensil
die Haushaltswaren household goods
die Haut *n* skin
heiraten *v* marry
heiß hot (temperature);
~e Quelle hot spring;
~es Wasser hot water
heizen *v* heat

die Heizung heating
der Hektar hectare
helfen *v* help
der Helm helmet
das Hemd shirt
der Herd stove
das Herz heart
die Herzkrankheit heart condition
der Heuschnupfen hay fever
heute today; ~ Abend tonight
hier here
die Hilfe *n* help
die Hin- und Rückfahrt round-trip
Hinfahrt- one-way (ticket)
hinter behind (direction)
hoch high
das Hockey hockey
die Höhle *n* cave
hörgeschädigt hearing impaired
die Hose pants [trousers BE]
das Hotel hotel
hungrig hungry
husten *v* cough
der Husten *n* cough
der Hut hat

I

das Ibuprofen ibuprofen
die Identifikation identification
die Impfung vaccination
in in

infiziert infected
die Information information;
~ information desk
inländisch domestic
der Inlandsflug domestic flight
das Insekt bug
der Insektenschutz insect repellent
der Insektenstich insect bite
die Instant Message instant
message
das Insulin insulin
interessant interesting
international international;
der ~e Studentenausweis
international student card;
der ~e Flug international flight
das Internet internet;
~café internet cafe
der Internet-service internet service
irisch *adj* Irish
Irland Ireland
italienisch *adj* Italian

J

ja yes
die Jacke jacket
das Jahr year
japanisch Japanese
der Jazz jazz; **~club** jazz club
die Jeans jeans
der Jeansstoff denim

der Jet-ski jet ski
jetzt now
die Jugendherberge hostel;
~ youth hostel
jung *adj* young
der Junge boy
der Juwelier jeweler

K

das Kabarett cabaret
das Kaffeehaus coffee house
die Kalorie calorie
kalt *adj* cold (temperature);
~ cool (temperature)
die Kamera camera
die Kameratasche camera case
der Kamm *n* comb
das Kanada Canada
kanadisch *adj* Canadian
die Karaffe carafe
die Karte *n* card; ~ map
der Kassierer cashier
der Kater hangover (alcohol)
die Kathedrale cathedral
kaufen *v* buy
das Kaufhaus department store
der Kaugummi chewing gum
der Kellner waiter
die Kellnerin waitress
die Kette necklace
der Kiefer jaw

das Kilo kilo;
~**gramm** kilogram
der Kilometer kilometer
das Kind child
der Kinderarzt pediatrician
das Kinderbecken kiddie pool
das Kinderbett cot
die Kinderkarte children's menu
die Kinderportion children's
portion
der Kindersitz highchair
der Kinderstuhl child's seat;
der Kinderwagen stroller
das Kino movie theater
die Kirche church
das Kissen pillow
die Klarsichtfolie plastic wrap
[cling film BE]
die Klasse class
die klassische Musik classical music
das Kleid n dress (clothing)
die Kleiderordnung dress code
klein small
der Kleintransporter van
die Klimaanlage air conditioning
die Klippe cliff
das Kloster monastery
das Knie n knee
der Knochen n bone
kochen v boil; ~ cook
das Kölnischwasser cologne

der Koffer suitcase
der Kollege colleague
kommen v come
die Konditorei pastry shop
das Kondom condom
die Konferenz conference
das Konferenzzimmer meeting
room
der Kongressaal convention hall
die Konserve canned good
das Konsulat consulate
kontaktieren v contact
die Kontaktlinse contact lens
die Kontaktlinsenlösung contact
lens solution
das Konto n account
das Konzert concert
die Konzerthalle concert hall
der Kopf n head (body part)
die Kopfhörer headphones
die Kopfschmerzen headache
der Korkenzieher corkscrew
koscher kosher
kosmetisch adj cosmetic;
~**e Gesichtsbehandlung**
facial (treatment)
kosten v cost; ~ taste
krank ill; ~ sick
das Krankenhaus hospital
die Krankenschwester n nurse
der Krankenwagen ambulance

die Krawatte tie (clothing)
die Kreditkarte credit card
die Kreuzung intersection
das Kriegsdenkmal war memorial
das Kristall crystal (glass)
die Küche kitchen
die Küchenmaschine food processor
der Kühlschrank refrigerator
die Kunst art
das Kupfer copper
kurz short; ~**e Hose** shorts
kurzärmelig short-sleeved
kurzsichtig near- [short- BE] sighted
küssen v kiss

L

laktoseintolerant lactose intolerant
die Lampe n light (overhead)
die Landesvorwahl country code
landwirtschaftliches Erzeugnis produce
lang adj long; ~**ärmlig** long-sleeved;
langsam slow; ~**er** slower
langweilig boring
der Laufstall playpen
lauter louder

leben v live
das Lebensmittelgeschäft grocery store
die Leber liver (body part)
lecker delicious
das Leder leather
leicht easy
das Leinen linen
leise quiet
die Lektion lesson
letzte adj last
die Liebe n love
lieben v love (someone)
der Liegestuhl deck chair (ferry)
der Liftpass lift pass
die Linie line (train)
links left (direction)
die Linse lens
die Lippe lip
der Liter liter
Livemusik live music
locker loose (fit)
der Löffel n spoon
löschen v clear (on an ATM); ~ v delete (computer)
die Lotion lotion
die Luftpost n airmail
die Luftpumpe air pump
lufttrocknen v air dry
die Lunge lung

M

das Mädchen girl
das Magazin magazine
der Magen stomach
die Magenverstimmung upset stomach
die Mahlzeit meal
der Manager manager
die Maniküre *n* manicure
der Mann man (male)
der Mantel *n* coat
der Markt market
maschinentrocknen tumble dry
die Massage *n* massage
mechanisch *adj* mechanic
das Medikament medicine
die Medikamente medication
medium *adj* medium (meat)
das Meer sea
mehr more
die Mehrwertsteuer sales tax [VAT BE]
die Menstruationskrämpfe menstrual cramps
die Messe mass (church service)
messen *v* measure (someone)
das Messer knife
der Messbecher measuring cup
der Messlöffel measuring spoon
das Mietauto rental [hire BE] car
mieten *v* rent [hire BE]

die Mikrowelle *n* microwave
mild mild
die Mini-Bar mini-bar
die Minute minute
mit with; ~ **Bedienung** full-service
die Mitgliedskarte membership card
mitkommen *v* join
mitnehmen give somebody a lift (ride)
Mittag noon [midday BE]
das Mittagessen *n* lunch
Mitternacht midnight
der Mixer blender
die Mobilität mobility
mögen *v* like
der Monat month
die Monatsbinde sanitary napkin [pad BE]
der Mopp *n* mop
das Moped moped
morgen tomorrow
der Morgen morning
die Moschee mosque
der Moslem Muslim
das Motorboot motor boat
das Motorrad motorcycle
das Mountainbike mountain bike
müde tired
der Mund mouth
die Münze coin

das Münztelefon pay phone
das Museum museum
die Musik music
das Musikgeschäft music store
der Muskel muscle
die Mutter mother

N

nach after
der Nachmittag afternoon
nachprüfen *v* check (on something)
die Nachricht message
nachschneiden trim (haircut)
nächste *adj* next
die Nacht night
der Nachtclub nightclub
der Nacken neck
die Nagelfeile nail file
das Nagelstudio nail salon
nahe *prep* near
die Nähe vicinity;
  in der Nähe nearby
der Name *n* name
die Nase nose
die Nationalität nationality
das Naturreservat nature preserve
die Nebenstelle extension (phone)
die Nebenwirkung side effect
nehmen *v* take
nein no
Nichtraucher- non-smoking (area)

nichts nothing
niedrig low
die Niere kidney (body part)
der Norden *n* north
normal regular
der Notausgang emergency exit
der Notfall emergency
die Nummer *n* number
nur only; ~ just

O

obere *adj* upper
der Oberschenkel thigh
offen *adj* open
öffentlich *adj* public
öffnen *v* open
die Öffnungszeiten business hours
ohne without
das Ohr ear
die Ohrenschmerzen earache
der Ohrring earring
OK okay
das Öl *n* oil
die Oper opera
das Opernhaus opera house
der Optiker optician
orange *adj* orange (color)
das Orchester orchestra
die Ortsvorwahl area code
der Osten *n* east

P

packen *v* pack
die Packung carton;
  ~ packet
das Paket package
der Palast palace
paniert breaded
die Panne breakdown (car)
die Pantoffeln slippers
das Papier *n* paper
das Papierhandtuch paper towel
das Paracetamol acetaminophen
  [paracetamol BE]
das Parfüm *n* perfume
der Park *n* park
parken *v* park
das Parkhaus parking garage
der Parkplatz parking lot [car
  park BE]
die Parkuhr parking meter
das Parlamentsgebäude
  parliament building
das Parterre ground floor
der Passagier passenger
die Passform fit (clothing)
die Passkontrolle passport
  control
das Passwort password
die Pediküre pedicure
das Penicillin penicillin
der Penis penis

die Pension bed and breakfast
die Periode period (menstrual)
die Perle pearl
der Pfad path
die Pferderennbahn horsetrack
das Pflaster bandage
das Pfund *n* pound (weight)
das Pfund pound (British sterling)
die Pille Pill (birth control)
die Piste *n* trail [piste BE]
der Pistenplan trail [piste BE] map
die Pizzeria pizzeria
der Plan *n* schedule [timetable BE];
  ~ map
planen *v* plan
das Platin platinum
der Platte flat tire
der Platz field (sports); ~ seat; ~
  am Gang aisle seat
die Plombe filling (tooth)
der Po buttocks
die Polizei police
der Polizeibericht police report
das Polizeirevier police station
der Pool *n* pool
die Popmusik pop music
die Portion *n* portion
die Post mail [post BE]; ~ post office
die Postkarte postcard
der Preis price;
  ~ **pro Gedeck** cover charge

preisgünstig inexpensive
pro per; ~ **Nacht** per night;
  ~ **Stunde** per hour; ~ **Tag** per day;
  ~ **Woche** per week
das Problem problem
Prost! Cheers!
die Prothese denture
die Puppe doll
der Pyjama pajamas

Q

die Qualität *n* quality
die Quittung receipt

R

das R-Gespräch collect call [reverse charge call BE]
ein R-Gespräch führen *v* call collect [to reverse the charges BE]
der Rabatt discount
das Radfahren cycling
der Rap rap (music)
die Rasiercreme shaving cream
die Rasierklinge razor blade
der Rastplatz picnic area
das Rathaus town hall
der Rathausplatz town square
rauchen *v* smoke
Raucher- smoking (area)
die Rechnung bill [invoice BE] (of sale)

rechts right (direction)
das Recycling recycling
das Reformhaus health food store
der Regen *n* rain
die Regenjacke raincoat
der Regenschirm umbrella
der Regenwald rainforest
die Region region
regnerisch rainy
der Reifen tire [tyre BE]
reinigen *v* clean;
  chemisch ~ dry clean
die Reinigung dry cleaner's
die Reinigungsmittel cleaning supplies
die Reise trip; ~ journey
das Reisebüro travel agency
der Reiseführer guide book
die Reisekrankheit motion sickness
der Reisepass passport
der Reisescheck traveler's check [cheque BE]
die Rennbahn racetrack
der Rentner senior citizen
reparieren *v* fix; ~ repair
reservieren *v* reserve
die Reservierung reservation
der Reservierungsschalter reservation desk
das Restaurant restaurant
der Rettungsschwimmer lifeguard

das Rezept prescription
die Rezeption reception
die Richtung direction
der Ring *n* ring
die Rippe rib (body part)
der Rock skirt
der Rollstuhl wheelchair
die Rollstuhlrampe wheelchair ramp
die Rolltreppe escalator
romantisch romantic
rosa *adj* pink
rot *adj* red
die Route route
der Rücken *n* back (body part)
die Rückenschmerzen backache
der Rucksack backpack
das Ruderboot rowboat
das Rugby rugby
die Ruine ruin

S

der Safe *n* safe (for valuables)
die Sandalen sandals
sauber *adj* clean
die Sauerstoffbehandlung oxygen treatment
die Saugglocke plunger
die Sauna sauna
der Scanner scanner
die Schachtel *n* pack; ~

Zigaretten pack of cigarettes
der Schal scarf
scharf hot (spicy); ~ sharp
das Schaufenster window case
der Scheck *n* check [cheque BE] (payment)
die Schere scissors
schicken send;
  per Post ~ mail
das Schlachtfeld battleground
schlafen *v* sleep
die Schläfrigkeit drowsiness
der Schlafsack sleeping bag
die Schlafstörung insomnia
der Schlafwagen sleeper [sleeping BE] car
der Schläger racket (sports)
schlecht nauseous; ~ bad
der Schlepplift drag lift
schließen *v* close (a shop)
das Schließfach locker
das Schloss castle; ~ lock
die Schlucht ravine
der Schlüssel key; ~ring key ring
die Schlüsselkarte key card
der Schmerz pain;
Schmerzen haben be in pain
der Schmuck jewelry
schmutzig dirty
der Schneeschuh snowshoe

schneiden *v* cut
schnell fast
der Schnellzug express train
der Schnitt *n* cut (injury)
der Schnuller pacifier [soother BE]
schön nice; ~ beautiful
schrecklich terrible
schreiben write
der Schrein shrine
der Schuh shoe
das Schuhgeschäft shoe store
die Schule school
die Schulter shoulder
die Schüssel bowl
schwanger pregnant
schwarz *adj* black
die Schwellung swelling
die Schwester sister
schwierig difficult
das Schwimmbad swimming pool
schwimmen *v* swim
die Schwimmweste life jacket
schwindelig dizzy
schwul *adj* gay
die Schwulenbar gay bar
der Schwulenclub gay club
der See lake
sehbehindert visually impaired
sehen *v* look; ~ see
die Sehenswürdigkeit attraction
die Seide silk

die Seife *n* soap
die Seilbahn cable car
sein *v* be
die Selbstbedienung self-service
selten rare
seltsam strange
das Seminar seminar
senden *v* send
die Serviette napkin
der Sessellift chair lift
**sexuell übertragbare
  Krankheit** sexually transmitted
  disease (STD)
das Shampoo *n* shampoo
sich scheiden lassen *v* divorce
sicher *adj* safe (protected)
die Sicherheit security
das Sieb colander
das Sightseeing sightseeing
das Silber *n* silver
sitzen *v* sit
der Ski *n* ski
Ski fahren *v* ski
der Skilift ski lift
der Slip briefs (clothing)
die SMS SMS;
eine SMS schicken *v* text (message)
das Snowboard *n* snowboard
die Socke sock
die Sonne *n* sun
der Sonnenbrand sunburn

die **Sonnenbrille** sunglasses
die **Sonnencreme** sunscreen
der **Sonnenstich** sunstroke
sonnig sunny
das **Souvenir** souvenir; **~geschäft** souvenir store
das **Sparkonto** savings (account)
spät late (time)
der **Spatel** spatula
später later
spazieren gehen v walk
der **Spaziergang** n walk
die **Speicherkarte** memory card
speichern v save (computer)
die **Speisekarte** menu
der **Spezialist** specialist (doctor)
das **Spiel** game; **~** match
spielen v play
die **Spielhalle** arcade
der **Spielplatz** playground
das **Spielzeug** toy
der **Spielzeugladen** toy store
das **Spirituosengeschäft** liquor store [off-licence BE]
die **Spitze** lace (fabric)
der **Sport** sports
die **Sportmassage** sports massage
das **Sportgeschäft** sporting goods store
sprechen v speak
der **Springbrunnen** fountain

die **Spülung** conditioner (hair)
die **Stäbchen** chopsticks
das **Stadion** stadium
die **Stadt** city; **~** town
der **Stadtplan** town map
die **Stadtrundfahrt** sightseeing tour
das **Stadtzentrum** downtown area
die **Stange** carton (of cigarettes)
die **Statue** statue
der **Staubsauger** vacuum cleaner
das **Steakhouse** steakhouse
die **Steckdose** electric outlet
stehlen v steal
steil steep
das **Sterlingsilber** sterling silver
der **Stich** n sting
die **Stiefel** boots
der **Stift** pen
stillen breastfeed
die **Stöcke** poles (skiing)
stornieren v cancel
die **Strafe** n fine (fee for breaking law)
die **Strähnchen** highlights (hair)
der **Strand** beach
die **Straßenkarte** road map
der **Strom** electricity
die **Strumpfhose** pantyhose [tights BE]
das **Stück** n piece; **~** play

(theater); **~** slice
der Student student
studieren *v* study
der Stuhl chair
der Stuhlgang stool (bowel movement)
die Stunde hour
der Süden *n* south
das Super super (fuel)
der Supermarkt supermarket
das Surfboard surfboard
das Surfbrett windsurfer (board)
süß cute; **~** sweet (taste)
die Süßigkeit candy [sweet BE]
das Sweatshirt sweatshirt
die Synagoge synagogue
synchronisiert dubbed

T

der Tabakhändler tobacconist
die Tablette tablet (medicine)
der Tag day
Tages- one-day (ticket)
das Tal valley
der Tampon tampon
tanken *v* fill (car)
die Tankstelle gas [petrol BE] station
der Tanzclub dance club
tanzen *v* dance
die Tasche bag; **~** pocket

die Tasse *n* cup
taub *adj* deaf
die Tauchausrüstung diving equipment
tauchen *v* dive
das Taxi taxi
das Team team
der Teelöffel teaspoon
der Teich pond
das Teil part (for car)
das Telefon *n* phone
das schnurlose Telefon wireless phone
der Telefonanruf phone call
die Telefonkarte phone card
die Telefonnummer phone number
der Teller plate
der Tempel temple (religious)
das Tennis tennis
der Termin appointment
der Terminal terminal (airport)
teuer expensive
der Text *n* text
das Theater theater
tief deep
die Tiefkühlkost frozen food
das Tier animal
der Tisch table
die Toilette restroom [toilet BE]
das Toilettenpapier toilet paper

der Topf *n* pot
die Töpferwaren pottery (pots)
die Tour *n* tour
der Tourist tourist
traditionell traditional
traurig sad
treffen meet
das Treffen meeting
trennen disconnect (computer)
die Treppe stairs
trinken *v* drink
das Trinkwasser drinking water
der Tropfen *n* drop (medicine)
das T-Shirt T-shirt
die Tür door
der Turm tower
die Turnschuhe sneaker

U

die U-Bahn subway [underground BE]
die U-Bahn-Haltestelle subway [underground BE] station
über *prep* over;
  ~ Nacht overnight;
  ~fallen *v* mug
die Übergröße plus size
überhitzen overheat (car)
übersetzen translate
überweisen *v* transfer (money)
um (die Ecke) around (the corner)

umändern alter
umarmen *v* hug
die Umkleidekabine fitting room
der Umschlag envelope
umsteigen *v* change (buses); ~
  v transfer (change trains/flights)
umtauschen *v* exchange (money)
umwerfend stunning
unbeaufsichtigt unattended
der Unfall accident
die Universität university
die Unterhaltung entertainment (amusement)
die Unterhose underwear [underpants BE]
die Unterkunft accommodation
die Unterlegplane groundcloth
unterschreiben *v* sign
der Untertitel *n* subtitle
die Unterwäsche underwear
der Urin urine
der Urlaub vacation [BE holiday]

V

die Vagina vagina
vaginal vaginal; **die ~e Entzündung** vaginal infection
der Vater father
der V-Ausschnitt V-neck
der Veganer *n* vegan
der Vegetarier *n* vegetarian

der Ventilator fan (appliance)
verbieten *v* prohibit
verbinden *v* connect (internet)
die Verbindung connection
die Vereinigten Staaten United States (U.S.)
verfügbar available
vergewaltigen *v* rape
die Vergewaltigung *n* rape
der Vergnügungspark amusement park
verheiratet married
verkaufen *v* sell
verlangen *v* charge (cost)
verlieren *v* lose (something)
verlobt engaged
verloren lost
verschlucken *v* swallow
verschneit snowy
verschreiben *v* prescribe (medication)
versenden *v* ship
die Versicherung insurance
die Versicherungsgesellschaft insurance company
die Versicherungskarte insurance card
die Verstauchung *n* sprain
verstehen understand
die Verstopfung constipation
verwitwet widowed

verzögern *v* delay
viel much; ~ a lot;
~**en Dank** thank you;
wie ~ how much
violett *adj* purple
die Visitenkarte business card
das Visum visa
das Vitamin vitamin
die Vitrine display case
der Vogel bird
die Volksmusik folk music
das Volleyballspiel volleyball game
Vollzeit- full-time
vor before; **Viertel ~ vier** a quarter to four
die Vorfahrt right of way
die Vorhersage *n* forecast
die Vorspeise appetizer [starter BE]
vorstellen *v* introduce (person)
vorübergehend temporary

W

wählen *v* dial
während during
die Währung currency
der Währungsumtausch currency exchange
der Wald forest
die Wanderroute walking route
die Wanderschuhe hiking boots
die Wanduhr wall clock

wann when (time)
die Ware n good; ~ product
die Waren goods
warm adj warm (temperature)
warten wait
der Warteraum waiting room
die Wartezeit n waiting period
was what
das Waschbecken n sink
die Wäscherei laundry (facility)
der Wäscheservice laundry service
die Waschmaschine washing machine
waschmaschinenfest machine washable
das Waschmittel detergent
der Waschsalon laundromat [launderette BE]
der Wasserfall waterfall
die Wasserski water skis
das Wechselgeld n change (money)
der Wechselkurs exchange rate
wechseln v change
die Wechselstube currency exchange office
wecken v wake
der Weckruf wake-up call
weich soft
das Weingut vineyard
die Weinkarte wine list
weiß adj white

das Weißgold white gold
weit adv far (distance); ~ adj loose (fit)
weitsichtig far [long BE]- sighted
das Wellness-Center spa
wenig adj little (not much)
weniger less
wer who
der Wert value
wertvoll valuable
der Westen n west
das Wetter weather
wickeln v change (baby)
wie how; ~ **viel** how much
wiederholen repeat
willkommen adj welcome
die Windel diaper [nappy BE]
die Wirbelsäule spine (body part)
wireless wireless
wo where
die Woche week
das Wochenende weekend
wöchentlich weekly
der Wohnwagen mobile home
die Wolle wool
wunder schön beautiful
die Wüste n desert

Z

der Zahn tooth
der Zahnarzt dentist

die Zahnpaste toothpaste
der Zeh *n* toe
der Zehennagel toenail
das Zeichen symbol (keyboard)
zeigen *v* show (somebody something)
die Zeit time
der Zeitraum period (of time)
die Zeitung newspaper
der Zeitungskiosk newsstand
das Zelt tent
der Zelthering tent peg
die Zeltstange tent pole
der Zentimeter centimeter
zerbrochen broken (smashed)
das Zertifikat certificate

ziehen *v* extract (tooth);
  ~ *v* pull (door sign)
die Zigarette cigarette
die Zigarre cigar
das Zimmer room
der Zimmerschlüssel room key
der Zimmerservice room service
das Zinn pewter
der Zoll customs; ~ duty (tax)
zollfrei duty-free
der Zoo zoo
zu *adv* too; ~ *prep* to
der Zug train
die Zunge tongue
zurückgeben *v* return (something)
der Zutritt *n* access

Berlitz®

speaking your language

phrase book & dictionary
phrase book & CD

Available in: Arabic, Brazilian Portuguese*, Burmese*, Cantonese Chinese, Croatian, Czech*, Danish*, Dutch, English, Filipino, Finnish*, French, German, Greek, Hebrew*, Hindi*, Hungarian*, Indonesian, Italian, Japanese, Korean, Latin American Spanish, Malay, Mandarin Chinese, Mexican Spanish, Norwegian, Polish, Portuguese, Romanian*, Russian, Spanish, Swedish, Thai, Turkish, Vietnamese
*Book only

www.berlitzpublishing.com